Engraved by John Sartain.

Rev. Josiah D. Smith D.D.

TRUTH IN LOVE.

SERMONS

BY THE LATE

REV. JOSIAH D. SMITH, D. D.,

PASTOR OF WESTMINSTER PRESBYTERIAN CHURCH, COLUMBUS, OHIO.

WITH A

BIOGRAPHICAL PREFACE

BY THE,

REV. JAMES M. PLATT,

PASTOR OF THE FIRST PRESBYTERIAN CHURCH OF ZANESVILLE, OHIO,

AND AN

INTRODUCTION

BY

M. W. JACOBUS, D. D.,

PROFESSOR IN THE WESTERN THEOLOGICAL SEMINARY.

"Speaking the truth in love."—EPHESIANS iv. 15.

PHILADELPHIA:
PRESBYTERIAN BOARD OF PUBLICATION,
No. 821 CHESTNUT STREET.

STEREOTYPED BY WESTCOTT & THOMSON.

TO

HER WHO SHARED THE SPIRITUAL ANXIETY, AND FAITH, AND HOPE, IN WHICH THESE DISCOURSES WERE FIRST PREPARED AND PREACHED;

AND

TO THE AFFLICTED FLOCK

WHO STILL REMEMBER THE WORDS OF THE PASTOR WHO

"PREACHED CHRIST UNTO THEM,"

THIS VOLUME

IS

AFFECTIONATELY DEDICATED.

CONTENTS.

SERMON IX.

SERMON X.

SERMON XI.

SERMON XII.

SERMON XIII.

SERMON XIV.

SERMON XV.

SERMON XVI.

SERMON XVII.

SERMON XVIII.

XIX.

ADDRESS.

INTRODUCTION.

THE late excellent and lamented Rev. Dr. F. Monod, of Paris, when addressing the students of the Allegheny Theological Seminary, a few years ago, remarked, that "A minister of the gospel, as he is true or not to his trust, is either the noblest or the most degraded of men." If he have no heart in his work,—a mere sermonizer, or scholiast or worldling, flippant, or perfunctory,—if he be a bitter disputant, as if that were, in the sense of the apostle, "to contend earnestly for the faith,"—if he be anything short of a gospelizer, and a winner of souls, he so far falls short of the shining mark. Dan. xii. 3. It is only as one is a *burning* light, that he can be a *shining* one. John v. 35.

It is a question of vital interest in what consists the proper *power of the pulpit.* Most men recognize it when they see it in some living example: and yet they may not be able to analyze the mysterious quality. Can we say, that what is called *pulpit power* is quite the same in all times, and in all cases, even in Whitfield and Summerfield, and Larned and Nevins, in Melville and Chalmers?

There are certain essential requisites for effective and successful preaching.

1. There must be *furniture.* Surely where the preaching is, in its main idea, a *message* delivered to men, everything depends

on the *matter*. What is the message? the substance of it, always, the whole of it, first or last—what is it? And the chief furniture is surely the message itself, well understood and arranged. Familiarity with the Scripture must lie at the basis of all true furniture, since it is the Scripture that is to be preached.

"All Scripture is given by inspiration of God," with all its profitableness, "that the man of God may be perfect," (*ready*, "αρτιος," αρτι.—now!)—*thoroughly furnished—thoroughly made ready*—(as a ship ready for the voyage) unto all good works."

The temptation of the day in some quarters, is to a parade of learned disquisition, not considering that Christ crucified, is "the power of God, and the wisdom of God unto salvation" though the Jews require a sign, and the Greeks seek after wisdom. Paul at Athens, is the model for the time. The Scriptural Cosmology, and Ethnology, are to be used to point men to the hastening judgment of Jesus Christ as the God-man Mediator. And the Scripture has in itself the living germs of all truth. John xvii. 17.

2. But the discourse is to be *practical and direct*. As this gospel is to be presented in its application to all the relations and duties of life, so it is to be brought home to the hearers. As "having such hope," we are to "use great plainness (openness) of speech," 2 Cor. iii. 12, 13, "and not as Moses, which put a vail on his face,"—only indirect and restricted and partial.

The dull rehearsing of the generalities and common-places of Theology, as if merely to fill out the hour, is not adapted to move the congregation. The most brilliant essay, exhibiting the preacher more than Christ, can never be expected to convert men. It is not so calculated, nor constructed. There is a manner of preaching which the Holy Spirit recognizes as fitted to issue the saving results. Paul and Barnabas, in that synagogue at

Iconium, "SO SPAKE, (THUS—*in such manner*, and to such effect) as that a great multitude, both of the Jews, and also of the Greeks, believed." Acts xiv. 1. How can a drawler or a drone do this? How can a learned trifler, or a frigid disputant, or a heartless essayist do it?

That "Paul may plant, and Apollos water," without any power to give *the increase*, is no proper excuse for not copying Paul and Apollos as preachers of the word—nor is it any proof that such Apostolic preachers will not get the increase which God alone can give.

3. But the directness is not fitting for the requisite effect without a *tender earnestness*. If the language and tone be harsh and dictatorial, how little does it become the service of Him who giveth wisdom liberally to all men, *and upbraideth not?* And just here it is that a vital distinction must be made. Here is the public call for a heartiness, which gushes forth in tenderness, and expresses itself in loving, earnest utterances. It is needful to notice how the *tongue of fire* is yet the symbol and secret of ministerial success, no less than at Pentecost. There must be *fervour*. The pulpit is no place for *cant*. Nor is it any place for *rant*. It is the place for a heart and tongue on fire with the love of God published in the heart by the Holy Ghost—for a glow such as shall be reflected upon the assembly—for an unction such as shall run down from the head to the garments.

And this is a requisite which can neither be gotten from books, nor bought with money. A heart alive to the Divine power of the truth, and burning with zeal for its dissemination, must be a heart in direct and lively communion with God. *Prayer*—or rather prayerfulness—the *praying spirit*—is not this the true *power of the pulpit?* Is not this the secret of the tongue of fire? —For "out of the abundance of the heart the mouth speaketh."

And only such a living conviction of the truth as leads to prayer, and such a conviction as prayer leads to, can be the well-spring of *the true Evangelistic zeal* that is advertised for in the churches.

It is herein that the great Apostle to the Gentiles makes his boast, that "*God hath qualified us ministers of the New Testament,*" 2 Cor. iii. 6. God will have *the living ministry*, not the *dead ministry!* The preacher must show his Divine anointing. This is the proper *unction.* The baptism of fire comes of earnest wrestling in prayer, as at the Pentecost—and thus occurs the true *directness*—that men hear the preacher speaking, "each in their own tongue, the wonderful works of God." And thus it occurs also, that "the Lord adds to the church such as shall be saved." The whole question of discourse, of delivery, of matter, and of manner in the pulpit finds its best solution in this "gift of tongues," which is the home-preaching to every man, and in that language which he recognizes as his own soul's vernacular. This is the proper *power of the pulpit.*

The author of this volume of Discourses was himself a happy example of these high qualities; and he illustrated, most strikingly, this combination of ministerial gifts in the pulpit at Columbus. He was, by all admission, a man of power, because he was a man of furniture, and of earnestness, of tenderness, and of prayer. None who knew him, will deny to him this fair tribute. His sermons speak for him this testimony. They glow with the burnished lustre of the golden candlestick when it is lighted up, and glorious in the reflection of its Divine beams.

Rich, spiritual discourse, that is also deeply intellectual, and shows the devotion of a strong mind to the noble themes of salvation, is the characteristic of Dr. Smith's pulpit history.

BIOGRAPHICAL PREFACE.

THE author of the sermons here presented was one whose praise is in all the churches amongst which his valued life was spent. And it seems natural to suppose that discourses originating in such a healthy, vigorous mind, and prepared with such devout care, and preached with so much acceptance,—though with very little of the grace of oratory beyond what still appears in the simple faith, and the earnest, affectionate spirit which they manifest,—should be adapted to a still wider usefulness through the press. For this reason, then, the preparation of this volume has been suggested and undertaken. And in order that the readers of it may be made somewhat acquainted with the man of God who thus preaches to them, the leading features of his life and character will here be given.

JOSIAH DICKEY SMITH was born in Western Pennsylvania in the year 1815. His father, William Smith, was a native of Edinburgh, and at the time of the son's birth was married to his second wife. In the spring of

1818 he removed to Franklin county, Ohio, not far from Columbus, where he purchased a valuable farm, part of which he devoted by his will to the education of this, his youngest child. In the summer of 1819 the father died, leaving his little son to be trained up under the mother's pious care. As he grew up and received his early education at the log school-house near by, she had the comfort of knowing that he was a good boy, an amiable, open-hearted, obedient son, and possessed of a mind which gave promise of substantial usefulness. He had no equal among the boys of his own age in his knowledge of the Bible and the catechism, or in his clear perception of Divine truth; and his schoolmates regarded him as a noble competitor for every honourable distinction, and a faithful umpire in every dispute. But notwithstanding the hopefulness of his early years, his mother was taken from him when he was but sixteen years of age, and before he had yet become a child of God. In after years, however, he showed in many ways his grateful memory and appreciation of her tender, faithful nurture.

In 1833 he entered college at South Hanover, Ind., where he was graduated in 1837. It was while he was a student here that he became a subject of Divine grace, under the influence of a powerful revival in the college, in 1836. This change of heart led to a change in his plans of life; and, giving up his former intention to study law, he turned his thoughts to the work of the gospel ministry. Accordingly he entered the Theological Seminary at the same place in 1837, and finished his preparatory studies there in 1840.*

In the spring of 1840, after having been licensed to preach the gospel, he visited the churches of Truro and Hamilton, in Columbus Presbytery, and in the same county in which his boyhood had been spent. After supplying these churches for a year as a probationer, he received a call, and was ordained to the full work of the ministry, Oct. 20, 1841. His two congregations were composed mainly of the farming population of the adjoining neighbourhood, among whom the "simplicity and godly sincerity" of the young pastor were held in very high esteem. Such plain, earnest, and powerful presentations of the gospel, coming from one so modest and so gentle, and yet so manly and uncompromising in his love of the truth, were well adapted to win souls to Christ. He laboured among them not only with a growing popularity, but with an increasing influence. In 1843 the church of Truro enjoyed a precious revival under his ministry, as the fruit of which some fifty persons were admitted to full communion in the course of a few months. Such, in fact, was the prosperity of this

* These details as to his academic training, with some others embodied in this narrative, are taken from an article in "The Presbyter," signed "G. L. K."

church, that they secured the labours of their pastor for three-fourths of his time, and afterwards,—in 1849 or '50,—they obtained his undivided services.

Under such influences as these, he was planted, and grew, and ripened as a Christian minister. But while his labours proved so acceptable as well as useful to his own people, his standing as a minister had become known in the Presbytery and elsewhere, and one so well fitted for eminent and more extended service in the church "could not be hid" in the quiet rural parish of Truro. He had been preaching to the same people for ten years when the first intimations were given that he must go elsewhere. The venerable Dr. James Hoge, who was himself as regular as any of his juniors in his attendance at ecclesiastical meetings, had had frequent opportunities for observing the development of this young pastor; and finding it necessary to secure a colleague in the pastoral office, in order that he might be more at liberty to engage in the new enterprise of establishing a Theological Seminary at Cincinnati, he brought the matter before his congregation, and a call was promptly extended to Mr. Smith. Here, then, was a direct appeal, not to his ambition, for this, in its ordinary sense, no one ever discovered in his character, but to that holy aspiration which always possessed him to make the most faithful and thorough use of all his capacities for the honour of his Divine Master. Modest indeed he was, and disposed rather to shun than seek a position of any prominence in the church; but he had, nevertheless, the consciousness of having an important trust committed to him, and in a spirit of humble, reverent obedience, his Christian manliness girded itself for every work that was given him to do. In such a spirit he accepted the call, and removed to Columbus, where he was installed as co-pastor, January 24, 1851.

Here he soon attached himself to a large congregation by his genial, friendly deportment, and by his peculiar adaptation to the work of comforting and counselling them from house to house, no less than by the spiritual fervour and intellectual force which characterized all his public ministrations. He had not been settled long, however, until his spirit began to be "stirred within him," as he observed the gradual growth of the city, and how little his own church was accomplishing in the way of aggressive Christian effort, in comparison with the extended field entrusted to them. The church to which he ministered had become quite overgrown, and families which would have preferred worshipping there were attaching themselves to other congregations, while the actual means and capacities of his own people were in nowise developed to their natural proportions. A few of his hearers were at last led, by means of his stirring discourses, to see that some increase of church accommodations ought to be provided to meet the demands of an increasing population; and a colony of thirty members prepared to go out from the old church and form a new organization. In committing themselves, however, to the responsibilities of such an enterprise, they desired to remain still under the same leader whose zeal had "provoked" them to such an undertaking, and he consented to sever his connexion with a church "where he was highly acceptable, and sure both of audience and support," and to cast in his lot with the younger and weaker branch. Accordingly, on the first of June, 1854, the Westminster church was organized, and Mr. Smith was called to accept the pastoral charge, over which he was installed on the fifth of August, following.

This little congregation secured for a temporary place of worship, the "theatre," of Starling Medical College, and for three years they continued holding their services in this unprepossessing place, where the pulpit was as if at the bottom of a great funnel, and the wall in the rear was hung with charts illustrative of anatomy and chemistry.

But notwithstanding the unedifying aspect of the place itself, as respects *spiritual* matters, the little flock of Westminster went on to increase year by year, and members were added to them as rapidly then as at any time afterwards. Meantime, the work of building was begun, and a commodious church of stone in the Norman style of architecture was seen slowly rising from its foundation, and made ready for the sharp slated roof. The interior was finished in a neat, plain style, with seats of varnished pine, and with a gallery for the choir only; and without waiting to complete the tower and spire, the church was dedicated for the worship of God, August 23, 1857. A few years afterwards, a spacious lecture-room was added in the rear of this main edifice, with apartments for the pastor's study, and for the social gatherings of the congregation.

Thus the new and difficult enterprise was crowned with success. In 1861, the number of communicants reported to the General Assembly, showed an increase from the original thirty, to *one hundred and thirty*, and by that time the church might be considered a strong and well-established organization. The pastor was surrounded by an efficient "staff" of officers, and by a bevy of helpers in every good work. His session was in more than an ordinary degree composed of intelligent, educated men, and they had a very high appreciation of his peculiar worth. While they could not fail to discern "that the oracles of God which from a child he had known, were the fountain from which flowed his peculiar power and pathos as a preacher of the word," they observed also how "his native vigorous intellect was so fully developed by patient study and discipline, and so richly furnished with the varied treasures of science and learning, and his heart so 'filled with the Spirit,' that he was enabled to analyze, expound, and enforce the principles, doctrines, and precepts of our holy religion, with a clearness and purity of style, and with a power of argument and illustration but rarely equalled in any pulpit."* These are in part the words in which they have recorded, since his death, the sentiments of profound admiration with which they were known to regard him during his life.

It was very seldom that Mr. Smith would undertake any literary labour aside from the preparation of his sermons. In two or three instances, however, he consented to deliver an address before some gathering of students, where he was heard with very great interest. In August 1858, he attended the commencement exercises at South Hanover, where he addressed the literary societies of the college on the "Conditions of Eminent Usefulness." This was requested for publication, and afterwards was inserted in Dr. Van Rensselaer's annual "Education Repository." It was at this time that he received from his Alma Mater the degree of "Doctor Divinitatis," a title which his friends esteemed as a well-merited compliment, and which he wore with remarkable modesty and meekness.

In the ecclesiastical meetings, which he attended with conscientious regularity, Dr. Smith was always a lead-

* Extract from record of Session, June 3, 1863.

ing member, not because he *took* such a position, but because it was generally *assigned* to him. Even there he shrank from any notoriety, and scarcely ever made what could be called "a speech," satisfying himself with clearing up a single point, or furnishing some desired information; but often in a few pithy well-chosen words he would show how earnestly his heart was enlisted in whatever affected the prosperity of Zion; and always at such times he displayed such fairness and good sense, and such freedom from all unworthy motives, that his opinion was possessed of great weight, and his character would shine out so pure, and manly, and noble, as to render him beloved by all.

There was, however, a power in this servant of God, which nothing but the preaching of the gospel could fully develop. In the pulpit his mind exhibited a clearness of discernment, and a firmness of grasp, and a breadth of view, and a freedom from conventional modes of thought, that would often surprise those who had observed only his quiet unassuming demeanour. His style of address at the beginning, presented very few attractive points to any one who was not in sympathy with the character of the man. The singular opening and closing of the eye, the somewhat prolonged utterance of an occasional sentence, and the unusual emphasis here and there given to some half-concealed, and yet forcible word, might have been accounted by a casual hearer, as among his rhetorical defect, and may, perhaps, have prevented his being more widely known and appreciated. But to his own people, these were merely the signals for some clear and finely-drawn distinction, or some expression that savoured of the very richest vein of evangelical thought and feeling. As he went on, he brought the minds of his hearers into sympathy with his own, and by some touch of genuine tenderness would win their confidence, while with some powerful argument and appeal he would bring them, for the time at least, to feel convinced of the high claim which God's own word had upon their loving, lifelong obedience. In the pulpit, as in the private intercourse of life, he despised none of the accepted formulas of correct taste, but he made no display of his gifts, and sought no rhetorical effect beyond what was necessary to commend and enforce the exact thought which he had in view. The general impression made by his preaching was that of having been brought into sympathy with the most solemn and important and powerful truths that man can present to his fellow-man, and of having had them urged upon one's attention with the utmost candour and tenderness, though with all the energy of a strong, masculine faith.

In the social circle, no one relished congenial company more than Dr. Smith, and no one excelled him in enjoying as much of the society of others as was *enjoyable*, and in letting the rest pass without any unkind remark. It was always wonderful to see with what natural grace he would put himself upon a level with his juniors and inferiors, manifesting no critical impatience, nor any conscious superiority, but listening attentively to whatever might be suggested, and in whatever blundering fashion it might be expressed, and replying as though he had a rare appreciation of the thought, detecting the exact point, and reproducing it, all enriched with his own solid acquirements and ripe spiritual culture, without seeming to suppose that he had actually communicated anything of value in doing so. With a fine vein of humour, and a keen sense of the ridiculous, he would show a hearty relish of anything that provoked an honest, good-natured laugh. And while this contributed a freshness and a *naturalness* to his ordinary conversation, it showed how his character retained all the cheerful, elastic, healthy spirit of his boyhood, combined with the noblest admiration of Divine truth, and a constant, devout regard to its precepts. The piety that was nurtured in the holy song and earnest supplication which could be often overheard in his retirement, seemed to flow out as a full deep stream of blessings to all that were acquainted with him; and every one who knew him could not but feel, while conversing with him, that he was indeed a man greatly beloved of God.

We need not attempt here to indicate in how many ways such a life as his had its due influence in his own denomination, nor. to what extent his fervent catholic spirit may have had its effect as "light," and "salt," and "leaven" upon society at large. Though the whole period of his regular ministry was spent within the radius of a few miles, his love to the cause of Christ was one which took the widest range, and embraced all who rejoice in a blood-bought reconciliation. In visiting among his brethren, it was his "meat and drink" to preach "the glorious gospel of the blessed God," and not the least of the effects of his ministry, away from his own people, has been the delightful savour of the knowledge of Christ which was manifested by him in every place.

Dr. Smith entered with a ready sympathy into all the practical aspects of life around him, whether relating to the family or the community, the church or the nation. On the right and duty of the pulpit to set forth the counsel of God concerning topics of great national importance, his views were very clear and decided, and always expressed with as much freedom from every thing like partisan prejudice and intolerance as could well be imagined. His character as a faithful servant of God was so conspicuous in the very act of speaking boldly against great national evils, that no one had the audacity to accuse him of being influenced by any of the grovelling aims of the demagogue, or by any fanatical frenzy. In the great national contest which is still in progress, he discerned the immense moral issues which lay imbedded beneath the turbulent surface, and with all the ardour of a Christian patriot he watched the shifting scene of alternate success and defeat, and in the darkest hours of the nation's peril could still commit all to Him who reigns in righteousness. During his last illness he was at one time told of some news that had just been received. As if reminded of some neglected duty, he said, "I had almost forgotten my country," and at once offered a fervent prayer for the government, making requests such as had often been heard from him in the sanctuary.

It was at a time when he thought himself more than ever qualified to labour in his Master's vineyard, that he was summoned to the chamber where a long and severe illness awaited him. At first he regarded it as an unwelcome interruption of his labours. But as soon as he found his disease assuming a more serious character he gave heed to the warning and set his house in order, arranging all his affairs with calmness and precision, committing his family again and again to the care of a covenant-keeping God, and trusting himself to the Chief Shepherd whom he had served. The last sermon he had preached in his own church was on the 15th of March, 1863,—(the text was Heb. xi. 18–20),—and from that time for ten weeks he had occasion to exercise the same faith of which he then spake, "Accounting that God was able to raise him up even from the dead." To an inquiry from Dr. Hoge as to the ground of his hope, he replied, "I have examined as thoroughly as I could the foundation of my hope, and there I find my Redeemer. I love Him—I adore Him—I trust in Him. I am content." And on one occasion, when his utterance was only in the feeblest whisper, there was one affectionate ear that caught a few words intended only for the Master. "The lowest place—the lowest place, dear Jesus." Such a prayer was soon answered by the invitation, "Come up higher." He departed to be with Christ on the 29th of May, 1863, in the forty-eighth year of his age.

"More years had made us love him more."

To speak of the sorrow occasioned by such a death would require us to go beyond the home that has been rendered so lonely—beyond the church where a plain marble tablet in the rear of the pulpit, commemorates the ministry of "their Beloved First Pastor,"—beyond the community and the Presbytery amongst whom so valuable a life was spent. In the Synod of Ohio, which met in October, a casual observer could not but notice the tenderness and deep affection which seemed to pervade the body as often as this bereavement was alluded to. It was evident, as their own record expresses it, that they had "lost one of their most honoured and beloved standard bearers,"—one who was "cut off at the very acme of his usefulness, when his mind was still developing in intellectual robustness, as well as in the choicest graces of the Spirit." And still, among those who knew him and found it so easy to confide in his goodness, his name calls up a throng of tender and hallowed recollections that must live on in many hearts, till all are united with him in a more perfect companionship, and a more enduring joy. Thus blessed is the memory of a disciple whom Jesus loved—of a servant whom the Father honoured.

> "Thrice blest whose lives are faithful prayers,
> Whose loves in higher love endure;
> What souls possess themselves so pure?
> Or is there blessedness like theirs?"

To the writer of the foregoing sketch, the work of preparing this volume for the press has been entrusted. After some necessary and unavoidable delay, it is now submitted to the Christian public for their approval, and it is hoped also for their edification. In the selection of discourses, regard has been had to variety, both in topics and treatment, and to the presentation of the intellectual and spiritual excellences of the author's mind, with the view of continuing after his death the precious influences of his life. May the same spirit which prompted these utterances pervade the hearts and lives of all who here peruse them. J. M. P.

Zanesville, Ohio, March, 1864.

TRUTH IN LOVE.

SERMON I.

THE FRIEND OF GOD.

JAMES ii. 23.—*And he was called the Friend of God.*

THIS means somewhat more than that Abraham *was* the friend of God. "*This* honour have *all* the saints." The appellation was *bestowed* on the patriarch as an especial distinction, and in the same pre-eminent and peculiar sense it belongs to no other man.

How it was at first conferred does not appear. It may have been by an express and formal act of God, like that which changed his name from *Abram* to *Abraham*, when he was made the covenant-father of a multitude; or it may have been accorded to him by the suffrages of pious men in view of the signally gracious relations into which he was brought with the Most High.

The presumption is, perhaps, in favour of the former suggestion: but, however this may be, it amounts to the same thing, since the title is recognized in Scripture as justly belonging to him, and, in one instance at least, is *directly* given him by the Spirit of God. Assuring Israel of his everlasting favour, and speaking by the mouth of Isaiah, the Lord said—"Thou art my servant, Jacob, whom I have chosen, the seed of *Abram my friend.*"

This, however, is not the first place in Scripture where the title occurs. *Before* the days of Isaiah we find Jehoshaphat, in a time of danger, pleading it in prayer as an argument in behalf of Israel. "Art not thou our God, who didst drive out the inhabitants of this land before thy people Israel, and gavest it to the seed of *Abraham thy friend* for ever?" These passages, in connexion with the text, make it plain, that if this title was not formally given to the patriarch during his life-time, it afterwards obtained currency among the chosen people, and had, in the end, if not in the beginning, the express sanction of God.

Under that old dispensation of Divine grace there were many others whose "ways pleased the Lord"—righteous Abels whose sacrifices he accepted—wrestling Jacobs to whose mighty importunities he yielded—Enochs and Elijahs whom for their piety he took up to heaven in a chariot of fire—and a Moses, with whom he talked face to face, as a man to his friend: yet from among all these, and a host of others equally deserving of mention, but one man obtained the honourable distinction of being called the "Friend of God." Between the Old Testament and the New there are many beautiful correspondences: and the point in hand is not without its parallel. In the olden times of the church there may have been men gifted with loftier genius and called to the performance of more splendid services than was this simple shepherd of Mesopotamia. The great hero and prophet of the Exodus may have outshone him in the brilliance and magnitude of his achievements; and the "sweet Psalmist" of Israel—the man after God's own heart—may have been his superior in poetic inspiration; but in all those moral and spiritual endowments which *endear* a man to God, Abraham seems to have had no peer. Him, and him only, did Jehovah name his *Friend.*

When the new economy was inaugurated, its Divine Founder

called to service and favour a company of men variously gifted with intellectual and spiritual qualities. *Peter* is always named first in the catalogue of the apostles, and though he certainly was not invested with the *primacy*, as Romanists pretend, he was a man of position and great excellence of character. And far above him and all the rest, in learning, genius, and eloquence, soared the great apostle of the Gentiles. Both of these were men greatly endeared to the Saviour; yet neither of them was "*the disciple whom Jesus loved.*" This honour was assigned to the loving John, whose distinguishing excellence was spiritual rather than intellectual. Under the old economy, which in its characteristic spirit was one of promise and preparation, requiring men to believe in and hope for a future good, the man of pre-eminent *faith* was "the Friend of God." Under the New, whose great characteristic fact was the actual appearance of Israel's hope and consolation, and in this, the most glorious and touching display of God's love to the world, the disciple who "dwelt in love" was its most exact and complete type, and he it was whom Jesus suffered to rest on his bosom and received to the embrace of his peculiar love. Before Christ came in the flesh, those servants of God pleased him best who looked with most assurance for the fulfilment of the Divine promises; now that he *has* come, those disciples are the especial favourites of Heaven who thank, love, and serve him most for his unspeakable gift: and thus there is set before us all an open door into which we may enter and attain to this high and blessed distinction; for, says Jesus, "Ye are *my friends* if ye do whatsoever I command you."

And though each of us may not be visibly singled out from the midst of others, as were Abraham and John, and formally named the friends of Jesus and of God, this high and holy honour is conferred without exception on those who give their hearts and bow their knees to the Lord Jesus Christ. "Henceforth I call you not servants, but *I have called you friends.*"

The title is descriptive both of *character* and *privilege.* It imposes duty and it confers dignity. Friendship is in its nature *mutual.* It *gives* as well as takes: and the proverb that "he who hath friends must show himself friendly" applies not less to the spiritual and Divine relationship of which we now speak, than to the earthly and human friendships of which it is the recognized law and condition. The friendship of God and his people is *reciprocal.* In the sense of the text, he is not the Friend of any but those who are friendly to him. There is, however, a vital difference between the attitude of the parties. The love is now *mutual*, but it was not so at first. We did not purchase nor *win* his love toward us by the demonstration of ours to him. It was just the other way. "We love Him *because* He first loved us." By the greatness of the love wherewith He loved us even when we were dead in sins, He conquered our enmity and gained our affections, and thus, while in the beginning, the love was all on one side, it is now both mutual and cordial, and with full consent the holy God and redeemed sinners have entered into a solemn league of perpetual friendship.

1. It presents, in the *first place*, the aspect of duty; and we may occupy a few moments in noticing the CHARACTER of those who are admitted to the dignity and happiness of being made and called the "Friends of God."

The apostle tells us, in very express terms, that the bestowment of this privilege upon Abraham was vitally connected with his character and conduct, and particularly with *the obedience of faith.* "And the Scripture was fulfilled, which saith, Abraham believed God, and it was imputed unto him for righteousness, and he was called the Friend of God." Ver. 23. The Scripture here referred to and quoted, describes the faith which Abraham reposed in the promise of a numerous seed, at a time and in circumstances which rendered the fulfilment of the prediction a natural impossibility. There was nothing for sense or reason to work on, and he was shut up to pure and absolute faith in God: and nobly did he sustain the trial. "And being not weak in faith, he considered not"—the natural impossibilities which seemed to fetter Omnipotence, "and staggered not at the promise of God through unbelief, but was strong in faith, giving glory to God——."* The peculiar significance of this case is, that while it involved a severe trial of faith, it involved *nothing more.* It did not jeopard his interests, or wound his feelings, or require him to do anything, except just to believe in the power and faithfulness of God. This he did, and the example is put on record for the instruction and the admiration of the world. "It was not written for his sake alone that it was imputed to him; but for us also to whom it shall be imputed, if we believe on Him who raised up Jesus our Lord from the dead." And this gives us *implicit faith in the promises of God,* as the first characteristic of Abraham's spiritual seed, and heirs with him of the Divine friendship.

And the second is like, namely this, the faith which shows itself *in unswerving obedience to the Divine commands.* In the context, the apostle James is arguing with holy indignation against those professors of Christianity who rested their hope of justification and salvation on an intellectual, barren, and dead faith in the facts and doctrines of the gospel, and perverted the Pauline doctrine of "justification by faith, without the deeds of the law."

* Rom. iv. 19–21.

Of this doctrine Abraham was brought forward as the most illustrious example and proof. It is highly instructive and specially interesting to observe how the apostle James meets and corrects this perversion of a great truth. He does not contradict Paul's doctrine; he does not, in fact, supplement it by teaching anything which that apostle had omitted: and so far from conceding that the case of Abraham gave any countenance to the formalists who hung their cause upon it, he boldly brings the patriarch forward as the most conspicuous pattern of an obedient, working, fruitful faith which the annals of redemption record. His faith, unlike that of these pretenders, not only believed promises, but obeyed commands: and the latter, at least in Abraham's case, was the harder of the two. It was hard to *reason* and sense to believe the promise of a son in his old age; it was no less difficult to reason, and infinitely harder to feeling, to sacrifice that son of promise, at God's command, for "a burnt-offering to the Lord." Never was there *such* a mandate given to a servant of the Most High: and the manner in which he bowed to it, stands and will stand till the end of time to challenge the admiration and excite the wonder of the world! *Though* the command appeared to be at war with the Divine character, and inconsistent with the Divine promises, and violative of the tenderest and most sacred affections of the human heart, he asked not a question, he uttered not a word, he delayed not a moment, but went quietly forward under the naked power of the one supreme conviction that God, in all things, must be trusted and obeyed!

He has reached the designated hill. The altar is built in sad and solemn silence. Taken and bound by paternal hands, the son of promise and prayer, more comely and endeared than ever before, awaits the fatal stroke!

The sacrificial knife gleams in the sun-light, and, to all intents and purposes, the command is as thoroughly obeyed as if the life-blood of Isaac had run down on the altar, and the fire had consumed his body to ashes. At the critical moment, the angel of the Lord arrested him, and said, "By myself have I sworn, that in blessing I will bless thee—and in thy seed shall all the families of the earth be blessed: *because thou hast obeyed my voice.*" It was not simply faith, but the *obedience of faith*, which crowned the "father of the faithful" with everlasting honour, and, as the apostle intimates, secured for him the title of which we speak: "Seest thou, how faith wrought with his works, and by works was faith made perfect?" as a cause is seen to be perfect in its effect. "And the Scripture was fulfilled, which saith, Abraham believed God, and it was imputed unto him for righteousness: and he was called the Friend of God."

And thus we have a vivid representation of those qualities and characteristics which, above others, please God and win the tokens of his peculiar love: and though this sublime example of heroic faith may chide our unbelief, and rather quench than kindle the hope of successful emulation, it is comforting to know that "like precious faith" *in kind*, is possessed by every true child of God, and that it is not only within the compass of possibility, but plainly within the range of our duty and privilege, so to have our faith "*increased*," that we shall implicitly believe every Divine promise, and bow in willing obedience to every Divine command: and when this attainment is made, each of us shall be esteemed and treated, even if we are not "called" the "*Friend of God.*"

Unlike man, God is "no respecter of persons." His friendship is not determined by considerations of *birth*, or *position*, or *talents*, or *learning*, but is absolutely and in every case controlled by *spiritual excellence;* and that—thanks be to his gracious and holy name—is within the reach of the *weakest saint.* Trembling, downcast, sorrowful Christian, thou mayest be as dear and lie as close to the heart of Infinite Love, as any who occupy the highest places in church and state. Nay—what hinders thee from resting with John himself in the bosom of Jesus? Nothing hinders thee, but thy own unbelief and disobedience, for, has he not said,—"If *any man* hear my voice, and open the door, I will come in to him, and will sup with him, and he with me."* And "if a man love me, he will keep my words, and my Father will love him, and we will come unto him, and make our abode with him."

For any of us here present, to aspire to the especial friendship of Queen Victoria, Louis Napoleon, or some of those persons who reign as kings in the Republic of letters, besides being a piece of ridiculous vanity, would be to attempt a simple impossibility.

But what is impossible to get from men is more than possible to obtain from God. It is not presumption and folly, but the duty and privilege of every one of us, to aspire to the intimate acquaintance and eternal friendship of the Sovereign of all worlds! And this, as we shall now, secondly, proceed to show, is a blessing worthy of our most fervent desires and highest ambition.

And I think it is this aspect of the subject which is most prominently suggested in the text. It seems to be set forth, not only or mainly as the character of Abraham, but rather as his privilege and distinction that he was called "*the Friend of God.*" It involves much—in fact, comprehends everything, even as the promise in the covenant that was made with him—"I will be *a God* to thee," said everything in a single word.

1. The peculiar value and preciousness of the privilege depend

* Rev. iii. 20.

essentially on the *character* of the being whose friendship the Christian enjoys.

To weak and dependent natures like ours, made up so much of wants, and sorrows, and sympathies, friendship is quite indispensable. Not alone in the sentiment and poetry of youthful minds, but in soberest reality, *human* friendship is felt to be the best of earthly blessings. A thought more bitter, a feeling more oppressive, never passes through the heart, than that we are without the love and sympathy of others! Ethereal and spiritual though it be—rather, just because it is so—the sincere and manifested friendship of a fellow-creature goes direct to the heart, and mightily helps us, in our greatest sorrows and heaviest burdens. At such an hour it is prized more than gold, even as it is a commodity which gold cannot buy. Sincere friendship is very precious, whether it be shown by those above, below, or on an equality with ourselves. God's friendship, in its general nature, resembles that which mortal men feel for one another, since it is only by means of this experience which passes within our own bosoms, that we rise to the conception of a corresponding attribute in the Godhead. But while this is so, the infinite difference and distance between God and men require that we should ascribe qualities and attributes to *his friendship* as much superior to ours, as in all *other respects*, God is above man. Even in its best estate human friendship partakes of human frailty—at the very least, it is always subject to the limitations of human *weakness*. Man's heart, in contrast with God's, is as a cistern to the boundless ocean; and man's *hand*, even when moved by warmest friendship, unlike God's, is "shortened that it cannot" bestow the needed benefaction: and it is in reference to the point now in hand, that the High and Holy One himself—proclaims—"My thoughts are not your thoughts,

—neither are your ways my ways, saith the Lord. For as the heavens are higher than the earth, so are my ways higher than your ways, and my thoughts than your thoughts."

There is not a single attribute of friendship in which God's is not infinitely greater and better than man's. It is more *true.* He professes much, and *feels* all he professes. It is not always so with men. Their protestations of friendship are sometimes heartless, and even when earnest, are apt to conceal a large infusion of selfishness. Their kind offices come to an end whenever they cease to be remunerated. The most of what passes current under the name of friendship is the base metal of selfishness, thinly gilded over with the courtesies of social life: and a *true friend*, who sticketh closer than a brother, is indeed a treasure, rare as he is precious. Such a friend is God. He loves truly, deeply, tenderly, infinitely, and *for ever!* The jealousies, and mutations of earth, which so often "separate chief friends," and leave but the memories of broken ties, never touch the relations of amity and concord which Jehovah has established between himself and the people of his covenant and his care.

Not even that common and sure destroyer of earthly friendship—the ingratitude and forgetfulness of its objects—shall ever occasion the end or abatement of his. As he bestowed it at first without merit in its recipients, moved by his own compassion and good pleasure alone, so for the same reason he continues it from age to age, even "to everlasting," and one of its most blessed exhibitions is seen in the patience with which it endures the ungrateful returns we make, and the pains it takes to hold us in its kind embraces. "The mountains shall depart, and the hills be removed; but my kindness shall not depart from thee, neither shall the covenant of my peace be removed, saith the Lord that hath mercy on thee."

2. Descending from the consideration of the essential attributes of the Divine friendship, we find many elements of value and endearment in its *particular fruits and manifestations.* Friendship among men, implies *mutual confidence* and *confidential communications.* In proportion to its depth and intimacy will be the freedom and the frequency of this communion: and, though no material and substantial advantage is given or received, there is no one privilege of friendship more valued. It is the honour and joy of the Christian to be made, as it were, the confidant of God: "The secret of the Lord is with them that fear him." And, said Jesus to his disciples—"Henceforth I call you not servants, for the servant *knoweth not* what his lord doeth: but I have called you *friends; for all things that I have heard of my Father, I have made known unto you.*"

A signal example of this peculiar phase of the friendship of God, occurs in the history of Abraham himself. For the wickedness of Sodom, the Lord had determined to destroy it: and without interference or question from man or angel, he might have proceeded at once to execute the righteous decree. But he did not. There was one man who stood in peculiar relation both to the guilty city and to its holy Judge. Him, Jehovah remembered, and said—"Shall *I hide from Abraham* that thing which I do?" The connexion shows that the consideration which moved the Lord to make the disclosure of his purpose, existed in the *character* and *covenant-relation* which the patriarch sustained. The alliance and the amity were too close to allow concealment. This obedient believer must be apprised of the peril which threatened the city where Lot his kinsman dwelt. The sequel of intercession and deliverance you know.

And thus the Lord dealeth with all his *friends.* New revelations he may not give you, nor disclose unsearchable mysteries in which you have no interest, but his tenderest and deepest thoughts of love, he will reveal, and give you those "manifestations" of his friendship which the world cannot receive, and, in due time, when you shall have "overcome" by the blood of the "Lamb," and the power of his grace, he will give you to eat of the "hidden manna," and entrust to you "a white stone, and in the stone, a new name written which no man knoweth, saving he that receiveth it." So intimately and profoundly confidential is the intercourse of God with the souls whom he loves and blesses with his friendship.

It is a further attribute of true friendship, and pre-eminently so of God's, that *its attentions and benefactions are multiplied the most in time of our greatest necessity.* The homeliness of the proverb should not cause us to discard it in this connexion:—"A friend *in need*, is a friend *indeed.*"

This is the test of all profession. The sorrow, the necessity which exposes and repels the false, attracts the true; and a man's real friends, like the brothers of his flesh, are "born *for adversity.*" They fly to him in his distress. And such is the friendship of God. At all times near, he is a "*very* present help in trouble." Not quite sure that our friends may not regard our drafts on their kind offices too heavy or too frequent, we study to avoid the application, and spare them as far as possible: but God says, "Call upon me in the day of trouble; I will deliver thee, and thou shalt glorify me," by seeking my assistance, and relying to the uttermost on my salvation. That was a true testimony which Eliphaz bore to the character of God, when seeking to console the man of Uz, he said—"Behold, happy is the man whom God correcteth; therefore, despise not thou the chastening of the Almighty. For he maketh sore, and bindeth up, he woundeth, and his hands make whole. He shall deliver thee in six troubles; yea, in seven, there shall no *evil* touch thee."

Suffer we may in the flesh and in the spirit; and our sorrows, like Job's, while having their root in sin, may have their commission from God; but they do not prove either the want or the weakness of his love. Rather they are its clearest proofs and dearest pledges. "Faithful are the *wounds* of a *friend.*" Those are our best friends, and should be so esteemed, who labour with humility and charity to correct our faults and improve our character. There are hundreds of persons who would rather give us money, or visit us in affliction, or weep with us in bereavement, than utter one humble, kind, faithful word for such a purpose as this. Only the truest and best of friends can do it. Harsh and proud *complaints* are plentiful; tender admonitions are rare, and are often the greatest favour which it is possible to confer. And in this matter we should judge of God as we do of one another. The smarting rod and the soothing whispers of his Spirit are expressions of the same love, and there is not a whit less of friendship in the one than in the other.

Friendship *delights to increase the happiness by promoting the advantage and honour of its objects.*

A person in the possession of riches and the enjoyment of place and power, is accustomed and expected to *provide for his friends.* He secures them positions, and exerts his influence to advance their interests. The friendship of God reveals itself in similar manifestations; and in view of his *resources* and his *power*, what may we not expect? What he *has* to give, that he *will* give—the adoption of sons—the inheritance of heirs—the honour and elevation of kings and priests. Now, for their own good, and because the purposes of God toward the world require it, they are kept under tutors and governors, and appointed to live in obscurity. But a day is ordained and hastening on for their glorious manifestation. Then he will publicly own them as his friends—will call them his "jewels"—and will satisfy his own love and theirs by taking them to his bosom for ever. With the friendship of God, now and to all eternity, what more does the Christian need? Beloved, rest satisfied with your portion. Why lament the loss of a drop, when the ocean of God's unchangeable and infinite love remains? If you had not another friend in the universe, *He is enough.* "Whom have I in heaven but thee? and there is none upon earth that I desire besides thee. My flesh and my heart faileth: but God is the strength of my heart, and my portion for ever."

It is sad to think and say that the relations existing between some of us and God are not those of *friendship.* It is beyond contradiction that some of you do not act a friendly part toward God. You spurn his *authority*—you disobey his commands—you refuse his salvation.

In the circumstances of the case, this open hostility betrays an unfriendly heart: and so far from being God's friends, you are his "*enemies;*" and so he accounts and calls you. This wicked enmity of yours to God necessitates on his part a *holy opposition* to you: and, in this respect, so far from being your *friend,* he is your *adversary.*

But notwithstanding this, he is willing to be *reconciled;* and with an ambassage of peace I am now come to you. "Now, then, we are ambassadors for Christ, as though God did beseech you by us: we pray you in Christ's stead, be ye reconciled to God." "Acquaint now thyself with him, and be at peace: thereby good shall come unto thee."

SERMON II.

THE LESSONS OF THE FLOWERS.

LUKE xii. 27.—*Consider the Lilies.*

SOME men walk through the world with eyes shut, seeing nothing and learning nothing. Persons, things, events with which they come in contact, are not studied—are hardly conceived of with any distinctness, and are, of course, forgotten. Others, from natural aptitude and from habit, not only see, but *observe* what passes. They note the causes and the consequences, the peculiarities and the relations of actions and events, and acquire a fund of practical philosophy, which is of the highest value in the affairs of life. That which is thus seen to be our wisdom, in relation to the interests of earth, becomes, in the higher sphere of religion, a *duty.*

God reveals himself in the books of Nature and of Revelation, and the same Divine Messenger who bids us "Search the Scriptures," gives this other command—"*Consider the lilies.*" These books are emanations from the same source—rays from the same sun—and if one shines with a fuller blaze, it is no reason why the mild radiance or the single beam of the other should be despised. "There is one glory of the sun, and another glory of the moon, and another glory of the stars," but all alike borrow their glory from the "Father of lights."

Inviting us to study the lilies, the Saviour only makes a special application of the general duty of considering the works of God. It is an act of piety, and a source of pure delight. "The works of the Lord are great; sought out of all them that have pleasure therein." The consideration of them which is inculcated in Scripture, is an exercise of devout meditation, which beholds *God* in his works, sees the Creator in the creature, and rises through the visible and the material, up to the unseen, the spiritual and the eternal.

Many consider the works of God in another manner, and for a different purpose. The man of science studies nature not as the workmanship of God, but precisely as a mechanic would study a curious machine which the hand of man had constructed, or as an artist would view a piece of statuary which human genius and skill had conceived and chiseled. Such a man sees nothing but matter and its laws; and instead of ascending through nature up to nature's God, many a naturalist loses himself in the labyrinth of that Divine mechanism which needs only the recognition of a living and personal Creator to reduce it all to perfect unity and order, and to make it radiant with the beauty of the Lord.

There is certainly no inconsistency between the scientific study of nature, and the exercise of faith and devotion. The natural sciences, as Botany, Geology, and Astronomy, furnish numberless and obvious proofs of creative power, and skill, and goodness; and nothing can account for the fact that the student of Nature fails to recognize and worship God, but that the human soul is "out of chord" with the harmonies of the universe. The study of nature tends to piety, and the Scriptures invite to it. The man of deepest learning and widest acquaintance with the works of God will, most likely, believe the teachings of Scripture, because he sees the harmony of nature and revelation

Professor Henry of the Smithsonian Institute, is reported to have said that he knew but one thoroughly scientific man in the United States, who was an avowed Infidel. "An undevout astronomer is mad." The man of sound mind and of right heart will rather exclaim with the Shepherd of Bethlehem—"When I consider thy heavens, the work of thy fingers; the moon and the stars, which thou hast ordained; what is man, that thou art mindful of him? O Lord, our Lord, how excellent is thy name in all the earth!"

While this transition from the study of nature as a Science, to the religious consideration of it, as a manifestation of God, is easy and natural, it is not *necessary;* and we advert to the difference, just to mark the various grades of interest and points of view from which men look, in studying the works of God. In some respects, the scientific study is the lowest. Next above this, is that admiration and enjoyment of nature which is experienced by persons endowed with poetic sensibility, and indeed by almost all persons at some period and in some circumstances of their lives. The dullest eye will brighten, and the coldest heart awake from its torpor, and rise from the routine of its commonplaces, when the beautiful, the grand, the majestic, or the terrible in nature is suddenly presented: and some minds of exquisite sensibility will dwell on scenes of material loveliness and splendour, with a tenderness of feeling, and a mysterious depth of emotion, and with blending and changing shades of thought, which no language, not even the dialect of loftiest poetry can express. The soul's response and sympathy in thus communing with nature in her varied forms of mild beauty, and majestic greatness, and terrible grandeur, bears a certain resemblance to *piety* and *worship;* and we admit that it is far higher and purer and more ennobling to the spirit, than the lower studies of natural science, which *analyzes* nature, and exhibits the bony skeleton of her naked laws; and which does even this for the material uses to which her laws and forces may be applied. But we must remind you that admiration of nature is a very different thing from *adoring* the *God* of nature. Dissevering the creature from the Creator, it is, at the best, a species of refined idolatry, which, like the ancient heathenism, burns incense to the gods of the mountains and the valleys, the groves and the streams, and adores the sun, the moon, and the stars, rather than the eternal and invisible God, who is above all, and through all, and in them all. In point of historical fact, idolatry had this precise origin. Not liking to retain the knowledge of a holy and personal God, the Ruler and Judge of men, and yet not able, and perhaps not willing, to relinquish all conception and belief of a Deity, men *began* by substituting for the invisible divinity, the greatest and most beneficent of his works, and ended the backward and downward movement, by worshipping "four-footed beasts, and creeping things." It would thus appear that the admiration and enjoyment of nature is not necessarily a *religious* sentiment: and those dreaming spirits deceive themselves, who put the excitement of their natural sensibilities in the stead of that devotion which makes the beautiful and the grand in nature mere stepping-stones for its ascent to the throne of God. The study of nature, to which the Saviour invites us, has express regard to the *relation* which all material things sustain to the *Author* of nature. The study of the *lily* as it is *in itself*, is *botany;* the study of it as it stands related on the one side to *God*, who made it, and on the other to *man*, for whom it is made, is *natural theology.* "Consider the lilies," not for the beauty they possess, but for that beauty as an adornment given them by a Divine hand. It is God who "*so clothes* the lilies." Hence their capacity and power to become our teachers. It is relationship to God that gives everything its meaning, and from this point of view must its significance and purpose be studied.

Descending from these generalities, we may remark *the exquisite finish and perfection of the lily.* The Scriptures tell us that the Son of God, who bids us consider the lilies, is their *Maker.* He is more than willing that his work should be scrutinized. It will bear inspection, and the severest test which even the microscope applies reveals no fault nor coarseness in the Divine workmanship. Not so with the creations of human skill! The most perfect thing which man ever made was not absolutely faultless. No book that was ever written, no picture ever painted, no house ever built, was in every minutest particular above criticism. The limitation and weakness of the creature is impressed on all that man does: and in like manner the signature of an infinitely wise and Almighty God is written on all his works, the least not less than the greatest. "As for God, his work is perfect." "Nothing can be put to it, nor anything taken from it; and God doeth it that men should fear before him." There are not, in all the universe, any unfinished works of God, nor any abandoned relics of experiments that did not succeed, nor is there any single thing which develops according to the law impressed by him, that is not perfect in its kind. The infinite and unapproachable godhead of the Creator is seen in the absolute completeness and perfection of his works. Not only cannot men suggest any improvement in anything he has made, but the highest achievements of their genius and art consist in a feeble imitation of the Divine patterns which are set before them in nature. How impotent is man to create a lily! What a botch is his best imitation! Without life, without fragrance, without growth. So true is the poet's lines—

> "There's not a flower
> But shows, in freckle, streak, or stain, the marks
> Of his *unrivalled* pencil."

Coming nearer to the specific theme of the text, we may "Consider the lilies" as *flowers*, and gather the lessons taught by their *exquisite beauty*. It is an obvious though very important remark of Dr. Paley, that God might have made this world far different from what it is, and yet made it good enough to support the human race in mere existence. Every touch might have been a sting, every sound a discord, and yet men might have existed. In that case, natural theology would have given us little or no proof of the Divine benevolence. But how different is the world in point of fact!

Beyond what is *necessary*, God has given what is *comfortable;* and above what is comfortable, he has added that which decorates the world and gratifies that sense of the beautiful which he has inwrought with our mental constitution. How pure this pleasure is, and how linked with our proper nature, is shown by the fact, that when God had made man in his own image, he placed him in a garden of material delights, where was found not only every tree that was *good for food*, but such as were "pleasant to the eye." Eden was decked with flowers, and when the sinless pair walked amid its aromatic groves, and regaled their senses with the fragrance they diffused, the incense of their devotions went up with more buoyant joy and holier gratitude. Our minds are familiarized with the argument for the Being and Character of God, which is derived from the palpable *uses* which are accomplished by the objects and the order of nature. The goodness of God in the shining sun, and the falling rain, and the flowing river, and the changing seasons, is recognized because it is so obvious. Not happiness alone, but life depends on these benign arrangements.

The use of the beautiful, which the Divine Architect has lavished on all his works, is not so manifest and obtrusive; it is more spiritual and subtle: yet who can for a moment doubt that the very same wisdom and love which placed the burning and glorious sun in the firmament are concerned in the creation of every insect that basks in his beams, and every flower that unfolds its petals to his light?

What, then, are the divine lessons that we read in the *beauty* of the lily? And first of all, the inquiry starts, does it teach us aught of the nature and character of God *as he is in himself?* Why does *beauty* emanate from God? Is it not because the archetype and ideal of beauty is in his own eternal mind? And all the material loveliness of the universe is but the efflux of what, from everlasting, was in the Creator. From the fact that God created man in his own pure image, we justly infer that he loves, and, to speak as men, admires the beauty of holiness: and may we not, by the self-same logic, reverently adopt the conclusion that the Maker of the flowers admires the beautiful creation of his own hands?

If any feel as if this were treading on questionable ground, we will not press the suggestion, and proceed to another in which all will agree: The beauty of the lilies, and of all the floral kingdom, and indeed, of all the visible creation, is an evidence of God's *paternal kindness, and of his desire that his creatures should have a happy and delighted existence.*

The beauty of nature makes a large contribution to the sum of our enjoyment, and would make more, if we entered more fully into the design of God. The lowest view of this argument is that which has respect to the *mere gratification of sense* which is derived from the fragrant odour and stainless beauty of the flowers. This delighted sensation is of no small value as an argument for the Divine benevolence, when it is considered how easy it would have been to Almighty power to have left all nature bare and barren of these adornments, and to have doomed us to pass through life without ever being permitted to gaze on the beauty or to inhale the scent of flowers. If no higher use were assigned them, the lilies were not made in vain. But have they not a nobler ministry, and are they not capable of imparting a higher good than the momentary sensation they excite? In the absence of express revelation on the subject, we infer the use for which anything is made from its *nature and adaptations.* For what use the fields wave with yellow grain, and the giant oak bares its head in the forest, and the orchards bend with luscious fruit, we know from the *fitness* of each and all. And in like manner we may know from their natural adaptation as well as from their experienced effect, for what end God has garnished the earth with flowers. Through that sense of the beautiful which he has given us, they speak to the heart, and *have a peculiar power over the affections.* Is there not a profound connexion between the beautiful in nature, and the beautiful in manners, and in morality, yea, and the higher beauty of holiness?

Does not the fragile nature and texture of the lily, the grace of whose fashion perishes in a day, and cannot bear the touch of rudeness, directly teach us the lesson of *gentleness?* and its robe of stainless white, the lesson of purity? With their meek modesty and quiet loveliness, flowers seem in natural affinity with "whatsoever things are pure and lovely, and of good report," and the "fruit of the Spirit which is love, joy, and peace," might be thought to flourish best, in those whose *hearts* are in unison with their sweet influences and suggestions.

In a word, flowers are clothed with a moral power, and are appointed to a humble ministry to our intellectual and spiritual nature.

This point is so admirably put by another, that you will more than pardon the quotation of his eloquent words: "Here is more than infinite skill. *Here is a moral power.* Here is an appeal to the most delicate susceptibilities of my soul. Here is a voice to my heart. As adjuncts, and scarlet-robed attendants of religion, these things are adapted to elevate my affections, and to educate my nature for the scenery of heaven. Let none misunderstand: nature is not revelation: beauty is not piety; *taste is not holiness.* Let India, and South America, and Bishop Heber witness to this:—

"What though the spicy breezes
Blow soft o'er Ceylon's isle,
Though every prospect pleases,
And only man is vile?"

Still I do affirm that the ministry of the beautiful is a reality; flowers have a mission, and the lesson of the lilies is one which Christian hearts will always love to study."*

The force of this argument is enhanced by the consideration that man has lost the primeval holiness in which he was created, and has been driven from the Paradise in which he was placed.

For his sake the world was cursed, so that it should bring forth thorns and briers, the remembrancers of his sin, to pain and trouble him. But surely, it is a significant fact, and not without the germ of a blessed hope, that the earth on the face of which he was sent abroad was not so blasted with the curse of Heaven, that its every aspect should frown the wrath of God upon him, and sink him in despair. If Paradise were never to be regained, the cherubim with flaming sword might have been seen in every

* Rev. F. G. Clark, of New York.

object that met the eye: but instead of this, what do we behold? The flowers bloom on every field, and by every dwelling, and even "waste their sweetness on the desert air," where not even the wandering Arab inhales their fragrance, or observes their beauty. The roses bloom amid the very thorns that sting us while we gather them; and what is the significance of this? Is it not that the earth is not irredeemably cursed? and that man is not abandoned of God, but is dealt with in a way of mercy for his recovery; and this, moreover, by the ministry of ten thousand agencies, from the mighty angels who camp around the just, to the lily of the field, which breathes to-day its gentle lesson, and to-morrow fades for ever?

That flowers do sustain such relations and fulfil such a ministry to the spiritual nature of man, is in agreement with the typical significance ascribed to them in the word of God. They are fit types of *moral beauty* and *Divine grace*, and are so used by the Spirit of inspiration. The first and highest use of the *lily*, is to image the beauty, and glory, and fragrant grace of the Lord Jesus Christ, who, in the gorgeous symbolism of that Song of songs, declares—"I am the Rose of Sharon, and the Lily of the Valley."

The image is infinitely below the glorious original; yet, addressed as it is to sense and to our inner sense of the beautiful, it conveys a vivid conception of Him whose name is as ointment poured forth. Portraying, in a special aspect, the character of the Divine pattern to which all Christians are conformed, the lily is also a scriptural emblem of the *church*. Believers have the same mind which was also in Him, and hence, "to express their residence in the world, and how he values them above others," he says—"As the lily among thorns, so is my love among the daughters."

And there is yet another relation in which they stand to Jesus. It is expressed in the words of his admiring Bride, the church: "My Beloved is gone down into his garden, to the beds of spices, to feed in the gardens, *and to gather lilies.*" What can this be? The owner of a flower-garden cultivates it for himself; he goes into it to inhale its sweet odours, and if he plucks a lily, it is to bring it nearer to himself, to carry it with him, and, perhaps, to weave it into a coronal of beauty, that, in its new setting, it may be the more admired and the more enjoyed. You can interpret the parable.

The Saviour came into his garden when he entered the congregation of his saints and the families of his redeemed, and took to himself at one time the buds of promise which had enshrined themselves in our affections; and again, those expanded flowers which had fulfilled their mission below, and were ready to be transferred to the brighter skies and balmier air where they might bloom for ever. Murmur not: *He* took them, whose they are, and he will restore them when he comes to garner the ripe harvest of the world. Then every flower that ever bloomed in the garden of his grace below, will find its appropriate place and use in the Paradise above. And this reminds us that *heaven* is *pictured* as a place of surpassing beauty, through whose broad avenues there flows the crystal river, on whose banks grows the tree of life, which yieldeth her fruit every month, and whose leaves are for the healing of the nations. An Eden of sensible delights, and much less a Mohammedan or Pagan Elysium of carnal lusts, is not the heaven prepared for the redeemed who shall follow the Lamb on the celestial plains: yet it is certain that in that glorious world the redeemed from among men will be clothed with *bodies*, and their dwelling will be a *place;* and why should we doubt that their *sense of the beautiful*, which God now cultivates and makes an instrument of their renewal, will find its perfect and ceaseless gratification in the material glory and loveliness of their eternal abode?

There yet remains to be noticed the lesson which the Saviour deduces. It is, in appearance at least, more obvious and practical than those of which we have been treating, though not more true and real. It is the lesson of *a peaceful and perfect trust* in the providential care of God. To learn this lesson, "*Consider the lilies;* how they grow: they toil not, they spin not, and yet I say unto you, that Solomon, in all his glory, was not arrayed like one of these." This is the premise of the argument. The lily's peerless beauty and unapproachable superiority to all the adornments of art, is a fact which all may observe, and, no doubt, had been observed a thousand times: but the *inference* remained to be drawn by Him who came to interpret at once both Nature and the God of Nature. The logic is irresistible. The reasoning is what books on logic call the argument *a fortiori*. It is reasoning from the stronger to the weaker case. If, in a given case, a thing which is difficult and unlikely to happen has been done, *much more*, in the same circumstances, will that which is *easy and probable* take place. It is the argument which Paul uses to assure the justified sinner of salvation, when he says, "He that spared not his own Son, but delivered him up for us all, how shall he not with him also freely give us all things?"

Thus in the context, the Saviour reasons in reference to God's providential care of men: "If then God so clothe the grass, which is to-day in the field, and to-morrow is cast into the oven; *how much more* will he clothe you, O ye of little faith!" *Reason* cannot resist the argument, and if our hearts were not filled with earthliness and unbelief, such a demonstration and assurance of the paternal care of God, would quiet every anxiety, and keep our souls in perfect peace. Are not ye of more value than the fading flower? If God, in the lavish expenditure of his resources and his skill, arrays it in tints of divinest beauty, will he deny to those who trust in him, the raiment that they *need?* Ye careworn souls, who destroy your own peace, and dishonour your God, by useless and unchristian anxieties,—"Consider the lilies," and let them preach to you the blessed lesson of trust in the providential government and fatherly love of God. Important at all times, the lesson is especially needed *now*, when the foundations of society are shaking, and men are tempted to even more than common worldliness of spirit, and distrust of Heaven. Cast the burden of your care on him who careth for you, that your heart may be light and free for his service in the things which pertain to the immortal soul, and the life everlasting.

"Seek ye first the kingdom of God, and his righteousness, and all these things shall be added unto you." Matt. vi. 33.

The general subject before us, opens a field of delightful meditation to the devout and thoughtful. It teaches us how to read the volume of that revelation which the invisible God has unrolled in nature, and shows us how to find treasures of wisdom and fountains of pleasure, and means of moral improvement in every creature that God hath made. Without either the telescope or the microscope, the naked eye and the unscientific mind has access to a world of wonders which proclaim the Creator's eternal power and goodness.

And the general reason is, that we should school ourselves to *study God in nature.* Then the brightness of every flower, and the carol of every bird, and the murmur of every brook, and the deep blue sky over-arching all, will speak to us of truth and piety, of God and heaven, and help the soul in its aspirings to a nobler and better life.

And let me say to our friends who have not yet "received the atonement," nor known by sweet experience the blessedness of reconciliation with God, that the highest and best enjoyment of *nature* is possible only to those who know and love its *Divine author.* To them it is said, "All things are yours:" and "Blessed are the meek, for they shall inherit the earth."

To the man of clean hands, and of a pure conscience, and of a heavenly hope, all creation shows the beauty of the Lord: and every natural object whispers peace. He sees and enjoys God in nature.

> "His are the mountains, and the valleys his,
> And the resplendent rivers, his to enjoy,
> With a propriety that none can feel,
> But who, with filial confidence inspired,
> Can lift to heaven an unpresumptuous eye,
> And smiling say,—'My Father made them all?'"

Be thou reconciled to God. Become a new creature in Christ Jesus, and when old things shall pass away, and all things become new, the world itself will seem a new creation, and you will have an earnest of what awaits the regenerated church, in "the new heavens and the new earth."

SERMON III.

ORPAH AND RUTH.

RUTH i. 14.—*And Orpah kissed her mother-in-law, but Ruth clave unto her.*

THERE is very much in the character and position of this little group, which appeals to the softer sensibilities of the heart.

They had been together in seasons of joy, and had all drunk of the same bitter cup of affliction. Each of them had for a limited period discharged the duties, and enjoyed the pleasures of married life: and each in her turn had felt the heart-crushing agony of bereavement.

One of them, advanced in life, was—in the sense of Paul's words, "a widow indeed," and "desolate,"—trusting in God, and continuing in prayers and supplications night and day.

The other two were *young*. Though their earthly prospects had been prematurely blasted, they might hope to live for many years; and at this point of time, might be regarded as starting out anew on their journey of life; and the circumstances in which they were now placed, were of such a nature as to impart to their action in the premises very great importance, and a decisive bearing on both their temporal and spiritual interests. It was, in fact, a *crisis*, from which an immortal career was to take its point of departure. The question which these two young women were then to decide, and which there is every reason to believe, they *did* decide, was not that of a continued residence in the country of *Moab*, the land of their nativity, or an emigration to the land of Israel. It was infinitely more profound and far-reaching. Essentially and really it was the question of their translation out of the kingdom of darkness into the kingdom of God—the same which meets every one of us as we journey through life, and which sooner or later is decided by us all, to our eternal joy or grief.—Shall I yield to the dictates of conscience, and the calls of God; cast in my lot with his people, and take his favour for my portion?

The different ways in which this question is disposed of, are palpably exhibited in the conduct of *Orpah* and *Ruth:* and we may very fairly regard each of them as the representative of a class; to which it may possibly appear that we ourselves belong. And without thereby limiting the application of the text to persons of any particular age or sex, it may, perhaps, awaken more interest in the minds of a portion of my hearers, to remind you that these individuals were *young women*, who have their antitypes in every congregation.

Let us, for a little season, meditate on the contrast which is here represented. 1. Our first point is *Orpah's return.* Her *kiss* was that of valediction and parting. Having at first, along with Ruth, expressed her determination to go with Naomi to Canaan, she afterwards changed her mind, and, though with evident sadness, and a degree of reluctance, went back to live and die in the land of her nativity. Her conduct presents very distinctly two phases of character and experience which are reproduced in every generation. It reveals, so to speak, that *dualism* in the soul—that struggle of conscience with corruption —of the religious sensibilities with the deep ungodliness of our nature—which is familiar to the experience of all who live under the ministrations and influences of the gospel. Who has not felt himself pulled in contrary directions? not only as to whether he should do or not do a given action, but as to the great and decisive question of surrendering his heart to God? Reason, conscience, and the fear of punishment urge to the surrender: aversion to holiness, and the love of a sinful life, hinder and prevent it. In the conduct of Orpah, these opposing forces are visibly depicted.

She *went a certain distance* with her mother-in-law. We will not strain a significance out of this which does not fairly belong to it. Doubtless it was personal attachment mainly which wrought with her, and there is no *positive* evidence that she had in mind the bearing her conduct might have on her spiritual interests and the salvation of her soul.

But when we consider who *Naomi was*—a Jewess—a worshipper of Jehovah—a woman of devoted piety, whose holy and consistent life had been making its mark on the mind of Orpah, for years together, in scenes of joy and sorrow;—and when we further remember that the simple act of removing her residence from Moab to Canaan involved a change of religion—and necessitated the renunciation of idol-worship—it is plain that a religious element must have blended with the personal affection which drew her after Naomi. Not her heart of natural love only, but her *conscience* led in that direction: and she went a certain distance, intending, as it would seem, to go all the way and have her part and portion with the people and God of her pious relative.

Not with the desire of turning them from their purpose, but, as we must suppose, for the sake of putting their sincerity and earnestness to the test, "Naomi said unto her two daughters-in-law, Go, return each to her mother's house: The Lord deal kindly with you, as ye have dealt with the dead and with me. The Lord grant that ye may find rest, each of you in the house of her husband. Then she kissed them, and they lifted up their voice and wept." At first suggestion, the thought of separation was too painful to be entertained; and they both exclaimed, "Surely we will return with thee unto thy people." As if determined to subject their characters and purposes to the most thorough probation, she then stated in detail the drawbacks and disadvantages involved in carrying out the resolution which they had just announced: and this occasioned a new outburst of grief; but it also brought on the crisis, and developed what before had been latent—the *difference* in their characters.

"Orpah kissed her mother-in-law," and departed. It cost her a struggle, but she *did* it, and there are many like her. It is a very common thing among the unconverted—especially the young, and most of all, perhaps, among young females, to feel tenderly and strongly attracted towards the people of God and a life of piety: and it is lamentably common with those who are the subjects of this experience, and have taken some steps Zionward, inquiring the way, to stop, halt a while between two opinions, and at last go back to the place of departure, and die and perish in the land of their nativity. A superficial conviction of sin, sympathy with the religious feeling which prevails around them, personal attachment to individual Christians, and motives less pure, may start a person on a course of external deportment and duty which gives promise of conversion and salvation. But he starts without "counting the cost;" and hence, when brought into contact with the difficulties and sacrifices involved in the undertaking, he turns back, and is seen no more in company with those whose faces are resolutely set toward the Zion of God. The life and ministry of Jesus Christ brought many such characters to light. Such was "a certain Scribe" who said—"Master, I will follow thee whithersoever thou goest;" but who immediately disappeared on our Lord's saying—"The foxes have holes, and the birds of the air have nests; but the Son of man hath not where to lay his head." Such were a multitude who, having begun to follow him from interested motives, presently stumbled at his "hard sayings," and went back and walked no more with him: and as an exact type of this class, and as a counterpart of the case in hand, we may mention the *young ruler* who came running to Jesus, and kneeling at his feet, inquired, What he must do to inherit eternal life. A more hopeful inquirer it would be hard to imagine. As to the letter, he had kept the commandments of God from his youth; his morals were pure, his manner profoundly respectful, his feeling deep! Surely he is just now taking the decisive step—entering in at the strait gate!

We should have thought so: but the Searcher of hearts judged otherwise, and applied a test which revealed to the man his heart: and, like Orpah, he *went away sorrowful*—with disappointment and grief depicted on his face.

What has now been said may suffice as to the influences and feelings which induced Orpah to go as far as she did: but here an important question meets us: Why did they not carry her forward? Why did she turn back? The inconveniences and hardships ahead, as represented by Naomi, had some influence on the result; but they were not insurmountable: a resolute and undivided heart could overcome such obstacles.

Ruth did it. There must have been at work a secret and powerful influence drawing her in the opposite direction. And what this was, we are not left to conjecture, or to infer from the general doctrine of Scripture, in regard to the sinfulness of the human heart. The narrative supplies the explanation. Just as Orpah turned to depart, Naomi made a last appeal to Ruth, to see whether example might not shake her constancy. "Behold, thy sister-in-law is gone back *unto her people*, and *unto her gods;* return thou after thy sister-in-law." These words, to our mind, assert not only the general nature and effect of Orpah's conduct, but the *motive* also which induced it.

It was *love to her sinful countrymen and kindred*, and *devotion to idols.* These were the two strong bonds by which Satan held her soul in captivity—the powers which counteracted and overcame the dictates of conscience, and sundered her connexion with those to whom she was nearly related and tenderly attached. And the same influences have had the same effect on multitudes besides. Domestic and social connexions, with those who fear not God, are among the most operative and powerful causes of continued impenitence.

Common topics of conversation, common sources of pleasure, and a common alienation from God, are their bond of union—a magnetic attraction which draws unbelieving minds and earthly hearts together. The love of such associations and friendships—the unwillingness to displease—want of courage to be singular—and the fear of ridicule and contempt, are powerful impediments to conversion. They are continually suppressing conviction, and quenching the Spirit in thousands of hearts. To make their operation palpable as possible, suppose the case of a young lady who is devoted to fashionable pleasures. She lives in *society.* Her most intimate friends, are, like herself, thoughtless on the subject of religion. She meets with them often—drinks into their spirit, and is never so happy as when mingling in the festivities of a party. The *dance* is her Elysium. Leading such a life, she is not a very likely subject of serious thought. Nevertheless, the gay votaries of pleasure do sometimes receive the visitations of God's Spirit. It thus happens to her. A sermon, a providence, the solemn appeal of a pious friend, brings the subject before her mind, and conscience and the Spirit unite to give it impression and power. She feels that she ought to be a Christian; that the life she is leading is neither right nor safe. And while these thoughts occupy her mind, she is half-persuaded to act on them, and "go" with the people of God. Like *Orpah*, she takes some steps in that direction, then stops, and at last turns back. Why does she act thus? I appeal to the experience of my hearers, especially of the young, and most especially of young women, if the consideration which first occurred and operated with greatest power, was not the thought that by becoming a Christian, you would be compelled to give up your intimacy with gay and godless companions—renouncing the pleasures of the ball-room, the card-table, and all the kindred practices in which undevout and earthly minds delight?

Your social connexions, enfolding you like a net-work, held you fast, and after an ineffectual struggle you determined—regretfully and sadly it may be—but still you determined, to give the matter of your soul's salvation the go-by, at least for the present, and to drink the cup of sinful pleasure a little longer.

You "*went back to your own people*," and you are an impenitent sinner to-day, because you *would not* separate yourself from those who were living in estrangement from God.

But it is further said of Orpah, that she "went *back unto her gods.*"

The gods of the Moabites were, of course, false deities—idols which had usurped the name, the place, the prerogatives, and the worship due to Jehovah, who alone is the Creator, Lord, and Redeemer of men. Of these the principal were *Chemosh* and Baal-Peor, of whose peculiar worship little is known, except that what was rendered to the latter, is said to have been emphatically an "abominable idolatry." To these impure rites and God-dishonouring altars Orpah returned, and gave to these vile usurpers the homage and affection of her soul.

And it was because she preferred to be an *idolater*, that she did not become a worshipper of the God of Israel. Her heart was fully possessed by that infatuation and blindness which ever characterize idolatry: and though she had seen the lovely fruits of a purer religion in the character and life of Naomi, she could not be won from it: and hence, after meditating a change, and for a season purposing to break away from its bewitching attractions, her resolution failed, and she went "back to her gods"—to live and die, and perish at their altars.

I need not inform you, my friends, that *idolatry* may exist where no temple or priest, image or victim, is seen. "There are gods, many," and idolaters many, where the light of revelation shines with fullest blaze. And I suppose that the guiltiest and most God-dishonouring idolaters on the face of the earth are those *among ourselves* who "are lovers of pleasure more than lovers of God," who "worship and serve the creature more than the Creator."

Spiritual idolatry is the common and fundamental wickedness of the impenitent in Christian lands; and it is the mightiest impediment to their conversion. It lies at the foundation of what we have before spoken of—the sinner's unwillingness to forsake Christless and worldly companions. This is the precise thing which hinders your salvation. Your heart is ungodly and *idolatrous.* You love the pleasures of sin more than the God who created you, and the Saviour who died for you.

You may make an idol of your *person*, of your *attire;* of *company*, of an *amusement*, of a *novel*, of any "trifle light as air," so fearfully atheistic is man's apostate nature. Many of you, perhaps, have often done already, and I greatly fear will do again to-day, the thing which Orpah did—*go back to your gods!*

But why will you do it? Why will ye die? I entreat you not to do it. I warn you against it. It is a *great iniquity*, though often committed by very *amiable persons.* We feel a great interest in Orpah. She possessed tender sensibilities, warm affections; and Naomi, who had reason to know, bore witness that she had been a dutiful daughter and a devoted wife. But—she was an *idolater.* She preferred to prostrate herself at the shrine of a filthy idol, rather than "compass the altar" of Jehovah, and join in the acts of a pure and sanctifying worship!

And I must tell you that amiability, sweetness of temper, grace of person and manners, dutifulness as a daughter, kindness as a sister, devotion as a wife, will avail you nothing, if over against it all is set an ungodly heart.

Orpah committed a great *error*, as well as a great sin, in going back. She chose what for the present was the more agreeable course—yielding to the impulse of feeling, rather than following the dictates of judgment and conscience. What became of her in life, death, and eternity, is not recorded. The natural presumption is against her. The probability is, that she lived and died in her sins, a worshipper of idols, and went to an unblest eternity—an eternity the more unblest, because, at one time in her history, she had been powerfully attracted towards God and salvation, and "almost persuaded" to cast in her lot with those who were going to Canaan and to heaven.

Her conduct is, therefore, our "ensample," not for *imitation*, but for *warning*—a beacon-light set up on a dangerous coast where multitudes have made shipwreck of faith and a good conscience, and lost their souls.

"Remember *Lot's wife*," whose lingering, regretful look at the accursed city cost her her life. Remember *Orpah*, who, after having actually started to the Land of Promise, lost heart, and drew "back to perdition." Keep these monuments of *unbelief*, *worldliness*, and *idolatry* ever in your view, and flee the danger which they indicate: and when your hearts are possessed with a salutary fear of going in the wrong direction, turn to the beautiful and persuasive example of *Ruth*, and peradventure, it may win you to the pleasant ways of wisdom, and put your feet in that path, the end of which is "glory, honour, and immortality."

II. "And Orpah kissed her mother-in-law, but Ruth clave unto her." The noblest examples of heroic faith, and of fidelity to God and conscience, are often raised up on the very scene of defection and apostasy: and they shine with a brighter lustre, and draw with a stronger attraction, because of the contrast in which they appear. They show that in the very same circumstances of trial and difficulty before which others give way, it is possible to hold fast one's integrity, and enter the kingdom of God. These parallels run through the Scriptures, and are constantly developed in the history of Redemption.

Of such classes, Orpah and Ruth are excellent types; and the example of the latter comes to us clothed with peculiar power, because we see it in the light of her sister's defection. Nothing could change her steadfast mind. Her courage grew with the obstacles it encountered, like *Bartimeus*, who cried the louder, when the multitude required him to hold his peace.

Three several times did Naomi propose that she should return—in the last instance citing the example of Orpah: "Behold, thy sister-in-law is gone back unto her people, and unto her gods: return thou after thy sister-in-law."

This brought matters to a crisis. Such a proposal was abhorrent to her soul. She repelled it, and *clave* unto Naomi; and her full heart gave vent to its overpowering emotions in those ever-memorable words, concerning which Voltaire is said to have acknowledged that there is "nothing in Homer or Herodotus that goes to the heart" as they do: "Entreat me not to leave thee, or to return from following after thee: for whither thou goest, I will go; and where thou lodgest, I will lodge: thy people shall be my people, and thy God my God: where thou diest, will I die, and there will I be buried: the Lord do so to me, and more also, if aught but death part thee and me."

Let me commend to you this admirable example of *decision.* Many fail of the grace of God, and lose their immortal souls, by halting between two opinions. They *wish* to be Christians, hope they shall be; have no thought of dying in impenitence; but they cannot bring themselves up to the point of an immediate and unalterable purpose to serve God, and to cast in their lot with his people.

To be saved, you must look the difficulties full in the face, count the cost, and, in the strength of God, *resolve* that, as for you, you will serve the Lord. If neighbours or kindred will not go with you, you must go alone, and, in the meaning of our Lord, "*hate*" and "forsake" them, for the kingdom of God's sake.

Without such a resolution, formed and acted on, you will vacillate all the days of your life, or else, after resisting the convictions of your conscience for a while, become so hardened through the deceitfulness of sin, as to feel no concern about salvation. I exhort you, therefore, to be decided. Determine now to be a Christian. Be resolute. "Strive to enter in at the strait gate: for many, I say unto you, will seek to enter in, and shall not be able."

Imitate Ruth, who *clave* unto a poor and pious widow, because she was the representative of God, of his people, and of his salvation. *Cleave* to your convictions. "Cleave to that which is good," and to those who are good. "Cleave unto the Lord your God." Say to the church—"I will go with you, for I have heard that God is with you."

To help, if possible, this good purpose to the birth in your heart, let me suggest how *morally beautiful* genuine piety is in the young; and, may I not add?—especially in *young women.* I am sure you admire the character of Ruth more than that of Orpah. Her very *name* is held in precious remembrance, and *given* to many a child of prayer and of promise. Godliness is not *un*becoming to any one. It dignifies and graces the character of a *man.* It "becomes the throned monarch better than his crown." "'Tis mightiest *in* the mightiest."

But surely, of all the adornments of a woman, this is the chief. "Favour is deceitful, and beauty is vain: but a woman that feareth the Lord, she shall be praised. Gold, and pearls, and costly array lose their brilliancy and beauty beside "the ornament of a meek and quiet spirit, which, in the sight of God, is of great price"—and in the sight of man also, even of those who are blind to the beauty of holiness, is not by any means despised. If you wish to put on the most "beautiful garment"—one woven by divine art, and woven in the colours of heaven, "put on the Lord Jesus Christ," and the graces of his Spirit. Love, joy, and peace; meekness, gentleness, and humility, will be "an ornament of grace unto thy head, and chains about thy neck."

In time of youth they will be more beautiful than the rose on your cheek, or the lily-whiteness of your hand: and in those "evil days" which are coming fast,—when the "daughters of music are brought low, and the windows are darkened, and you have no pleasure in them,"—these flowers of Paradise, early planted in the garden of the heart, will put forth their comeliest colours and emit their sweetest odours. "The righteous shall flourish like the palm-tree; he shall grow like the cedar in Lebanon." "They shall still bring forth fruit in old age; they shall be fat and flourishing."

And finally, the example of Ruth is commended to your imitation, by *the happiness, blessing, and honour which resulted from her choice.*

From the hour she took for her *own*, the people and God of Naomi, a benignant providence attended her steps. She found in Canaan far more and better things than she left in Moab. The reproach and sorrow of widowhood, she presently forgot in the house of an affectionate, honoured, and pious husband. And the temporal blessings enjoyed were the least part of her recompense. She lived and died according to her wish, in communion with the people of God; and with them now awaits a glorious resurrection. She proved, experimentally, that "godliness hath the promise of the life that now is, and of that which is to come."

If you imitate her example, you will share her blessedness. "Wisdom's ways are ways of pleasantness, and all her paths are peace."

"Every one that hath forsaken houses, or brethren, or sisters, or father, or mother, or wife, or children, or lands, for my name's sake, shall receive an hundred-fold, and shall inherit everlasting life." Matt. xix. 29.

SERMON IV.

BEARING THE YOKE IN YOUTH.

LAM. iii. 27.—*It is good for a man that he bear the yoke in his youth.*

THOSE things which are best for us, are not always the pleasantest: and many things which the Bible represents as blessings are looked on as quite the reverse.

In regard to the government and discipline which God exercises over mankind, we sustain the same kind of relation that children do to the control and care of their parents. So ignorant are they of what is best for them, and so utterly incapable of entering into the views of those who have at heart their highest happiness and welfare, that it often seems to them as if their parents' will and authority were the greatest evil they had to encounter. Their appetites and passions are clamorous for indulgence, and they can neither see the wisdom nor the kindness of denying them what they crave.

In their case we can readily see that it is inexperience and ignorance that beget unhappiness, and make them restive under parental control. The best blessing to a child, next to the care and love of the Great Father in heaven, is that of "the fathers of our flesh:" and there is nothing for which a man is more devoutly thankful than for the very restraint which, while it annoyed and chafed his youthful spirit, was the effectual means of turning his feet from the paths of danger, and forming those habits of self-control and industry which have led to temporal success, and even to the salvation of his soul.

What parental discipline is to a child, as a means of preparing it for the labours of mortal life and of this present world, the gracious government of God is to us all, as the heirs of an immortal existence. Its object is our ultimate welfare, and not our present gratification; and its wisdom and love are vindicated not by the pleasure of present experience, but by the preciousness of its final fruits. What is "good" for us may not be agreeable, and what is agreeable may not be good. Left to ourselves, like children, we instinctively choose what is pleasant, thoughtless or ignorant of consequences, and if no higher wisdom than our own were brought to bear in the premises, we should be our own worst enemies.

A child cries for sweetmeats when it needs medicine, and a boy clamours for liberty when his safety and salvation demand government; and there is not one of us who is not guilty of follies and errors, equally injurious to our welfare as accountable and immortal creatures. Many of us have lived long enough to see that Divine checks and interferences with our wishes and purposes have subserved our interests, and given us greater blessings by far than would have been the gratification of our desires.

The statement of the text should not therefore encounter our prejudice. Not to insist on its authority as a Divine oracle, it is supported by many analogies and abundant experience. "It is good for a man that he bear the yoke in his youth."

The nature and significance of the "yoke," and the reasons why it is good to bear it in the days of our "*youth*," are the points presented, and to which I now invite your attention.

I. And first, we are to inquire for *the nature and meaning of the yoke* referred to.

In general, a yoke is the emblem of service and subjection—as where the apostle speaks of "servants under the yoke."

It may be galling and oppressive, amounting to intolerable slavery, like the "yoke of bondage" to Jewish ordinances, of which Peter said, "neither we nor our fathers were able to bear." Or, it may be the light and pleasant yoke of the "reasonable" and willing service which Christ requires, and of which he says, "My yoke is easy, and my burden is light."

As the language of the text is *general*, and there is no limiting or descriptive epithet which shows the application designed, we are left to *infer* the nature of the yoke spoken of from the declaration that it is good for a man to bear it in his youth: and I have no doubt that in this case, the highest sense is the truest. It is the yoke of *religion*—the *subjugation of the soul* to the will and employment in the service of the Lord Jesus Christ. The declaration of the text is true, however, in all its applications,—the lowest not less than the highest. The yoke of a child's subjection to its parents; the yoke of a lad's apprenticeship to the master who teaches him a mechanical trade, and the yoke of a school-boy's discipline by which he is taught the lessons of submission to rightful authority and patient and painful application, are earthly and secular senses in which the principle announced holds good. The truth is, it is a fundamental principle of human well-being, and inseparable from the existence of creatures at once dependent and accountable. If religion is a *yoke*, it is put on necks which are made to bear a yoke, and which, in all other respects, are not "unaccustomed" to do so.

In the prosecution of worldly undertakings men draw, like the veriest oxen, in the yoke of a real or a self-imposed necessity, taking up their daily cross of self-denial. Ease, pleasure, society, are constantly sacrificed to what they regard as a higher interest: and religion is but acting on the same principle in its application to the highest concerns of immortal beings. And the Bible is both frank and fearless in calling it by its proper name. It *is* a yoke. It involves obligation, service, and subjection. It is not an opinion, a sentiment, a feeling, or a profession. It is a loving obedience to God. It is discipleship in the school of Jesus, taking him for Teacher, Lord, Pattern, not less than as Redeemer and Saviour. If this *is* the nature of religion, and these the terms of salvation, we should not hesitate to set it forth in its true colours. Jesus did so. He met men at the very threshold of their inquiries with the *cross* and the *yoke*. To the old and the young, he said alike:—"If any man will come after me, let him deny himself, and take up his cross, and follow me." And even to those whom he saw fainting and falling under the burden of their sins and sorrows, he said, "Take my yoke upon you, and learn of me: for I am meek and lowly in heart; and ye shall find rest unto your souls."

I am well aware that a *mistaken idea* of what the yoke of Jesus is, exists in the minds of men, and operates with peculiar power on *the young*, as a hindrance to their conversion and salvation. They see in religion nothing but restraint, and their exact conception of it is that of a "yoke," which limits their freedom and fetters their powers. Hence they refuse it, and resolve to enjoy the largest liberty. There is, perhaps, no single objection which has more weight with persons in the earlier periods of life. In the hope of neutralizing its power, we offer two or three remarks.

The first is, that unrestrained liberty is *impossible.*

Our freedom to do as we please, is confined on every side, by impassable barriers. The relations we sustain to one another in the family, in society, in the state, and the rules of conduct imposed by public opinion and civil authority, prevent men from doing many things which they might wish to do: while the moral obligations which rest upon us as the accountable creatures of God, are inseparable from our existence. If we disregard, we cannot annul them. They must bind us still, as we shall find, in the day of final retribution, and in the miseries which sin begets even in this present life.

Creatures cannot be independent. Subjection to law and authority is the condition of their existence.

In the second place, let it be considered, that every one is certain to wear the yoke of some master. If we do not serve God, we will serve mammon, or appetite, or some of the "divers lusts and pleasures," which enslave the votaries of the world. Our choice is between being the Lord's freedmen or Satan's slaves: between a voluntary, rational, and manly compliance with the dictates of conscience and the demands of reason, and an ignoble and slavish subjection to the blind importunity of appetite and passion. It is a master-stroke of Satanic subtlety and falsehood, to make men believe that in choosing the latter branch of this alternative, they are making sure of personal freedom and independence! To set reason and conscience at defiance, and give one's self up to the dominion of appetite, lust, and worldly pleasures, involves a deeper moral degradation, and a more abject bondage, than is found among the slaves of a Southern plantation.

Is the drunkard free who cannot withstand the fascination of the wine-cup? Or the adulterer, who is unable to pass by the house of her whose ways take hold on hell? Or the "companion of fools," who has not the moral courage and manliness to say *No* to their guilty and shameful enticements? Or the gay devotee of fashionable pleasures and amusements, who continually suppresses the voice of conscience and the strivings of God's Spirit? One and all these are miserable slaves, and none the less so because their bondage is *voluntary*. A man is none the less a *slave* because he *chooses* to abide with his master, and these "servants of sin" are made slaves by the *power* of their *master*, and the *degradation* of their employment and condition: and rightly considered, their voluntariness is but an element of their bondage, even as the contentment of a slave proves how utterly the spirit of genuine manhood has been extinguished in his heart.

Once more:—Let those who dread and shun religion as if it were a "yoke of bondage," listen to the testimonies of Scripture, and the experience of Christians as to the nature of experimental and practical religion. Though the Bible calls it a "yoke," good care is taken to tell us in *what sense* the word is used. If it implies service and subjection, all that is repulsive and forbidding in this conception is dissipated when we are informed that Christ is our Master, and hear from his own gracious lips this sweet call to discipleship—"Take my yoke upon you, and learn of me; for I am meek and lowly in heart, and ye shall find rest unto your souls." So far is discipleship in the school of Christ from being a condition of *bondage*, that the Scriptures present it under the image of a blessed emancipation from servitude, and an introduction of the soul into a state of "glorious liberty." To the Jews, Christ said—"If the Son shall make you *free*, ye shall be *free indeed*." The apostle James describes the rule of a believer's obedience as "the perfect law of *liberty*," and expatiates upon the blessedness of the man who, in heart and deed, is conformed to it. Christians are temples of the Holy Ghost, and "where the Spirit of the Lord is, there is *liberty*."

Still, perhaps, it seems a mystery that men should be *free*, while yet they are under a sacred and imperative *obligation* to "serve the Lord Christ." But what *is* liberty in any true and practical sense of the word? It is not unbridled license to do whatever caprice, interest, or passion may impel us to do. It is freedom from oppression and compulsion, and is all the more perfect and secure because it is regulated, defined, and defended by laws and constitutions which are supreme over all individual wills.

As American citizens are we not *free?* Liberty is our boast and glory: and yet every one of us is subject to the authority of laws which we dare not violate, even if we were disposed to. We obey "every ordinance of man for wrath or for conscience' sake," even though it may not be wise or just, and yet we account ourselves a free people.

The Christian's liberty resembles this, but is far more perfect. The law to which he is subject, is "*holy*, and *just*, and *good*," insomuch that his obedience to it, in every jot and particular, is promotive of his well-being and happiness. Furthermore, it is not engraven on tables of stone, nor printed in statute books, but "written" on the fleshly tables of the heart, and in the experience of every believer, is "the law of the Spirit of life in Christ Jesus," making him "free from the law of sin and death." He loves it and obeys it from choice, moved thereto not by the fear of threatened perdition, but by gratitude and love for a present and promised salvation.

And what the Scriptures represent concerning the nature of the yoke worn by the disciples of Christ, is found true in their actual experience. They bear it "with delight." They would not, if they might, be released from it. If it were taken off, they would put their necks under it again, the next moment. They are all in sympathy with him who cried—"O Lord, truly I am thy servant, and the son of thy handmaid: thou hast loosed my bonds."

The suggestions now offered are sufficient, as it seems to me, if they were duly attended to, to remove the prejudice and misapprehension which exist in the minds of men, and particularly in those of the young, in regard to religion. It is *not* the yoke of bondage which they take it to be, but the easy and pleasant service which a ransomed sinner and renewed soul renders to the glorious Redeemer whom he adores and loves.

II. And if this be so, it goes far to prove the truth of the proposition laid down in the text:—"It is good for a man that he bear the yoke in his youth."

It is good for a man to bear it at *any time*, even though it were in his old age, and in the decay of all his powers. If he had but the last of his threescore and ten years to live, it would be good to put his neck under Christ's yoke, for that short period. But while this is *true*, it is not the thing which is *said* in the text: nor is there any such thing said in express terms, anywhere in Scripture. And that, my friends, is a very significant and solemn fact—a *silence* of the Scriptures quite as impressive as their utterances! From the Bible we gather, that *all* sinners, and therefore *old* ones, may be converted and saved, but we are not thus left to infer from general principles, the relation which the *young* sustain to the service and salvation of God.

On this subject, revelation is explicit and full, and here is one of its blessed oracles: "It is good for a man that he bear the yoke *in his youth.*" It is good for any, for all, but pre-eminently good for the *young*. This is the precise truth announced.

It is good in every sense of the word. It is *morally* good, right in the sight of God. It meets the approbation of conscience, of heaven, and of all good men: and it is good in the sense of being *beneficial*. It promotes the welfare and happiness of men to bear the yoke of Christian service, and especially to bear it in their youth:—and for this there are some special reasons; and

1. It *is easier* then than afterwards, to be *broken in to the yoke of Christ*. The animals which serve us with submissive meekness and docility, are "broken" and trained to the harness and the yoke while *young*. If suffered to run at large unbridled and untamed till they have grown old, it is almost impossible to subdue them. If done at all, it is accomplished with great difficulty, and they are seldom or never brought to the perfect subjection and usefulness which are attained by an earlier training.

A bullock "unaccustomed to the yoke," till he has grown strong and stubborn, is a true type of the sinner, who has "hardened his neck" against the authority and restraints of religion, till he has grown gray in the indulgence of his own will, and in the practice of iniquity. His conversion and salvation are not impossible, but are commonly effected with a peculiar difficulty and severity of discipline. And after he is fairly yoked as a disciple of Christ, he does not usually *draw* with that steadiness and strength, or with ease to himself and pleasantness to others, which characterize those who from childhood were "trained up in the way they should go."

Youth is the time for education and discipline. The young mind and heart is docile and plastic—readily taking on the forms which the moulds about it impress.

It is then that principles are deeply rooted, habits firmly fixed, and the powers of nature developed in almost any required direction. True in general, this is pre-eminently so of religion. It is the highest education and the noblest development of man. It implants the strongest as well as the holiest principles in the heart, and forms the soul to habits of piety and virtue, which become so entirely a "second nature," that what may have been felt at first, as a cross and a yoke, is borne without the consciousness of pain or difficulty. Comparatively speaking, it is easy to become a Christian in childhood and youth: though even then, it requires the exertion of omnipotent grace.

If this favoured season is suffered to go by without improvement, the probabilities of conversion rapidly diminish, and in old age—if we should live to see it—there is almost an impossibility of salvation. Such is the representation of Scripture. When the Ethiopian can change his skin, and the leopard his spots, then those who have been accustomed to do evil, may learn to do well.

It is a fact that cannot be too often repeated, or too solemnly pondered, that an overwhelming majority of all who ever *are* converted, begin to bear the yoke of Christ in their youth! Here and there, now and then, a gray-haired sinner like *Manasseh*, is made a monument of redeeming love, but the cases are so few as to be manifestly *exceptional*, while hosts of young Samuels, Josiahs, and Timothys, Ruths and Marys, rise up to show the love that God hath to the young, and the greater readiness with which the youthful heart yields to the loving importunities of the gospel.

2. A second reason and proof of the proposition laid down in the text, exists in the *peculiar usefulness* which is attained by those who bear the yoke of Christ in their youth.

Enlisting early, they have more time to serve under the Captain of salvation. Those who enter the vineyard at the *eleventh* hour, may be useful and accepted labourers, but they accomplished little in comparison with others who begin their work in the morning, consecrating to it "the dew of their youth," and the best energies of their meridian years.

And besides the length of time employed, these have opportunity of becoming trained and disciplined in the school of Christ for increasing usefulness; while those converted late in life find their habits so firmly rooted, that they are unable to adapt themselves to their new circumstances, or at least experience great difficulty in doing so, and always labour at great disadvantage. And, in addition to this, there is a peculiar charm in youthful piety which tells with saving effect on the hearts of men. When the heart is full of the new joy of existence, buoyant with hope, and running out on every side to embrace the delights which a benignant Providence has prepared, how beautiful and how precious the offering which is presented to God, when this fresh and youthful spirit yields itself to the sweet and sovereign sway of Jesus Christ!

Upon those who have passed through this summer season of gracious visitation without effectual attention to the soul's concerns, how startling the impression of such a spectacle! And with what soft and sympathetic persuasion does it draw those of their own age!

"The young love to follow the young," and often has it happened that the conversion of a young man or a young woman has been the means of awaking conviction in the heart of a companion, and drawing him to the same blessed choice and consecration. If an aged person, who visibly stands on the verge of life, is converted, men think that religion is a very proper and necessary thing in one so circumstanced, and quietly make up their minds to defer the matter till they are in like need. But when *a youth* bows his neck to Jesus, this speaks a different lesson. It proclaims that religion is as good in life as it is in death, as necessary in time as in eternity.

In the former case, it is looked on as a necessary evil to which one is compelled to submit; in the latter, as a blessing which we are glad to embrace.

Bow to Jesus, my young friends, and thus shall you save yourselves and those who are influenced by your example: and giving your whole life to Him who redeemed you, you will be spared the bitter regrets on a dying-bed which many have expressed?

3. A third consideration going to prove the truth and illustrate the sense of the text, is *the peculiar happiness which youthful piety never fails to secure to its possessor.* This thought, somewhat involved in what has gone before, deserves more express mention. Religious experience, ever pleasant and satisfactory, is peculiarly so in the young. The natural joyousness of the youthful heart, when sanctified by the grace of God, and having infused into it the element of spiritual delight, is such a pure and perfect bliss, as renders every unhallowed pleasure insipid, and imparts unknown endearment and sweetness to those which are lawful and innocent. *Love-tokens* of peculiar preciousness does God give to those who "remember their Creator in the days of their youth." Of such He declares—"I love them that love me: and those that seek me early shall find me." These, above others, find that "wisdom's ways are ways of pleasantness." For every earthly and simple gratification which they surrender, God opens a fountain of "holy delight" incomparably better, and all things in nature, providence, and redemption, are commissioned to minister peace and pleasure to the new-born soul.

The experience of President Edwards, who was converted while a *young man*, has been substantially reproduced in many a youthful heart. It is given in his own words:

"The appearance of every thing was altered; there seemed to be, as it were, a calm, beautiful appearance of divine glory in almost every thing. God's excellency, his wisdom, his purity and love seemed to appear in every thing; in the sun, moon, and stars; in the clouds and blue sky; in the grass, flowers, and trees; in the water, and in all nature, which used greatly to fix my mind. I often used to sit and view the moon for a long time; and in the day spent much time in viewing the clouds and sky, to behold the glory of God in these things; in the meantime singing forth, with a low voice, my contemplations of the Creator and Redeemer."

This surely is heavenly happiness, and now, by the promise of the "peace which passeth all understanding," and the "joy that is unspeakable and full of glory," I exhort you to come to Jesus and be blessed. Take his yoke upon you, for it is good for a man that he bear this yoke in his youth.

4. On this theme of wide extent, I only add, in conclusion, that *early piety prepares for an early death*, if such should be the ordering of God's providence.

For the reasons already mentioned, "the fear of the Lord would be the beginning of wisdom" to each of you, my young friends, if you had a revelation from God that your days would be prolonged half a century. But you have no such revelation, nor any sure defence against an early death. The bloom on your cheek, the bounding pulsations of your heart, the elasticity of your step, do not assure you that in one short week you will not be sleeping in your graves. Many and touching examples prove this to be true: and in the *death*, not less than the conversion of the young, God calls you to the service and salvation of his Son. For you they sicken, and for you they die. Oh, let not the dear-bought lesson be lost on any of you! "Seek the Lord while he may be found, call upon him while he is near." And be ye therefore ready also, "for in such an hour as ye think not, the Son of man cometh."

SERMON V.

HARVEST TIME NEGLECTED.

JEREMIAH viii. 20.—*The harvest is past, the summer is ended, and we are not saved.*

THE pathos of Jeremiah's lament over the sorrows and perils of his country and of the church of God, is scarcely exceeded by anything in Scripture. Loyal devotion to the land of his birth, and fervent zeal for the honour of religion, glowed in his heart, and in view of the impending and visible calamities from which there was now no escape, called forth these melting expressions of pious and patriotic grief. The case was desperate.

Already he saw the invading host of the Chaldeans; the "snorting of their horses was heard from Dan, and the whole land trembled at the sound of the neighing of their strong ones." In their previous history, Israel had ofttimes been exposed to like dangers; but through the intervention of judges, prophets, and kings, had been brought to repentance, and had thus obtained deliverance. In signal instances, God had directly interposed to break the yoke of their oppressors, and to defeat the hostile designs of their heathenish foes. But in the prophet's estimation, their present case was not of this character, and fell under a different law. It appeared to him to be without remedy: and this not because the enemy was so powerful and so near.

The situation was not so threatening as in the days of Hezekiah, when Sennacherib, king of Assyria, was encamped before the gates of Jerusalem, with a mighty host of warriors. On all grounds of mere human and worldly calculation, there was no prospect or possibility of deliverance: but this vital difference then existed. The king and his people had access to God. They had recently reformed his worship, and returned to the observance of his ordinances and his law. With a clear conscience and a strong faith, Hezekiah spread the case before the Lord, and sent a message to Isaiah the prophet, saying, "This is a day of trouble and rebuke and blasphemy—wherefore lift up thy prayer for the remnant that is left." At once an answer of peace was given, and the same night an angel of God, with invisible hand, destroyed the arm of flesh in which his enemies had trusted. Here was an example most encouraging, for Jeremiah to imitate. But he seems to be without hope. Instead of praying, he only weeps, and vents his sorrow in touching lamentations over calamities which were now inevitable.

But why inevitable? Not because their Almighty deliverer was less able to succour and save, but because Israel had sinned against him in such a manner, and for so long a time, and up to such a point of aggravation, that he would not, and according to his established methods of dealing with men, could not, interfere, to save them from evils which were of their own procuring. Hence the prophet sought in vain for any ground of hope or source of consolation. "When," says he, "I would comfort myself against sorrow, my heart is faint in me:" and that which in particular distressed him, was the thought that these terrible and destructive judgments might have been averted by timely repentance, and were now become certain, only through the thoughtless and wicked unbelief of Israel. A day of merciful visitation had been afforded, but instead of filling it up with works of piety, and virtue, they had spent it in self-indulgence, and now they must take the consequences of their folly and wickedness. "The harvest is past, the summer is ended, and they are not saved."

The parallel between the circumstances of the Jewish people, and the condition of men who have sinned away their day of grace, is so obvious that this passage which bewails the hopeless misery of Israel, has been commonly applied to the latter subject; and it suggests to the mind of almost every one who reads or hears it, this high and solemn application. That its primary and intended reference was to a temporal deliverance, and not to a spiritual and eternal salvation, there is little or no reason to doubt, and we are not in any such need of proof-texts as to be even tempted to press this into a service which it was never meant to perform.

All we want and design to use, is the principle it recognizes, of a probation allotted to men, in which they act a part that tells influentially and for ever on their condition: a "summer" in which they may lay up in store a good foundation against the winter of their necessity; a "harvest" season, whose brief and earnest reaping may garner fruit unto life eternal. The point of view from which it is regarded in the text is one, which, through the mercy of God, we have not yet reached, and the only possible reason we could have for carrying you forward to it in thought is to prevent you ever coming to it in fact. To look back with vain regrets, and keen remorse, on opportunities unimproved, time misspent, faculties and powers unemployed and undeveloped, and above all, to survey, from the verge of our earthly existence, a whole life that has failed of the very end and object of our creation, is the saddest of all possible experiences. In apprehension and fear of such a dreadful failure, let us dwell for a little, on the nature and characteristics of the harvest-time and summer season which God affords us for the purpose of our salvation; the liability and temptation we are under to let it pass without improvement; and the extreme and remediless misery of those who yield to this temptation, living for another purpose than that which God designs.

In the mercy of Heaven, we have a season of gracious visitation—a period of wondrous possibilities and blessed opportunities—a portion of our immortal existence, in which a brief fidelity insures unending bliss, or an equally short neglect of duty leads to incurable and everlasting sorrow.

This probation, we say, is given to men in mercy. It was goodness in God to put the angels on trial, for a limited period after their creation, instead of keeping them for ever on a footing of trial, and, of course, of uncertainty, being liable to fall and perish, as a part of them did. It was goodness that ordained the probation of Eden, which, though it involved the possibility of a fearful lapse, limited the possibility to a narrow space, and gave the opportunity of securing a holy and happy life by the obedience of an hour, and fidelity in a single instance.

If it was love to his creatures which moved God to give them a probation in their estate of holiness for its confirmation and perpetuity, it is nothing short of tender and infinite mercy that assigns to fallen and condemned sinners a state and period of gracious trial for their recovery and salvation. Our natural condition—"by nature children of wrath"—is that of creatures who have failed under a previous probation, and who might be justly left to suffer the consequences of that old forfeiture. To such it is that God, in the riches of his grace, gives a new trial under the gospel and through Jesus Christ. The first trial in paradise was given to man as a creature; the second is given him as a sinner, and is accompanied with abundant indications and express statements of its being the last he will ever know. Its essential idea, as is that of all probation, whether on principles of law or principles of grace, is that the fleeting present may be made to govern the unchangeable and eternal future; that a little portion of our existence at its beginning shall stand in such a connexion of influence and power with what remains, as to determine its character, whether of weal or woe, and that thus all possible motions to well-doing should converge upon the manner of life we lead while in the flesh. That this method of dealing with voluntary agents and responsible creatures has its foundations laid deep in the principles of God's moral and natural government we know, from finding that life, in all its relations and interests, is subject to its control. The general laws by which the world is governed, are a continual discipline and probation of mankind. They create "times and seasons" for every purpose under the sun; times and seasons when that purpose may be accomplished, but carry for ever away in their flight the possibility of doing the work, or securing the advantage which belonged to them.

Such a law is that of the seasons, to which the text has reference. The image presented is that of a field of grain ready for the sickle. Like the field for spiritual husbandry, of which the Saviour spoke, it "is white already to harvest." For months it has been maturing; through all vicissitudes of weather it has advanced to its present point of peculiar interest and critical importance. It is now not only ready to be gathered, but imperatively requires the reaper's toil. A few days, or, at most, a few weeks of neglect, and it utterly perishes; and with it is lost the blessing which the kindness and care of Providence had placed within the farmer's grasp. Time may come to him afterwards, but those weeks of harvest-time will never come again. The loss is irreparable; and cultivators of the earth, knowing this, make diligent improvement of this golden season.

When the summer ends, all its opportunities and possibilities end with it. Such is the law, fixed as the everlasting hills, with which we have to do: and of its operation none have any reason to complain, and none, in fact, do complain but the man who violates it. The industrious and prudent husbandman who, when the summer is ended, and the winter with its desolateness has come, finds his barns filled with plenty, blesses the beneficent law of the seasons; and only the sluggard complains—and he without cause—when he suffers the penalty of indolence and folly. Another natural analogy is found in the kind of relation which exists between youth and age.

The latter is what the former makes it. The beginning of life shapes its middle and its end.

It is the seed-time in which the germs of character are planted; the moulding period in which habits take their abiding shape; the school-days in which the education of our whole existence is received. At this plastic period, a month leaves deeper traces on the character, than a year of middle age, or a score of years next the close of life.

As the rivulet, which rises on the mountain-top, takes, within a little distance of its source, the general direction in which the mighty river shall flow for thousands of miles, so it is with the stream of human existence. The acts, the impulses, the incidents, and the influences which determine its course and prepare its channel, are located near its commencement, where alone it is possible to exert so great a power. Human skill and strength might control and change the course of a stream on the sides of the Alleghanies, but what power less than that of Omnipotence, could arrest the flow or alter the direction of the Mississippi, or the Amazon? It is the same with the course of human character and life. Its beginnings are everything. If these are in the right direction, they ensure an endless career of well-doing, and of happiness: but who shall cure the fatal mistake of early misdirection?

Who shall bring back to the idle and truant school-boy, who has doomed himself to a life-long ignorance, the opportunity of education; the leisure of childhood, the quick discernment, the tenacious memory, the eager curiosity, which render the youthful mind susceptible of discipline and development? The thing is naturally impossible, and requires a miracle which God has never been known to perform.

A law which thus operates in external nature, and in human life, yielding only beneficial results to those who regard it, might be presumed to have scope also in the sphere of morals and religion, and to exert a decisive influence on the future and eternal destiny of the soul. What experience thus renders probable, revelation declares to be true: and there is no reason at all to doubt, that the law in question is just as necessary, benevolent, and holy, in this last connexion, which we know by faith, as in the former relation, which we know by experience. There is, then, a harvest-time, and a summer-season, in which salvation may be secured, but after which this blessed possibility is gone for ever.

As youth, with its capabilities and freshness, never returns in the life of man; and opportunities—the rare conjunctures of many conditions—once knock at our door, and then vanish; so the day of salvation, the accepted time of Heaven's love, is of short continuance. Short, not because that love is small, but because it is great.

Born and destined to an existence which shall never end, the character of that existence, whether of purity or of sin, and the condition of that existence, whether of happiness or misery, is dependent on the hand-breadth, yea, in comparison with eternal duration, the hair-breadth, of time which we spend on earth! If this announcement startles you, and you feel perplexed in your attempt to reconcile with Divine goodness a method of procedure which leaves no room for repentance through everlasting ages, for a sin that was committed in time, and shuts men up at the very outset of their being to the choice of the path they will travel for ever;—there are two or three things which it would be wise and well to consider. If they fail to give complete satisfaction to the understanding, they may at least indicate the course of duty and safety. The first suggestion I offer is, that *if such be the law of our condition there is no manner of use in cavilling at its existence.* We cannot annul the law, nor escape from its operation. Whether we will or not, it will fix our condition in a future life, according as we improve or neglect present opportunities. What a wise man cannot alter or remove, he conforms to, adjusting his conduct to his circumstances. There is no advantage in quarrelling with facts, or struggling against necessity. If a man runs against a natural law, it will hurl him to death with remorseless violence.

And there is no reason to doubt, but, on the contrary, many reasons to believe that this great moral law and principle of a short earthly probation, will deal in like manner with those who either disbelieve or despise it. It is our wisdom just to accept the conditions of life and of salvation under which God has placed us.

Another suggestion, which goes far to vindicate this feature of the Divine government, and especially to show its consistency with a dependence upon the mercy and goodness of God, is the obvious truth, that *a short probation strengthens and intensifies, in proportion to its brevity, the motives and helps to a holy life.*

If the benumbed conscience of a sinner will ever awake from its torpor, and the regard a man has for his own well-being, will ever rise above the sphere of his animal wants and earthly necessities, and entertain the question of what is to become of him when he goes to the world of spirits; and if in any circumstances the fear of God will stir the soul to action, it must assuredly be when men are told that their eternal salvation depends upon their manner of life in these fleeting years of an earthly existence! What an amazing concentration of moral power does this secure, and bring to bear on heart, conscience, reason, sensibility!

As the lens converges the rays of light, and brings them together in a blazing focus, so does this gracious principle of a short probation for immortal creatures collect and pour upon their souls "the powers of the world to come"—the attractive influences of a blessed and holy immortality—the flashing terrors of the death that never dies! As it is, delay is the fatal snare of unwary souls: procrastination, the commonest and deadliest of all the sinner's temptations!

Even now, when he knows that his end is near, and may be at the door, he says in his heart, "My Lord delayeth his coming," and accordingly resigns himself to carnal indulgences and the neglect of his duty, and is surprised by the coming of death and judgment at an hour when he thinks not. With what augmented power would this temptation assail him, if, instead of threescore and ten, his probation were ten thousand years; and into what a profound slumber of sensuality and ungodliness would he sink, if it were known or believed that the sins and errors of the life that now is might be repented of and repaired in that which is to come! If sinful men are ever to be recovered to holiness and God, and started on a career of immortal happiness, it would seem as if it must be done by bringing the whole power of the eternal future to bear upon the fleeting present, and causing them to feel that they are in the crisis of their destiny every moment of their lives. It is, therefore, not justice, but mercy which gives to man a probation on earth; and there is as much mercy in making it short, as in granting it at all.

Our third suggestion on this point regards the *peculiarly gracious nature* of the probation which men enjoy under the dispensation of the gospel, and through the mediation of the Lord Jesus Christ. It is gracious in its continuance. Though short, it is long enough for its purpose. Life is given to men to secure an interest in Christ, to work out their salvation, and it affords ample time and abundant opportunity. Some prosecute this work for nearly a century: others complete it in the days of their youth, and go up to the glories of heaven very soon after they have tasted the joy of salvation.

To both, the day of grace was long enough. And not in its duration only, but with respect to all those acts and provisions on the part of God, which constitute life a harvest and a summer with regard to the future, it is a day of gracious visitation.

You rejoice in the benignant care of Providence which ordains the seasons, brings, in its time, the genial warmth of spring, with its shining skies, its refreshing showers, and its balmy air: and when you see how earth, and clouds, and sun, with all their subtle agencies, conspire to make the easy possibility of a harvest, to any man who heeds the suggestion and concurs in the working of the Creator, you feel an honest indignation at the sluggard who neglects to use this kind and wonderful provision for the supply of his wants and the improvement of his condition.

Many persons who perceive and appreciate this, do not see so clearly, nor consider so well, that the God of salvation has pursued the same method in the sphere of man's spiritual nature, and encompassed him with ordinances of religion and means of grace, which put within his reach blessings of infinite worth and eternal duration. Just as we incline to overlook the goodness revealed in the greatest natural blessings, such as the light, the air, and the seasons, because our enjoyment of them is constant: so, from frequent repetition and its perpetual presence, the glorious mystery of redemption which is disclosed in the gospel and made visible in the church, fails to impress us with its real character. It seems a thing of course, and so, a thing of naught. Through this inconsideration, men are little aware how much God has done and is doing every hour of their lives, to open before them a door of hope, and give them a day of grace.

As to means, what more could they have or wish than those already given; the throne of grace, always accessible to all sinners, by night, by day, at home, abroad, in the closet, or on the street: the Scriptures, in the tongue wherein they were born, revealing the mind of God in terms and style level to the understanding of a child, and making the way of life so plain that the wayfaring man, though a fool, need not err therein; the Sabbath, returning every week to break the chain of worldly thoughts, and lift the soul to a purer world, and lead it forward to the everlasting rest; the ministry of reconciliation, commissioned to offer, in Christ's stead, salvation to sinners, and by doctrine, warning, persuasion, and reproof, beseech them to accept it.

And with means and above them, the mediation and intercession of the Lord Jesus Christ, on his priestly throne, and the influence of the Holy Spirit, sent forth to convince of sin, to convert the soul, and reveal the Saviour's glory! Such are the condition and surroundings of the sinner every day and every hour of his life-time, under the dispensation of heavenly love. Is it not a day of merciful visitation, radiant with bright tokens of the love of God?

But while all its parts and stages are precious opportunities of salvation, there are times and seasons corresponding to those critical portions of the natural year, in which more may be done in a day of seed-sowing, or of harvesting the ripe grain, than during a much longer period in different circumstances. Such an auspicious opportunity is the season of youth, when the religious sensibilities exhibit a tenderness which, if it be trifled with and resisted, rapidly disappears.

Such an occasion is the hour of affliction, when the hand of God presses heavily upon us, disappointing our earthly hopes, or smiting the idol of our affections: and such, peculiarly and pre-eminently, is the time when the Spirit of God is poured out on the church and on our fellow-sinners, and, in sovereign love, upon our own hearts, awakening the conviction of sin, and the desire to be saved. This is God's nearest approach! the direct, personal, urgent persuasion of Divine grace. It is a moment of unspeakable solemnity—of infinite value! It is the "harvest" time—the summer season—of an immortal existence.

It is in such aspects and elements of our probation as these, that the evidence of God's love appears, and the grounds of his justification are finished, when he leaves the sinner who fails to improve it to the inevitable results of his own folly and wickedness. And of all conditions and experiences, none is more distressing than that of him who at length awakes to the fact that the day of his visitation has gone, and, along with others like himself, takes up the bitter and fruitless plaint: "The harvest is past, the summer is ended, and we are not saved." His cup of wo lacks no element of sorrow. Worse than the positive infliction of Divine justice, is the ever present memory of wasted probation and a slighted Saviour. He remembers the time when the door of mercy and of heaven, now shut, stood invitingly open: when celestial voices called, and Divine attractions drew, and his own faithful conscience urged him to choose the better part. He recurs to the days of his youth, and to seasons of revival, and sacred communions, when he could scarcely refrain from following his companions into the kingdom of heaven, so pressing was the importunity of the Divine call: and along with this comes the recollection of that fatal act and hour in which he put away the offer of life, and destroyed for ever the possibility of salvation. The conviction that he has "destroyed himself" will penetrate his soul, and this will be the acme of his wretchedness. The blame of his perdition will settle eternally upon himself. The cavils and excuses by which this solemn truth is now disguised will vanish in the light of eternity, and amid the stern realities of the judgment-day. The Bible, the church, the cross, the mercy-seat, the Holy Spirit will not suffer him to impute his ruin to God, and conscience will charge it home upon himself with an authority which he will not even try to resist.

Living men think they will never come to such a condition as this; some, through unbelief in the reality of future and eternal retribution; others, and these a great multitude, from the persuasion that they will make a better improvement of that portion of their day of grace which remains, than of the part which is past. If you are yet in your sins, I acknowledge that your only hope of salvation depends on so doing; but I must remind you that many, with the same thought in their hearts, have lived and died in impenitence. It is one of the commonest things in the world, for men not to know their opportunity. In reference to worldly interests,

> "There is a tide in the affairs of men,
> Which, taken at the flood, leads on to fortune;"

but how few discern the exact time, and go up with the swelling stream! How often we hear men regretting that they had not acted differently at some former time, and in a critical conjuncture! Yet, in a comparative view, men are keen-sighted in reference to secular concerns. Notwithstanding frequent oversights, they are wise in their generation as men of the world, but strangely blind to the wondrous opportunity which the mercy of Heaven puts directly in their pathway, and obtrusively urges on their attention.

This, my friends, is your greatest danger. While the hours of your probation are flitting by, and carrying up the witness of your continued unbelief to the book of remembrance, you are seeking to quiet the fears and silence the remonstrance of heart and conscience, by the promise of acting a different part at another day, and making a portion of your probation accomplish the purpose for which the whole of it is not too much.

To act thus, in any other connexion, would expose you to the suspicion of insanity, and would be the height of folly. It is shamed, as the prophet teaches in the very connexion of the text, by the instinct of birds, and, according to Isaiah, by the dumbest of the brute creation. "Every one turned to his course, as the horse rusheth into the battle. Yea, the stork in the heaven knoweth her appointed times: and the turtle, and the crane, and the swallow, observe the time of their coming: but my people know not the judgment of the Lord." In fable and history, the ass is the symbol of stupidity: but God, in the importunity of his desire to rouse men from the sleep of their death-like torpor, even rates their folly below this stigmatized creature. "The ox knoweth his owner, and the ass his master's crib, but Israel doth not know: my people doth not consider."

One of the most affecting incidents in the life of our blessed Redeemer was occasioned by the exhibition of this folly carried to its highest and last degree. In point of privilege and opportunity, Jerusalem was nearer to God and heaven than any other city of earth: and the day of its grace was longer and more precious than is wont to be accorded to mortals. There stood the temple in its material glory, and there were clustered the emblems and exponents of the presence and grace of God. To this people had come the prophets in long succession, and now, He to whom the prophets bare witness. But all in vain; and already, the vengeful cloud of wrath is seen gathering over the doomed city. Over this, it was, that "Jesus wept," and while his tears flowed, exclaimed,—"If thou hadst known, even thou, at least in this thy day, the things which belong unto thy peace! but now they are hid from thine eyes. For the days shall come upon thee, that thine enemies shall cast a trench about thee, and compass thee round, and keep thee in on every side, and shall lay thee even with the ground, and thy children within thee: and they shall not leave in thee one stone upon another; because thou knewest not the time of thy visitation."

By the errors and sufferings of others, be admonished. Probation may be wasted: and, if you are yet in your sins, there is imminent danger of wasting yours, and of losing your soul. "Behold, now is the accepted time; behold, now is the day of salvation."

SERMON VI.

THE SIN OF NOT LOVING CHRIST.

1 Cor. xvi. 22.—*If any man love not the Lord Jesus Christ, let him be Anathema, Maran-atha.*

These words stand at the close of one of Paul's longest epistles. Without any special relation to what precedes, they have an intimate general relation to the whole gospel of Jesus Christ. They give the impression that a devout and enlightened mind receives from the contemplating the glorious mystery of redeeming love, which, while it bestows on men infinite blessings, lays upon them unspeakable responsibilities. The passage, instead of being weakened by want of logical connexion, is the more impressive on account of its seeming isolation. It was at this point, the venerable man of God took the pen from his amanuensis, who had been writing at his dictation, and, to certify the genuineness of the epistle, appended the salutation with his "own hand." In three brief sentences, he gives his Christian greetings to his brethren, the apostolic benediction to the church, and utters this woe against every man who loves not the Lord Jesus Christ. The circumstance that the original words were traced by the apostle's own hand, though it does not render their truth more certain, nor invest them with any higher authority, throws around them a certain interest; and the fact of their finding a place in these few closing sentences, carries with it an impression of their pre-eminent importance.

But why gather extrinsic proofs when the passage shines in its own effulgent light? Without comment or illustration, its clear, simple, solemn meaning goes right to the heart and conscience: and even those foreign and untranslated words at its close, are sufficiently illuminated by what precedes, to assure us that they can mean nothing less, or else, than something most terrible and awful. In approaching a theme like this, it is vastly important that we should be governed by the same spirit which influenced the apostle in penning the text. Though he uttered a fearful truth—in fact, pronounced a malediction, he did not dip his pen in wormwood and gall to write it, nor was there one drop of bitterness in his spirit.

It was said with the same melting compassion for souls, in which, at another time, he said that he "Could wish himself Anathema from Christ, for his brethren," if such a sacrifice were either useful or admissible. It was spoken from the stand-point of one who was labouring to save sinners from the curse of God, not from that of one sitting upon a throne of judgment, and allotting to men the award of final retribution. In this temper of humility and tenderness, let us now endeavour to handle and heed the subject before us. It breathes love, yet speaks of wrath. Its power as a warning, depends on the terrors of the Anathema denounced against "any man" who commits the sin, and bears the character, and stands in the relation to Christ, which is here expressed. Though the case is put contingently, it is not because it never had occurred, in fact, and was only possible in the future. It is an expression like that of the apostle John, when to introduce and commend the intercession of Jesus Christ, he puts an "if" before the universal fact of human sinfulness—"If any man sin, we have an advocate with the Father," where the logical supposition is really the positive assertion of a well-known fact. Thus, when the apostle speaks conditionally of any man's not loving the Lord Jesus Christ, it does not imply that such characters had not yet appeared in the world, or were barely possible to exist.

The truth is quite the reverse: and there is no sort of injustice or impropriety in saying of some persons that they do not love the Lord Jesus Christ. They do not *profess* to. They admit the fact, and what is more, in making the admission, they do not feel as if they had confessed a deadly crime.

Others, however, may join issue on the question of *fact;* and, before proceeding to illustrate the wickedness of not loving Christ, we may advert to some of the *indications* that no such affection has place in the soul. Without intending so much, men often *acknowledge* this to be the case. When a man says that he feels no particular interest in the subject of personal religion; that he thinks of it at times, and expects to give it more consideration in future, the true rendering of all this is, that he does not love Christ; but, since to confess this in words, would be to let out a startling and fearful truth, it is softened by circumlocution and qualified phrases. Want of love to Jesus is the meaning of every excuse for the neglect of religion, and the root of that entire life of prayerless impotency which multitudes lead. And there are those, no doubt, who, shocked at the utter depravity of having no love at all for such a person as Christ, persuade themselves that their hearts are not wholly destitute of the feeling. A dim and shadowy image of his Divine-human perfection floats before their minds, and they admire it. They listen to the precepts of his heavenly morality, and their conscience assents to them as good. They read the record of his pure and blameless life; his unselfish devotion to the relief and salvation of suffering humanity; and when they gaze upon the mysterious sorrows and sublime heroism of his last hours, their sensibilities are touched, and they accord him the praise of a philanthropist and a martyr: and this they bring forward to qualify, if not to refute the accusation of being without love to him. But what is there in it all, more or different than the admiration which men feel in reading the history and listening to the wisdom of Socrates, or the emotion awakened by the virtue and the sufferings of any of those martyrs to the cause of human rights and liberty who are immortalized in the pages of the world's history? Nay, I might even ask, How much does it rise above that sentimental admiration of virtue and sympathy with suffering which is often lavished on the heroes of a fictitious story? To *admire* virtue is a very different thing from practising it, and to approve what Christ has said, and done, and suffered, falls infinitely short of that adoring and clinging love to his glorious *Person* which the apostle intends, and which is the beginning, the middle, and the end of personal religion. The Christian who claims this love is not a doctrine, or a fact, or an example which belongs to the history of a past age, but a living and Divine person who sustains to us the most intimate and sacred relations—coming to us as really and directly as to Simon Peter, at the sea of Galilee, with the home-thrusting inquiry—"Lovest thou me?" The nature and the reality of the love are determined by the nature, the character, and the claims of Him to whom it is due. The love in question is that which rightfully belongs to our incarnate God and Saviour. It is not a superficial and fruitless sentiment of admiration for something He has said, or something he has done, but it is an *adoring reverence* for his Divine Majesty, a complacent delight in his spotless purity, a confiding dependence on his truth and grace, and such a grateful sense of his redeeming mercy to the soul as "constrains" to worship, obey, and follow him! Is there such a passion in your soul? Be assured that love to Christ is as real, conscious, warm, and practical an affection as is any other love, and only differs from our earthly loves by being unutterably more profound, sacred, and enduring. In the sense of such an affection as this, can you say that you do love the Lord Jesus Christ? If still you think so, then let me ask for the visible and convincing proofs of its existence; or, rather, let me invite you to reconcile the idea of its existence in your heart, with certain facts which stand out boldly to view in the life of many who show outward respect to the ordinances and institutions of religion.

The proverb says that "Open rebuke is better than secret love," for the reason, I presume, that love, which is so secret as never to show itself in word or deed, is presumed to have no existence, or, at the best, to be of a very suspicious quality. It is not the nature of love to be silent and motionless. It is essentially demonstrative. It seeks occasion to express itself to the object of its admiration and delight: and especially is this true of that absorbing love to Jesus which the Spirit of God sheds abroad in the believing heart. Can such an affection possibly have room and free activity in the souls of those who never seek to have private, intimate, and, as it were, confidential intercourse with him in prayer? Who even repel his advances, and when he knocks, wishing to come in and show his love, shut the door in his face, and bid him depart? And when he spreads his table, with the memorials of his passion, and bids his disciples receive them in thankful remembrance of his sorrow, and as the pledges of mutual and everlasting friendship, is it love to Christ that occasions your absence?

or is that absence capable of being reconciled with the existence in your soul of true love and loyalty to his person and his cause?

Jesus is not so much an object to be contemplated as an example to be followed, and a *Master* to be *served:* and his own test of love and fealty is obedience to his commandments. "He that loveth me not, keepeth not my sayings." One of his sayings is—"Enter into thy closet and pray." Do you? Another is—"Repent and be converted." Have you any experimental knowledge of godly sorrow and the repentance which is unto salvation? Over the gate-way to his kingdom, he has inscribed "*Self-denial,*" as the condition of discipleship, and the way to heaven. Is this the manner of life which, for Jesus Christ's sake, you are leading? Or, is it a fact, clear to your own consciousness, and evident to those who observe your conduct, that *self-indulgence* is the regulating principle of your behaviour? From points like these, mankind divide and diverge —the few defiling into the "narrow way" of self-denial, in obedience to Christ; the multitude keeping on in the "broad road" of self-gratification, walking in the ways of their own hearts, and in the sight of their own eyes: and because such a life is forbidden by Jesus Christ, those who thus live are guilty of persistent rebellion against his authority, and stand convicted of,—at least, the want of his love.

From such facts, we might proceed to arraign many persons on a graver indictment, than even this which is expressed in the text. Beyond the negative crime of not loving Christ, we might charge them with being under the power of an opposite feeling. We might argue, that in a case like this, if there be no love, there can be no indifference, and must be enmity. We might quote the Saviour's own decisive declaration, that whosoever is "not with him, is against him," and show that in the conflict between the church and the world, truth and error, good and evil, Christ and the devil, there neither is nor can be either indifference of feeling or neutrality of position: but this is unnecessary, and we forbear.

The text speaks not of such as hate and oppose, but of those who love not the Lord Jesus Christ, and we need not transcend the letter of the proposition. And it may be admitted, that while there is no possibility of a man's being wholly neutral in spirit and attitude toward Christ and his cause, there may be, and manifestly there are, degrees of that sinful state of heart, which causes multitudes to stand aloof from Christian vows and church fellowship.

In some, it is *indifference*, in others *aversion*, in a third class, open and unrelenting *hostility*.

Some "care for none of these things," some cavil at the doctrines, and spurn the restraints of Christianity, and some, like Saul of Tarsus, persecute its professors, and seek its extirpation from the earth. It would be altogether unjust and untrue to charge without discrimination, all these degrees and forms of opposition to Christ, upon all unconverted persons; but it is neither untrue nor unjust to lay at their doors, and on their consciences, the accusation, that they do not love Jesus! This, they cannot deny, and there is not one among all the multitudes of the unbelieving of whom it is not true.

And here, I drop the question of fact, and leave each of you, under the convictions of truth, and the sense of your responsibility to God, to find the place which belongs to you, among those who say with trembling and with tears, "Lord, thou knowest all things; thou knowest that I love thee;" or with such as feel in all their souls that up to this day Christ has not been an object of love and a source of joy. Do I address any who have now taken this latter position? Who, under the constraints of truth and conscience, have confessed to themselves the fact that love to Christ has no place within them?

That it should cost you a struggle to make, or even approach such an acknowledgment is very natural, both because the thing confessed implies so much sin, and exposes you to so great danger, but, on the other hand, it is to be considered, that confession of the truth does not render the facts of the case any worse, and removes, at least, one impediment out of the way of your salvation. "He that covereth his sins, shall not prosper; but whoso confesseth and forsaketh them, shall have mercy."

2. To forward, if possible, this blessed result, join with me in giving your close, patient, and impartial attention to *the "exceeding sinfulness" of not loving Jesus Christ.* The text throws this idea forward in high relief, by threatening the curse of God against those who are guilty of this particular sin: yet, in the whole catalogue of acts and omissions which the Scriptures condemn, there is none of which it is so hard to fix the conviction in the conscience. And we encounter this singular feature in the spiritual character and condition of men, that the one sin which the Bible holds up for especial reprobation, and delivers over to the severest punishment which God inflicts on any class of transgressors, is the one offence in reference to which they feel the slightest compunctions, and scarcely rate themselves a degree lower on the scale of morality because they are guilty of it. Their natural conscience condemns *vices* which war on their own bodies and minds, and crimes which war against the rights of others and the welfare of society; they "approve the things that are excellent," and, according as they were guilty or innocent of the impeachment, their cheeks would mantle with shame, or

burn with indignation, if accused of violating these fundamental moralities of life and society. But observe them under the charge, or when they make the frank acknowledgment that they have no love for Jesus Christ! Do they blush, as at the confession of a great moral delinquency? or grow indignant, as if the imputation were deeply damaging to their character? Nothing of the sort. They treat it as the merest peccadillo, less, immeasurably less, than the utterance of a lie, or the theft of a dollar.

In fact and experience, *not loving Christ* is no sin, according to their habitual modes of thinking and rules of action. But if, according to the teachings of Scripture, it be not only a sin, but the very essence and aggravation of human wickedness, it is a question of interest, why a conscience which, with promptness and power, condemns immorality and vice, bears so faint and unfelt a testimony against the sin of withholding our hearts from the Son of God.

This inquiry opens a wide field of remark, on which our purpose does not allow us to enter; and we will only suggest, as a key to the solution of the problem, the fact that *sin*, by its *very nature*, extinguishes, tôtally, and completely, every spark of love to God in the soul, while it leaves the personal and domestic, social and public, moralities of human nature, if not undamaged, certainly *undestroyed.* Total depravity is *total ungodliness.* Publicans and sinners who love their friends very much, do not love God at all; and this is the reason, in its root, why, when God comes to men in the person of his Son, they see in him "no beauty," and turn away with indifference or aversion. We cannot, then, conclude that, because the conscience of men does not anathematize the sinner who has no love to Christ, therefore *God* does not. We must consult truer oracles than our own blinded hearts. If you have read the New Testament with any care, you must know that *sins against Jesus Christ* are those which it signalizes as exposing the sinner to the deepest displeasure of God, and as consigning the soul to the most intolerable of the woes of eternity. You remember how Jesus himself upbraided the cities in which his mighty works were done, because of their unbelief and impenitency, and how he declared that, in the day of judgment, it would fare worse with them than with Sodomites and heathens; and, having once heard, can you ever forget the solemn declaration, that "he that believeth not is condemned already, because he hath not believed in the name of the only-begotten Son of God;" and that "the condemnation" which will burn its blasting curse most deeply into the soul, is the fact that "light has come into the world, and men have loved darkness rather than light?" The man who, by impenitence and unbelief, turns his back on Christ, and thus counts himself unworthy of eternal life, is appointed to "severer punishment" than befel the sinners of a past dispensation, or will overtake idolaters in the day of judgment. Such is the estimate in which God holds the sin of which men make so little. To ask *why* the want of love to Christ is so great an iniquity, is much the same as to inquire why sin *against God* is an evil so crimson in its guilt, so mortal in its effects.

Yet there is a difference which may be rendered plain and palpable.

God in Christ sustains new and peculiar relations to men, and these relations are evidently such as to enhance the guilt of those who do not act in conformity with their nature and purpose.

And here all that is special and peculiar clusters about, and, in one relation or another, depends upon the unique and glorious character of Jesus, as *the mediator between God and men.*

It implies and requires the mystery of his *incarnation:* the coming down among men in human form and earthly manifestation of Him who dwelt from everlasting in the bosom of the Father, and who thought it no robbery to be equal with God. If in this we saw nothing more than the *coming nigh* of God to man, revealing himself under forms and conditions better adapted to our feeble apprehension, does it not even then bring us under a special obligation to recognize and love the *manifested and present* God? If we see in it the grace of a boundless condescension, in that He who was "rich" in celestial glory allied himself with the deep poverty of a lapsed race, does not this, his voluntary humility, claim the grateful acknowledgment of all for whose sake it was submitted to?

And if love returned be the right response for love shown; and if its degree is to be measured by the intensity, the pains, the sacrifices of the love by which we are saved, then tell me, O ye, who hide your faces from the Son of God, with "what manner of love" you ought to regard him, who endured the cross, and despised the shame for you?

Or, if love is to be grounded upon and measured by the value of benefits conferred or offered, estimate, if you can, how much of it is due to Him whose blood washes away the guilt of ten thousand iniquities; whose Spirit—free as the air you breathe, or the water you drink—purifies the heart from pollution; and whose all-powerful mediation brings the sinner back, and up from his apostasy and death on earth, to everlasting life and unutterable bliss in heaven? With a redemption in his hands—the price of his labour and travail, of his tears, and his blood, "The mighty God," in the humility of man's flesh, stands without, and knocks at your heart's door, for no other purpose than to bless your precious soul, with this Divine and infinite benefaction! Or if we have respect to that element in the nature of love, which consists in the admiration of a character for its intrinsic excellence, does not Jesus rise pre-eminent above all the sons of men, and the angelic natures of heaven, in his title to your affections?

The glory of the invisible God shines effulgent in his face; grace is poured into his lips, and distils in words of unmatched sweetness from his tongue. "His heart is made of tenderness." His life is beautified with super-human virtues. He is "altogether lovely."

Saints on earth bless him; the spirits of just men made perfect in heaven, cast their crowns at his feet, and look up to his unveiled face with love and joy unspeakable and full of glory; while an innumerable company of angels kindling with sympathetic adoration, join the alleluia that ascends around his throne, and shout—"Worthy is the Lamb that was slain to receive power, and riches, and strength, and honour, and glory, and blessing."

Such a Being as this it is, who claims your love, and only your love. He does not wish to make you servants but friends, taking you into his confidence, and preparing you to share his heavenly throne. "Give me thy heart,"—this is the sum of all his demands: but you will not give it, and this is the sum and aggravation of your sin. You love him not. You neither delight in his character, nor thank him for his salvation. You forget him, neglect him, disobey him, and perhaps, would be ashamed to have any one suppose that you were even seriously thinking of the duty you owe to him. This is a grievous wrong. In a world that hates him, and dishonours him, you refuse to enroll yourself under his banner, and never open your lips to repel the aspersions which are cast on his blessed cause and holy name.

And, think you, my dear unconverted friend, that this may be done with safety? Will a sin so great—so utterly without excuse—so contrary to the most sacred obligations, be allowed to pass with impunity?

It is a sin unto death, not only because it rejects the only redemption, but because of its own inherent criminality. It, above other forms of transgression, "deserves the wrath of God, both in this world, and that which is to come." It exposes you even to "the wrath of the Lamb." That meek sufferer, who was led as a sheep to the slaughter, and opened not his mouth to resent the blasphemous revilings of the wicked, will, one day, arise to avenge the injuries he has suffered, and to wipe away the reproach of his truth and grace. The salvation or the anathema of Jesus, is the dread alternative to which every one of us is shut up. "If any man love not—let him be anathema."

A person or a thing is anathematized, when devoted to God for destruction. It does not hurt one to be thus dealt with by a false and apostate church, as the faithful have been in the ages past. Its curse is a blessing: but "it is a fearful thing to fall into the hands of the living God;" and the anathema of Incarnate Love, if that be extorted from him by our sins, will torture and blast the soul for ever! The fruitless fig-tree, withered immediately away under his curse, and was doomed to perpetual barrenness and death. The curse which the sin of man entailed on the earth, is so dire and destructive, that the whole creation travails in pain beneath its awful pressure.

When our blessed Lord was nailed to the cross, he himself was anathema! for it is written,—"Cursed is every one that hangeth on a tree."

See how it tortures the soul of immaculate innocence; and hearken how the incarnate God cries out under its dreadful bitterness! And if this was done in the green tree, what will be done in the dry? Can you bear to be accursed of God? Can you endure even to hear Jesus say,—"Depart from me, ye cursed, into the fire prepared for the devil and his angels?"

And terrible as the punishment is, it is certain to be inflicted. The holy apostle, who sacrificed himself for the salvation of men, wrote the words of the text with calmness, and gave his consent in advance to the doom of those who love not the Lord Jesus Christ; and when the day of reckoning arrives, the judgment which delivers them over to the curse, will be approved by every human conscience, and every holy creature, and most of all, by Christ himself. Not in a spirit of vindictiveness, nor because he is less merciful than when he wept over the coming woes of Jerusalem, but because the eternal righteousness of God demands it, Christ will, from his judgment-seat, anathematize every one that loves him not! Nothing is more certain: and in assurance thereof, the apostle adds the mystic words,—"MARANATHA:"—"The Lord cometh."

Because he has gone away out of the world, and we see him no more, men are emboldened in sin, and seem quite at ease in their unbelief. Their inward thought is that he will either never come at all, or not for so long a time that the event is unworthy of present attention. Against such a ruinous and wicked thought, these words are directed. "The Lord cometh." "The day of the Lord will come as a thief in the night." "The Judge standeth before the door." And who may abide the day of his coming; and who shall stand when he appeareth? "Behold, he cometh with clouds, and every eye shall see him, and they also which pierced him; and all kindreds of the earth shall wail because of him. With all his holy angels, he will come, descending in chariots of fire, "taking vengeance on them that know not God, and that obey not the gospel of our Lord Jesus Christ."

In that immense assembly of a congregated world, you will be present: and it will seem to you, as if the eye of Jesus were withdrawn from every other creature, to concentrate its piercing gaze and holy scrutiny on yourself.

Are you ready for the meeting? If you love him now, that will be the day of your redemption. If you love him not, and live on to the day of your death without loving him, it were good for you, if you had not been born. When your slumbering dust awakes, and you meet him in mid-air, you will cry to the rocks and mountains to cover and hide you from his face. There will be none to help you then. The wife, the sister, the parent, the pastor who now prays for you, and weeps over you, will then have finished each one his work: and even Jesus, who now "with melting heart and bleeding hands," offers you salvation, will turn away from your cry of anguish and despair! O ye, that love him not, consider this, lest ye perish. *Why will ye die?* Jesus died to save you. He is this moment ready to save you: and he is able to save them to the uttermost, who come unto God by him, seeing that he ever liveth to make intercession for us. Beyond anything you have ever believed or imagined, Christ is urgent in the matter of your salvation. He yearns over you with tender compassion. He is waiting to hear you pray. He sues for admission to your heart. "Behold," he says, "I stand at the door and knock." Hear his voice then, and open the door, that he may come in to you, and sup with you, and you with him.

SERMON VII.

ABSALOM'S DEATH.

2 SAM. xviii. 14, 15, 17.—*And he took three darts in his hand, and thrust them through the heart of Absalom, while he was yet alive in the midst of the oak. And ten young men that bare Joab's armour compassed about and smote Absalom, and slew him. And they took Absalom, and cast him into a great pit in the wood, and laid a very great heap of stones upon him.*

THE Scriptures abound with the record of men who walked with God on earth, and were afterward received into glory. And parallel with these, and perhaps, not less in number, we have the biography of those whose character deserves only execration, and whose "latter end," so far from being a thing to be desired, inspires only sentiments of fear and horror. They are not patterns, but warnings; not models for imitation, but monuments reared upon the place of danger, "pillars of salt," that put us in remembrance of the sins which have ruined others.

What these warnings lack therefore, in presenting nothing positive for imitation, they make up by appealing to sentiments and principles which exist in the hearts of all men. The examples of the good and holy act with effectual power, only on those who have in some degree a corresponding character, and aspire to the same excellence; while the example of sinners, the history of whose crimes and judgments makes them a warning to men beset with like temptations, addresses itself to feelings which exist in every heart. All men dread evil, and desire to escape it, and when they see that sin entails misery and ruin on those who practise it, the depravity of their hearts is in a measure restrained, and in some instances, this fear may prove the germ of a thorough reformation, and eventuate in the conversion and salvation of the soul. In this view, we propose, as the subject of our present meditations, the death of Absalom, with such reflections as the facts of his life may suggest. He did not die the "common death" of men: and it is not upon any of the common aspects of death, as a fact in the history of our mortal race, that we propose to speak, but only of the special lessons of this particular death.

Its tragical nature, and the very peculiar manner in which it was brought about, besides investing it with an air of romance, fasten attention upon it as an act of Providence, and connect it with the antecedent life which came to this sad and sudden close. We cannot but look upon it as the punishment of a great crime; and when we consider who Absalom was, and the circumstances in which he was placed, his character and career may supply a useful and interesting study. The instruction it affords appears to lie mainly in two directions. His death may be considered in its relation to his own conduct and character, and also as it stands connected with that of his royal father, the king of Israel. Both aspects, taken together, may give us some insight into the principles and methods of Divine Providence.

I. In the first place, view the death of Absalom *as the natural termination of a vicious career, and the just punishment of a great crime.* "The wages of sin is death," and, sooner or later, they are certain to be paid. Sin, as a moral cause, operates with the same infallible certainty and irresistible power as physical agencies do. A cannon-ball which strikes a man on the head, a mortal poison received into the stomach, or a consumption which feeds upon the most vital organs of the human system, is no more sure to work the death of the body, than sin is to effectuate that of the soul. In some of its forms it destroys both soul and body, and so manifestly begins the work of ruin in the present world, as to inspire fearful apprehensions of what it will accomplish hereafter, when it is "finished" in death eternal. The case of the "young man Absalom" illustrates this position. It shows the connexion between sin and suffering—crime and punishment. Knowing his history, we naturally look for some signal expression of the Divine displeasure, and are not surprised at the swift and terrible retribution which overtook him.

His crime was great. It involved many elements of turpitude and circumstances of aggravation. He was a conspirator and a rebel against the best government in the world. Not only was it a good and righteous government, but, in a high and peculiar sense, it was a Divine government. Its constitution and laws were enacted *by God*, revealed on Sinai, and, as to their essence, written by his own finger on tables of stone. And not this only, but the actual administration of it was sanctioned by the same high authority. The reigning king was designated and anointed by an inspired prophet. To resist *him*, was, in a special sense, to "resist the ordinance of God;" and the attempt to subvert his authority, was, in effect, rebellion against the covenant-God of Israel. A second element and aggravation of his sin exists in the *motives* which prompted the guilty attempt to revolutionize the government and usurp the throne. The whole scheme proceeded from *personal ambition.* He had no wrongs to redress, no grievances to complain of, no great abuses and oppressions which he sought to remove. His aim was not to make a better government, but simply to get the reins of power into his own hands. David was growing old, and must needs soon resign the sceptre to other hands, and Solomon, by the appointment of his father, and the higher intimations of Heaven, had been already indicated as his successor. To defeat this purpose, and to place the crown on his own head, was the whole scope and object of Absalom's undertaking. His motive was purely selfish, and his aim unlawful and unholy. Having a wicked *end* in view, he would not, of course, scruple to pursue it *by means of the same nature;* and in these we have an added element of his crime, and a further exhibition of his character.

With a view to render himself popular, he played the demagogue, and was as genuine a specimen of the class as any age or country has ever produced. He affected regal state, beginning to act the king, that men might think of him as one fit to fill the throne.

He stationed himself in places of public concourse, and sought the acquaintance of the people. Without directly charging that the government was badly administered, he plainly hinted that such was the fact, and professed a very special and peculiar interest in persons whom he had never seen or heard of before: "And it was so, that when any man that had a controversy came to the king for judgment, then Absalom called unto him, and said, Of what city art thou? And he said, Thy servant is of one of the tribes of Israel. And Absalom said unto him, See, thy matters are good and right; but there is no man deputed of the king to hear thee. Oh that I were made judge in the land, that every man which hath a suit or cause might come unto me, and I would do him justice. And it was so, that when any man came nigh to him to do him obeisance, he put forth his hand, and took him, and kissed him: so Absalom stole the hearts of the men of Israel." To these low arts of the demagogue, he added the baseness of the hypocrite. When his plans were matured, and the conspiracy was ready for development, he pretended that, years before, when he was an exile in Geshur, a town of Syria, he had made a vow to worship and sacrifice unto the Lord in Hebron, in case he was brought again to his own country. It would seem the vow had lain lightly on his conscience for a long time, but now he pleads it as a pretext to ask permission to visit Hebron—a royal city where David himself had begun to reign—that, with the prestige of its fame and eminence, he might declare himself king, and rally the people to his standard. Pleased with his seeming piety, the request was readily granted, and the plot proceeded to its consummation. The particulars thus far gleaned from the history are enough of themselves to prove the badness of his heart, and to stamp his name with infamy. *Ambition, hypocrisy, trickery, and falsehood*, culminating in *open rebellion*, constitute a crime of no ordinary dimensions; but we have not named or adverted to the circumstance which imparts to the proceeding its chief malignity and wickedness: *It was directed against his own father!* It was highly criminal to make the attempt which he did, supposing that he intended simply to prevent Solomon from succeeding to the throne to which he had been chosen according to the forms, and in the spirit of their theocratic constitution. And for *any* man to have attempted the dethronement of *David*, who had now grown gray in the service of his country, and beneath whose wise and benign administration its people had been happy, and all its interests had prospered, and by whose martial prowess and victorious sword the territory of the kingdom had spread from the Mediterranean to the Euphrates,—for any man to have unfurled the standard of revolt against such a monarch, would have been a most wanton outrage, and an enormous crime. But for *Absalom* to do it, made the crime unspeakably greater. It was a contemptuous violation of the honour and duty which belonged to the best of fathers, as well as the best of kings.

Against the father whose bone and flesh he was, of whose endearment and fond hopes he had been the object, and from whom he had received for previous faults a free and cordial forgiveness, he devised a plot, and set in operation a revolt which endangered not only his throne and his honour, but his very life, and was in every way calculated to "bring down his gray hairs with sorrow to the grave."

In heart and purpose he was a parricide, guilty of the foulest murder and the most unnatural of crimes. The climax of his guilt was reached when he gave ready and delighted assent to the counsel of Ahithophel, which contemplated not the slaughter of the people, but only the assassination of the king. "I," said this wily warrior, "will come upon him when he is weary and weak-handed, and will make him afraid, and all the people that are with him shall flee, and *I will smite the king only.*" That Ahithophel ventured to make the suggestion, shows that he knew his man. "The saying pleased Absalom well." There is no intimation that the atrocity of the act gave him one moment's "pause," or occasioned even a twinge of conscience. If the object of his unhallowed ambition could have been reached without this horrible deed, no doubt he would have chosen to avoid it; only the malignity of a fiend could have found pleasure in it for its own sake. That he did not shrink from it, proves the remorseless cruelty of "vaulting ambition," and shows with what perfect ease and reckless determination it pursues its aim, trampling on all obligations, and plunging into the most unnatural and diabolical crimes.

Few chapters in the annals of the world are so black with infamy and guilt as those that record the conspiracies, cruelties, and murders which ambition has resorted to for the purpose of displacing those who stood in its way, and of mounting thus to thrones of power. It has made men "murderers of fathers," and of brothers, and of innocent children; and it has transformed the tender heart of woman into marble hardness. And at this hour, it has as much to do, perhaps, as anything else, among the immediate causes of our national troubles, in shaking the foundations of our government, and filling the land with distress and bloodshed. It is a crime of gigantic magnitude, and in its outworking cruel and relentless as the very spirit of the pit.

II. Having thus traced the character and crime of Absalom at their point of fullest development, a natural curiosity prompts us to inquire whether there is anything in the early history of this man which goes to explain the obliquity of his riper years—anything which marks a gradual departure from the ways of piety and uprightness, and which may be turned by ourselves to practical account.

His mother's name was Maachah, the daughter of Talmai, king of Geshur, a heathenish town of Syria. It is not to be supposed that she practised idolatry; as the wife of David, she doubtless became a proselyte to the Jewish religion, and was at least an outward and apparent worshipper of Jehovah: nevertheless, it would not probably trench on charity or the probabilities of historical truth, to suppose that she may not have been a very suitable person to train her son to the practices of virtue and religion. But, as often happens in fact, it might be suggested that the lack of service on the part of one parent was supplied by the fidelity of the other. We know that a father's dereliction in parental duty is not seldom counteracted, and in a good degree overcome by the spiritual wisdom, deep devotion, and holy life of a Christian mother: and, on the other hand, there are not wanting examples in which children who are denied her plastic powers to mould their characters, are well and successfully trained by a father's example and authority. Whatever may have been the character of Maachah, we know that David was a man of exemplary piety, and one that felt a profound and tender interest in the spiritual and eternal welfare of his children. After he had brought up the ark to Jerusalem with public ceremonies and rejoicings, we are told that he "returned to bless his household." His duty as king was immediately followed by that of a father—the priest of his family. The pious charge he gave to Solomon at his inauguration, discloses the same trait of character. The burden of it was, that he served God while he ruled the people: "Thou, Solomon, my son, know thou the God of thy fathers. If thou seek him, he will be found of thee; but if thou forsake him, he will cast thee off for ever." From these and like indications we might seem precluded from the attempt to trace any sort of connexion between the misconduct of Absalom, and the shortcomings of David in his parental relations.

And it must be admitted that there is nothing expressed in the history which proves any delinquency in respect of this particular child. Two or three circumstances, however, suggest the surmise that Absalom may have been a spoiled child, in whom the germs of tyranny and rebellion were planted at an early age by parental neglect and indulgence. It would seem that he was a darling child to his father, standing to David somewhat in the same relation as Joseph to the doting heart of Jacob. This might be gathered from the manner in which he yearned over him while in banishment*—from the charge given to the chiefs of his army as they went forth to quench so unnatural a rebellion—"Deal gently, for my sake, with the young man, even with Absalom;" and more especially from the irrepressible and overpowering grief occasioned by his death. Parental love is an implantation of the heavenly Father, and is like his own: and its truest manifestation and highest use are seen in seeking the spiritual and eternal welfare of our offspring; but that blind and foolish fondness which "spares the rod" when it is needed, according to an inspired oracle, is "hatred of the child." It may be that the starting point of Absalom's course to ruin lies just here. It is not an uncommon fault of good men. Faithful in other respects, they are lamentably remiss in this: they neglect the religious training and government of their children. Eli the priest was a good man, and "trembled for the ark of God," and glowed with patriotic devotion—but he did not govern his children. "When his sons made themselves vile, he restrained them not," and they rushed on to perdition.

Another circumstance which heightens the probability that the religious discipline and education of Absalom may have been in some degree neglected, is the fact that David was greatly occupied with affairs of state, and oppressed with business. He had the administration of a kingdom on his hands. It is true this would neither justify nor necessitate the neglect of his family; but we all know the absorbing nature even of our own out-door and public engagements, and how strong is the tempta-

* 2 Sam. xiii. 39.

tion they offer to omit home duties. The king of Israel may have felt, and, to some extent, yielded to a like, but immensely greater pressure. If he did, he committed a great mistake—he neglected a primary duty—and so laid the foundation not only for the most pungent parental sorrows, but for the subversion of his kingdom. Nothing whatever, come in what guise it may, whether of public and professional duty, or of urgent business, by which our children are clothed and fed, can justify the neglect of their religious education and constant training in the ways of the Lord.

A third circumstance, tending even more strongly to confirm the suspicion that lack of early restraint had nurtured the spirit of filial insubordination in Absalom, and made him at last a traitor, a rebel, and a parricide, is the recorded fact that in reference to another of his sons, David did pursue a course of uniform and weak indulgence, and with substantially the same results as were produced in this case. After the rebellion of Absalom had been suppressed, and David was old and bed-ridden, Adonijah, a younger son, "exalted himself, saying, I will be king; and he prepared him chariots, and horsemen, and fifty men to run before him." After this announcement, it is added, in significant proximity—"And his father had not displeased him at any time, in saying, Why hast thou done so?" The youth had done as he pleased, had gone where he chose, and no doubt had practised the petty tyrant over those whose condition was inferior, and thus had grown rapidly up to the full stature of a rebel, who was not afraid or ashamed to imbitter the last hours of his too indulgent father. If a similar course was pursued with Absalom, his precocious wickedness and filial impiety are sufficiently explained. "A child left to himself bringeth his mother to shame," and his father to grief: so natural and strong is the bent of an evil nature—so great the power of temptation—so fundamentally requisite is the wise, firm, and loving control of parental government. While we thus collect from the biography of this unhappy and erring youth a lesson of instruction and warning for parents, and a powerful stimulus to the performance of a great duty, we may learn something as to the danger of temptation, and the progress of sin. The last and fatal crime which cost Absalom his life, was not, by any means, his first lapse from virtue. He did not fall, nor does any man fall, at once from innocence and uprightness into the depths of infamy and guilt. His rebellion, with all its aggravations, was not the sudden outbreak of the native depravity which is common to all men, but rather the result and full-blown development of an advancing degeneracy which had been going forward for many years, and which had, on certain occasions, revealed itself in outward and palpable forms. The bloody vengeance he took on his brother Amnon, for the crime he had committed against Tamar, the sister of Absalom, may be, in some degree, extenuated by the provocation which moved him to it; yet the fact, and especially the manner of the deed, shows him to have been a man of vindictive spirit. He cherished the grudge for two whole years, and then carried his wrathful purpose into effect on a festive occasion at which his brother was present by his own invitation. This occasioned his flight to Syria, where he remained in exile for the space of three years: but the punishment does not appear to have wrought any improvement in his character, and the whole affair left him in a more hardened condition than ever.

We have already adverted to the connexion between ambition and cruelty: may not a like relationship be traced between this latter quality and personal vanity and pride? A man who is filled with self-conceit and puffed up with vain-glory, whatever its particular basis may be, will commonly be found regardless, in an equal degree, of the rights, the interests, and the feelings of others. Self so completely fills the sphere of his vision, that he scarcely discerns the existence of anybody or anything else, and is a cruel Moloch, to which every thing that comes in its way must be sacrificed. If we ascribe a character like this to Absalom, we do not go beyond the record. Beauty is generally deemed the snare, as it is the common endowment of the gentler sex. Doubtless many are too conscious of the possession, and from the fairness of the face, receive a blemish on the soul. The weakness and folly of their vanity, while quite without excuse, and far from being either innocent or harmless, are probably less so than when the same qualities are found in men, and are based upon personal attractions. The moral sense of the world, in reference to members of the sterner sex who pride themselves on the possession of personal beauty, is signified by calling them *effeminate* (or like women.) This, without doubt, was a snare to Absalom. He was famed throughout the nation for his comeliness. His hair was observed with admiration, and was probably "cultivated" with an assiduity not surpassed by any of the moderns. "In all Israel there was none to be so much praised as Absalom for his beauty: from the sole of his foot, even to the crown of his head, there was no blemish in him: and when he polled his head, (for it was at every year's end that he polled it; because the hair was heavy upon him, therefore he polled), he weighed the hair of his head at two hundred shekels, after the king's weight."

The admiring eyes that were turned upon him, and the incense of universal laudation which greeted his ears, flattered his vanity and nurtured his pride, till he became a very god in his own eyes; and when he reached that point, all generous and noble sentiments were paralyzed, and he was an easy prey to whatever temptation most powerfully addressed the ruling passion of his nature. The great crime which finally revealed his character and destroyed his soul, sustained a close relation to the vanity and selfishness which had long been growing up in his heart. As a tree stands erect, after its heart has been consumed by a slow decay, until the sweeping tempest lays it low, so he maintained his position till the course of events presented a temptation which found no principle or power within him to resist it, and he fell to rise no more.

This lesson of his life and history is, that a thoroughly depraved character is the result of a gradual process of moral deterioration—that a fatal issue of one's career is reached not at a single bound, but by many steps—and that "out of the heart are the issues of life." And the practical duty is, "Keep thy heart with all diligence."

The review of his whole character and life, connected with his melancholy and tragical death, leaves a profound impression of the evil and folly of sinful courses, and is a solemn comment on those Scriptures which assure us that the "way of transgressors is hard," and the "end of it death." His career is a warning to young and old, to parents and children, and especially to young men, who are so often ruined in body and soul, in time and eternity, by the indulgence of their passions and appetites. To those who are tempted to give themselves up to the promptings of ambition, the dishonoured grave of Absalom, and the great heap of stones thrown rudely upon his body, preach a sermon of touching eloquence. Such is the end and monument of those who would climb to thrones and chairs of state over violated constitutions and ruined nations. "Pride goeth before destruction, and a haughty spirit before a fall." "He that exalteth himself shall be abased."

It had been our purpose to inquire what relation the crime and calamity of Absalom sustained to the one great fault and error of his father's life—David's sin in the matter of Uriah the Hittite—but this we must pass over with a bare reference to the circumstances. Sinning against the family of another, he was sorely punished in his own. Because he killed Uriah with the sword of the children of Ammon, it was said to him, "The sword shall not depart from thy house." Thenceforward, to his dying day, domestic sorrows oppressed him; and many a dirge-like Psalm was made the vehicle of his bitter griefs. God remitted the penalty of damnation, but chastised him with temporal judgments: so strict and holy is he in dealing even with his saints. It is a principle of his government to punish the sins of parents in their children, "visiting the iniquity of the fathers upon the children unto the third and fourth generation."

The Lord smote the unconscious babe of Bathsheba with a mortal sickness for its father's sin. The real blow and judgment fell not on it, but on him. It was well with the child, and ill with the father. This only seems severe: it is beneficent and kind. It calls in, as a help and stimulus to piety and well-doing, the parental instinct—one of the strongest in our nature. If you sin, your children will suffer.

The grief of this poor afflicted father is one of the most affecting spectacles which any history, sacred or profane, records. Waiting with trembling heart for tidings of the battle, the sad fate of Absalom is at length reported. The slain youth was his deadliest foe, but then he was his son! and the king is completely merged and lost in the father. His heart breaks, and his piteous lamentations melt all beholders to tears; and at this distance we weep with him. Many like him have cried—"O my son Absalom! my son, my son Absalom! would God I had died for thee, O Absalom, my son, my son!"

May God avert, or long postpone, from you and me this piercing grief!

SERMON VIII.

THE FINISHED WORK.

JOHN xix. 30.—*When Jesus, therefore, had received the vinegar, he said, It is finished:* (Τετέλεσται). *And he bowed his head, and gave up the ghost.*

IT looked as if not his work, but his cause, were finished! The superscription fastened on his cross, in derisive mockery of his pretensions, proclaiming, in letters of Hebrew, and Greek, and Latin, to all beholders, "This is the king of the Jews," might have been deemed an epitaph, rather than a prophecy, and brought to mind the fatal hand-writing on Belshazzar's palace—"God hath numbered thy kingdom and finished it." Never, in all the history of the world, did the thoughts of God move in a plane farther above the thoughts of men and the subtlety of devils. At the moment the dying Saviour uttered these words, the plans of both were hasting to their maturity; *theirs* apparently, *his* really.

What wicked men did, under the instigation of Satan, to suppress the voice of truth, and to get rid of One who had disturbed their guilty repose, and set the terrors of the Lord in array against them, subserved, in a manner, the most direct, the merciful and holy designs of God. The murderous purpose, which for months had been waiting its opportunity, was now blindly fulfilling an older purpose of Heaven, and, in its infatuation, sapping the foundations of that unholy power which it thought to establish. How far Divine Wisdom exceeds human craft and hellish cunning, was never proved with such overwhelming demonstration as when Jesus, "delivered by the determinate counsel and foreknowledge of God," was taken, and, by the "wicked hands" of men, was "crucified and slain." No providential mystery which has ever cast its shadow on the church, has been so dark as that at which hell rejoiced, and the hearts of disciples were filled with anguish and despair, but out of which God has brought forth light, and hope, and joy, and salvation. If the "wrath of man," when vented against the Redeemer himself, and not restrained until it had accomplished his death, was made to praise God and bless the world, much more may we expect its feebler manifestations against the truth and the church to fail of their aim, and to redound to the greater furtherance of the faith which they seek to destroy.

But our design is not to interpret these dying words of Jesus in the sense of those who may have heard them, or in the light of the sad and gloomy appearances of that hour, but rather from the point of view—so far as it is possible for us to gain it—of him by whom they were spoken: and to gather and bring to bear on our hearts the lessons which they most obviously suggest. They have a peculiar interest and tenderness, from being one of the utterances which fell from his lips on the cross; and one of the last of these,—if we had no record but that of John,—the very last.

These expressions are a study of unspeakable interest. They were his dying words. His bodily pain was excruciating: his mental anguish was awful and mysterious: yet he was singularly self-possessed, and, until the moment when he bowed his head and gave up the ghost, observant of the scenes about him, and intent upon the object of his wondrous mission. He spoke repeatedly. We treasure the words of the dying, because we desire to know what is passing in the mind at this solemn and heart-searching hour. If the words of Christ in death are not possessed of more inherent weight than those he spoke in life, the circumstance of their being uttered when the waves of the dark river were surging about him, and the burden of a world's guilt was crushing his soul, must greatly enhance their impression, and we listen to them with tearful and sacred interest. It would seem that after he had been nailed to the cross, and then with rude violence it had been dropped into the earth, the first utterance was that heart-melting prayer for his murderers, "Father, forgive them, for they know not what they do." Then, inclining his ear to one who prayed to him for salvation, he said, "Verily, I say unto thee, to-day shalt thou be with me in Paradise." Seeing her standing by in whom old Simeon's prophecy was receiving its bitter fulfilment, that "a sword should pierce through her soul;"—the disciple whom he loved being also near—he cried—"Woman, behold thy son," and then calling the disciple by his name, said,—"Behold, thy mother." And, as the sorrows of his soul deepened, and a horror of great darkness fell upon him, he first exclaimed,—"My God, my God, why hast thou forsaken me," then, with calm self-recollection, declared, "It is finished," and at last, with a confidence in God, which even that mysterious shadow that hid his face could not impair, devoutly said,—"Father, into thy hands I commit my spirit," and then,—to show how literally exact were the words he spake when he said, "No man taketh my life from me, but I lay it down of myself,"—he bowed his head and gave up the ghost; asserting even in death that he was the Lord of life.

From these half-dozen dying expressions of our gracious Redeemer, we select the shortest, but, in a doctrinal point of view, perhaps, the most significant:—"IT IS FINISHED." The word bears the sense of *completeness.* A house is finished, not when its foundations are laid and the walls reared, but when it has received the last touch of the mechanic's tool, and nothing remains to be done before it is fit for occupancy. In this sense, the work was done to which our Lord referred, when he used the language of the text. The force of the term, and the facts of the case, necessitate a restricted application.

It cannot include anything which, as Mediator, Christ afterwards did, and is doing now, and shall do, until the economy of grace is closed, and the kingdom shall be delivered up to the Father; except it be in the modified sense that, as his death involved all this, he might be said to have virtually accomplished it. His work as a Saviour, however, will not be finished until the last of his redeemed ones shall have been called and santified, and the whole church, with glorious bodies and sanctified spirits, "without spot or wrinkle, or any such thing," shall be presented to God, "with exceeding joy."

His work as a Priest will not be finished as long as there is a sinful worshipper on earth to need his intercession; and he will sit on the throne of his kingly mediation, till the "last enemy" shall be trodden under his feet, and a risen church shall shout, "O death, where is thy sting? O grave, where is thy victory?" "Then cometh the end, when he shall have delivered up the kingdom to God, even the Father; when he shall have put down all rule, and all authority, and power." Redemption in its application to the souls of men runs through all the ages of human history, and will not be "finished" till it is proclaimed from heaven that "time shall be no longer."

The nature of the case thus leads us to fix upon some particular aspect of Christ's work which was finished at the moment he expired on the cross. Though the ground of our inquiry is narrowed, the interest of the theme is not diminished. Our view is confined to what is the very heart and centre of redemption. The words before us are true in a manifold sense. We do not impose it upon them from our own choice and fancy, but collect it from Scripture.

1. The immediate connexion of the passage leads us to view it first of all, in its relation to the prophecies which were fulfilled in the death of Christ. Upon no fact of his history, and upon no part of his work, do so many types and predictions converge as upon his death. It was prefigured by every sacrificial victim that bled from the beginning, and was the burden of many a psalm and prophecy which not only foretold the fact, but minutely detailed its circumstances. The paschal lamb, fastened on transverse pieces of wood, and roasted whole, without the breaking of a bone, was an annual and standing type both of the fact and manner of his death. When the soldiers came and found that he was dead already, they brake not his legs, and thus unconsciously fulfilled the Scripture, which said, "A bone of him shall not be broken."

When, according to the custom, his executioners sat down to divide his clothes among them, and declined to rend his seamless coat, but cast lots whose it should be, an ancient oracle they wot not of was verified: "They parted my garments among them, and upon my vesture did they cast lots." In the clustering sorrows and indignities which were crowded into his last hours, predictions that were made ages before, received in quick succession, and with amazing precision, their exact accomplishment. At length, one only remained without its verifying sorrow. "The things concerning me," said Jesus, "have an end," and this must be fulfilled, even though he himself make the occasion. "Knowing that all things were now accomplished, that the Scriptures might be fulfilled, he saith, '*I thirst.*'"

That was no fiction, but an awful fact; the burning, anguished thirst of one dying slowly by torture. At the commencement of the execution, he had been offered "vinegar mingled with myrrh,"—a beverage provided for criminals doomed to capital punishment, and designed to deaden their sensibilities. He refused it! The cup which his Father gave him, should he not drink it? Every nerve must writhe in pain, and every inner sense of the soul suffer up to its full capacity: but now, when this has been endured, he tastes the draught, and bows his head in death, and that other prediction passed into historic verity, which said,—"They gave me also gall for my meat; and in my thirst, they gave me vinegar to drink." If any inquire, Why this concern for the fulfilment of Scripture? the answer is, not only that the truth of God might be established, but that the evidence of his Messiahship might be placed beyond all doubt, and a sure foundation be laid for the faith and hope of a perishing world. In the matter of our eternal salvation, we cannot afford to be left in doubt, and God does not require us to believe in his Son without evidence. "Him hath God the Father sealed," by miracles wrought, and prophecies fulfilled, and voices spoken from the heavens, saying, "This is my beloved Son; hear him." "Believe on him, and you shall live for ever."

2. In the second place, we may connect these dying words of

the Saviour, with the ceremonial law and typical worship of the Old Testament, which foreshadowed his divine and glorious priesthood.

For four thousand years the blood of lambs, and goats, and bullocks, had been streaming from Jewish and Patriarchal altars: and priests of families and tribes, and of the united Israel of God, had performed this sacred but ineffectual function. Acceptable they were, because of Divine appointment; but their use was to foreshow and teach men to trust in the only real and availing priesthood which God has ever instituted, even that of the Lord Jesus Christ, begun in the outer court below, and carried on in the holy of holies above. The priest, the altar, the victim, the sprinkling of blood, the burning of incense, and all else that entered into the complex and orderly detail of the Jewish temple service, pointed to answering facts and realities in the person and offices of Jesus. All these, as the Apostle says, were "A shadow of good things to come," but "the body," (that cast the shadow) is Christ. And as their only use was to herald his coming, and meanwhile enable sinful souls to hope for and rely upon a redemption yet future, they ceased, as a matter of course, when Jesus appeared and performed the priestly offices which they had so long represented.

In so far as those ceremonial institutions were a system of laws, they expired by virtue of a limitation contained in themselves, being only "imposed until the time of reformation." Regarded in the light of types, they were displaced by the substance, in the room of which they had stood. As means of grace, they were no longer required nor useful, when "grace and truth" itself came by Jesus Christ. "Think not," said he, "that I am come to destroy the law or the prophets. I am not come to destroy, but to fulfil."

Every good thing of which the ritual of the Jewish worship gave pre-intimation, was realized in his coming, and in token that these typical institutions had accomplished their purpose, and were done away; an invisible hand rent the vail of the temple in sunder from top to bottom, in the moment that Jesus said —"It is finished," and resigned his spirit to the Father. Thus was the neck of his disciples freed for ever from the yoke of "carnal ordinances," useful once, but now injurious to those who have passed from the discipline of childhood, to the liberty of the sons of God.

This "hand-writing of ordinances which was against us, and was contrary to us, he hath taken out of the way," and, in the manner of a cancelled obligation, "nailed it to his cross."

The ceremonial law died with Jesus, and with respect to it, he might say—"It is finished."

3. A third and obvious application of these words, is that which refers them to the SUFFERINGS of *the Saviour.* He had now filled up the appointed measure of his sorrows. The last drop of bitterness had been drained from the cup which the Father had put into his hands: and we read here both a lesson of sadness and of joy—of sadness, that he suffered so much; of joy, that he should suffer no more. The humiliation of the Son of God—may we not say it reverently?—is the strangest chapter in the history of divinity. "The man Christ Jesus" was a *sufferer*—yea, the very prince of sufferers. His whole earthly manifestation was one of sorrow, deepening from the beginning to the end. Never were there so many, or so varied, or such peculiar sorrows allotted to any member of the human family. He was a *man of sorrows*, "acquainted with grief." "His visage was so marred more than any man; and his form more than the sons of men." It was an infinite humiliation to veil his Godhead

in our weak flesh, and take the nature of man into personal union with the nature of God. And this he did, and from choice, in circumstances of peculiar lowliness. He was "born, and that in a low condition," the child of an obscure virgin, beholding, at first, the light of day, not in the abodes of men, but in the habitation of brutes! In his infancy, persecuted with murderous intent; in his youth, "meekly subject to his parents;" in his manhood, following the humble and laborious trade of a carpenter; and during his public ministry of three years, greeted with contempt, cavils, and sneers, by nearly all who gave tone and direction to public opinion. Reviled of men and tempted of the devil, he keenly felt the sting of these trials, and none the less because he was also God. But great as were the sorrows of his life, they were not to be compared with those of his death.

Then he suffered in every conceivable way, and from every possible quarter; in his body, in his soul; from friends, from enemies; from man, from devils, from God! Behold him a prostrate suppliant in the garden, "with strong crying and tears, addressing his prayer unto Him that was able to save him from death, and gauge the depth of his anguish by the pleading importunity with which he cries, by the nature of the petition he urges, by the agony and bloody sweat into which he has fallen!" "Exceeding sorrowful, even unto death," was Jesus in that hour, the point, perhaps, of deepest depression, when his human nature shuddered and shrank back from that mysterious suffering which atones for human guilt! An angel appears from heaven, strengthing his fainting humanity, and he is prepared for the ordeal of the cross.

Hanging there in agonies unutterable, the moments pass sluggishly by, and his life's blood trickles from his hands and his feet. The reproach of sinners hath broken his heart, and when the load of man's iniquity which he bore projects its dark shadow to heaven, and covers with total eclipse the light of that face which had never before been clouded, that sinking of soul came over him which none know but those whom *God forsakes.* The cup of his sorrow is now exhausted, the last pang is endured, and it only remains for him to say "It is finished," and yield his freed spirit unto God.

While this touching declaration thus points to the fact and the greatness of his sufferings, it gives the sweet assurance that they were then ended for ever. They were *finished*, both in the sense of being *completed* and *terminated.* Though his death-bed was a cross, he fell sweetly asleep, and in Joseph's new tomb enjoyed untroubled repose. At the time appointed, he awoke and came forth with the freshness of a new-born immortality, joyful and triumphant. Thenceforward, his body never felt a pain, nor his heart a grief. Raised from the dead, he dieth no more, and weeps no more. The night of his humiliation is over, and the morning of his glory has dawned. Into "the joy set before him, for which he endured the cross, despising the shame," he has entered, and through eternal ages he will never shed a tear or know a sorrow. And what has already happened to the Captain of our salvation, is that which awaits ourselves. The moment of our last sorrow hastens on, and God, from his throne, will say, concerning us, "It is done," and we shall go to the blissful land where "there shall be no more death, neither sorrow nor crying, neither shall there be any more pain."

4. A fourth application of these dying words of our Divine Lord, and the most vital of all, is that which refers them to the completed atonement for the sins of men, which was made when he died on the cross.

The humiliation of his life, and the sorrows of his death, were the satisfaction which the law and justice of God required of those whose sins he bore in his own body on the tree. Deep as is the criminality of sin, countless as were the transgressions of a guilty world, aggravated as were the offences of many, and infinite as was God's abhorrence of evil, the precious blood of Christ was absolutely all that was needed or demanded to atone for sin.

When he died, justice did not ask, and could not accept anything more. When the last drop of his blood was shed, and his dear life went out a sacrifice to God, the atonement was made, completely made—incapable for ever of being impaired by lapse of time or sin of men, or of being supplemented by human works. In the most absolute sense of the words, it was "finished," and henceforth it belongs to men, not to repeat it, as the Romanists pretend to do in the sacrifice of the Mass, nor to add to it by uncommanded and vain austerities, but by humble faith to embrace it, and with grateful joy to commemorate it in the Sacrament of the Supper, till Jesus shall come the second time, without sin unto salvation. In common phrase, we sometimes speak of doing a thing "once for all," meaning thereby, that we do it effectually, and remove all occasion for ever doing it over again. In this sense precisely, it is said by the Apostle, "We are sanctified by the offering of the body of Jesus Christ, once for all." The Jewish sacrifices, because they possessed no inherent efficacy to atone, and only typified the coming expiation, were repeated day by day, and from age to age.

"But this man, after he had offered one sacrifice for sins, for ever sat down on the right hand of God,—for by one offering, he hath perfected for ever them that are sanctified." So certainly as the death of Christ is an accomplished fact, the atonement is a completed work. In the moment his life was extinct, the penal demands of God's broken law were satisfied, "all righteousness was fulfilled," and no impediment remained in the way of that impatient mercy which made for itself a channel through the mangled flesh and pierced heart of God's dear Son.

In that hour, the evangelic prediction of Daniel passed into actual history. "Messiah was cut off, not for himself," but "to finish transgression, to make an end of sins, to make reconciliation for iniquity, and to bring in everlasting righteousness." The gospel, therefore, which we preach to you this day, is not that an atonement for sin is promised. That were to remand you back to the twilight and shadowy grace of a by-gone dispensation. Nor that a partial and incomplete sacrifice for sin has been made by the sufferings of Jesus, and needs to be filled out by works of righteousness and tears of penitence; but the good news we bring you is, that redemption is finished, and for its actual power in your pardon and peace, requires nothing at all but naked acceptance. "The uttermost farthing" of your enormous debt of ten thousand talents has been cancelled by one who, "though he was rich, for your sakes became poor." It was liquidated in his streaming blood; the bond has been taken up by your "surety," and, if we may compare the mysteries of redemption with the transactions of earth, the gospel is God's written discharge from the penal claims of law and justice against all believing sinners. "A just God and a Saviour" is he: and his covenant name, "Jehovah Tzidkenu, The LORD OUR RIGHTEOUSNESS." Do ye, my brethren, comprehend well this glorious mystery? Is it dear to your understandings, and does it pour divinest consolation into your hearts, that you, who are unholy and guilty, and hell-deserving sinners, are freely and completely, now and for ever, "accepted in the Beloved?" justified by a righteousness not your own, exactly as if it were your own, being made over to you by the gracious act of God? Do you know and feel that your standing in his sight depends not on your fitful frames, imperfect obedience, and sin-defiled works, but on the "obedience unto death" of the Lord Jesus Christ?

Until you receive this central truth of the gospel into your heart of faith and love, "the spirit of bondage again to fear," will be ever and anon returning to you, and you will have but small experience of the liberty wherewith Christ has made us free.

Believe it then, ye sad and downcast disciples, that the one only sacrifice of Calvary, avails for your present and eternal justification! That for the righteousness' sake of Jesus, God not only pardons but accepts you; not only tolerates you in his dominions, and suffers you to live out of hell, but adopts you into his family, loves your person, approves your weak but sincere obedience, and destines you to the glories of heaven and a blissful immortality! The atonement was finished the moment Jesus died; and your justification was finished the moment you first believed with a true faith and a penitent heart. "Believest thou this?" Then let your joy be full, and your "songs abound," and the peace which passeth all understanding fill your hearts!

In this faith, come to the memorial supper which sets before you the finished sacrifice of Jesus, and while the sight

> "Dissolves your heart in thankfulness,
> And melts your eyes to tears,"

with sweet affiance your soul will embrace and magnify the Lord, and along with the profoundest sense of personal unworthiness, will blend the sense of your Saviour's merit, and you will sit in peace "beneath the droppings of his blood."

And while this foundation-truth of the Redeemer's completed atonement ministers comfort, inspires hope, and lifts a crushing burden from the hearts of Christians, it presents the gospel to those who are strangers to its peace and pardon, in an aspect of greatest encouragement and most persuasive power. If men are thoroughly indifferent on the subject of religion, it will, of course, awaken no interest, and be dismissed with less attention than more superficial phases of truth, just because it is the innermost and holiest of gospel doctrines. It is not to be expected that unawakened and unconvinced sinners will heed the announcement that an all-sufficient atonement has been made and finished by Jesus Christ.

But I do expect and believe that this declaration will be glad tidings of great joy to any among you who feel your sins and are aware of your danger. I tell you, then, in the name of Him who made the sacrifice, that it is finished and complete; of virtue, such, that "though your sins were as scarlet, they shall be white as snow; and though they were red like crimson, they shall be as wool;" and so absolutely universal in its adaptation, sufficiency, and offer, that "whosoever believeth in him shall not perish, but have everlasting life."

If you feel that you are guilty, and need pardon—that you are a sinner, and need salvation—consider, I pray you, how exactly a finished atonement suits your case. If it were incomplete, who could "finish" it? Could you? Your works, your tears, your prayers, your blood could not be blended with the sacrifice of the only-begotten Son of God. They have no atoning virtue, and they are not needed. If, therefore, you desire to be saved, you may be, and saved now! The burden of your guilt you need not bear for another hour. "Behold the Lamb of God" taking it away; and in this, your act of faith, the condemnation of sin will be taken from your conscience, and the sense of forgiveness will rise in your heart.

It is the spirit of self-righteousness and unbelief which prompts you to wait for deeper conviction, more bitter repentance, and a certain routine of duties and ordinances before you come directly to Jesus for salvation. This is ignorance of the very gospel. Not you, but Christ is the Saviour. Trust in him, and live. Look to him, and be saved.

> "On the bloody tree behold him,
> Hear him cry, before he dies,
> It is finished!
> Sinner, will not this suffice?"

There are men who, without avowing it as a theory of salvation, entertain a vague notion of finding acceptance with God, on the ground of their good character. In that view, what becomes of the finished redemption of the Lord Jesus? If courtesy, and decency, and morality, and philanthropy, and ritual worship, are an adequate righteousness for the justification of men, and they can do all these things "without Christ,"—as it is plain they can,—then why did he die at all? Their Christianity, if they call it such, leaves out the cross. God's judgment and theirs, as to the way a sinner may be saved, are wide as the poles apart. He holds up a crucified Redeemer; they hold up what they complacently term good works. They think these works a beautiful robe; God accounts them "filthy rags." They go about to establish their own righteousness: the word of faith proclaims "Christ the end of the law for righteousness to every one that believeth." We read of some imperfect and erring Christians who build upon the true foundation, but because they build with "wood, hay, and stubble," are "saved as by fire," narrowly escaping the damnation of hell, but there is no revelation that those who build the house of their hopes on such materials will meet with anything else than bitter and eternal disappointment.

And then, finally there is a class of persons (and we grieve to say it is a large one) who are profoundly indifferent to the subject of their personal salvation, many of them made so by a conception of the Divine mercy, at once unscriptural and fatal to the soul that entertains it. They are at ease, and imagine that God is too merciful to reckon severely with them for their short-comings and imperfections, as they softly name sins. The light that shines from the Saviour's finished redemption, dissipates this refuge of darkness and of lies. If, in all the actual or possible emergencies of the Divine government, there ever was an instance or an hour when justice would relax its rigours and remit its claims, it was when the dear Son of God was called upon to pay the forfeit of human guilt. But was it so? Was he spared one pang at the pleading of mercy? Did the Father's infinite love take from the poisoned chalice that was put to the lips of Jesus one of its bitter ingredients, or say, "It is enough," before he had received its last drop? In a sense, the Father himself—like the typical father of old, who bound his son—was the executioner. He bade it proceed, saying—"Awake, O sword, against my Shepherd, and against the man that is my fellow: smite the Shepherd, and the sheep shall be scattered." In the light of such an example, what becomes of the hope loosely based on your own notion of his mercy? "If these things have been done in a green tree, what shall be done in the dry?" "If God spared not his Son, who is holy, harmless, undefiled, separate from sinners, and made higher than the heavens," how shall he spare you, whose heart is a stranger to his love, and whose life is in open revolt and rebellion against his government? You are guilty; he offers you pardon through his Son.

If you refuse this, "there remaineth no more sacrifice for sins, but a certain fearful looking for of judgment and fiery indignation, which shall devour the adversaries." "As though God, therefore, did beseech you by us; we pray you in Christ's stead, be ye reconciled to God. For he hath made him to be sin for us, who knew no sin; that we might be made the righteousness of God in him."

SERMON IX.

HOPING AND WAITING.

LAM. iii. 26.—*It is good that a man should both hope and quietly wait for the salvation of the Lord.*

THIS book of Lamentations is a kind of supplement to the Prophecies of Jeremiah. It describes as realities the sorrows which had been before predicted; seeks to awaken repentance for the sins which had occasioned them, and encourages the suffering people of God, to hope in his mercy, and wait for his salvation. The situation of the captive Israelites is substantially reproduced in the experience of believers, and in the history of the church: and there being a book of Lamentations in Scripture, accords with the truth of our condition: and there is comfort in the fact, that the anguish we suffer, and the trials we endure, have such a recognition in the pages of inspiration. It gives assurance that God "knows our sorrows," and provides the needed succour and relief. The lamentations which grief extorts from our hearts, and with which it fills our habitations, find in the heart of Jesus a sympathetic response, and in the revelations of the Bible, all that is needed for comfort and instruction. When the children of Zion breathe their woes in threnodies and tears, the tender compassions of their Lord are deeply moved, and the strong consolations of his grace are imparted. Their condition is one of "distress," but not of "despair." What they suffer is discipline, not destruction, and the duty and privilege of their situation are those which the text presents.

I. In developing the lesson of the passage, and applying it for edification and comfort, it falls first in our way to notice the OBJECT proposed to our hope and quiet waiting. "The SALVATION of THE LORD."

In its widest significance, salvation includes every form of Divine deliverance of which men are the subjects or the objects. Properly, it is the soul's deliverance from the power and curse of sin. It is justification by the blood, and inward redemption by the grace of Jesus Christ. In this sense, believers are already saved. Their sentence of condemnation is reversed, and the dominion of sin is broken. Accepted and made new creatures in Christ Jesus, believers are now in a state of salvation, and in so far as it is a present possession, it cannot be an object of hope; for, "what a man seeth, why doth he yet hope for?" But while this is true and very comfortable, it is equally true, and revealed in Scripture with equal clearness, that salvation though begun is not complete, but is gradually progressive towards a glorious consummation which will not be reached till the earthly house of this tabernacle is dissolved, and the soul is clothed with its house which is from heaven. Nay,—the Scriptures carry us forward to the end of all things, and teach us not to expect the perfection of our being and the fulness of joy, till Christ shall come the second time without sin unto the salvation of the body: and, accordingly, his appearing in glory, coming in the clouds of heaven and with his mighty angels, is held up as the grand and final object of Christian hope. Believers are exhorted to "gird up the loins of their mind, and wait for the grace which is to be brought unto them,"—(not at death)—but "at the revelation, (αποκαλυψει) of Jesus Christ. While in this world, they are "kept by the power of God, through faith unto salvation, ready to be revealed in the last time." The date of this "last time" is fixed by the apostle Paul, who links with it, the resurrection of the body, and makes that the full harvest of salvation, compared with which all that is enjoyed on earth is no more than first fruits. "We ourselves, who have the first fruits of the Spirit, groan within ourselves, waiting for the adoption, to wit, the redemption of our body." It thus appears that in the proper sense of salvation, it is a future good, and so an object of hope: and we shall not do any violence to the text, if we find, in this connexion, one of its applications. It is good that a man should both hope and quietly wait for the salvation which the Lord shall give him in the end of his earthly pilgrimage when his soul is taken to Christ in Paradise; and in the end of time, when his body is rescued from the dishonour of the tomb, and made glorious like that of his Divine Redeemer. It is possible there may not be the same necessity for patient hope and quiet waiting in this case as in reference to another sense of salvation which we have yet to notice. Still we judge it is not useless to any Christian, while it is of the utmost importance to some.

There is no danger that any will hunger and thirst for perfect holiness with excessive longings, or too eagerly desire the beatific vision of Jesus Christ; but it is possible, and there is very great danger that even the best of men may grow impatient of the burdens and toils of life, and unconsciously murmur against the providence of God, by wishing to die before their time, and thus escape from trials which it is both their duty and their interest to bear.

However natural the feeling, it is not quite certain that the Psalmist uttered a purely spiritual desire when he sighed for "the wings of a dove, that he might fly away and be at rest." When Job, stript of property, bereft of children, and covered with loathsome ulcers, took a potsherd to scrape himself, and said, "I am weary of my life: I loathe it; I would not live alway," it is very evident that the feeling which predominated in his mind was intense disgust and dissatisfaction with the life that now is, rather than a holy longing for communing with God, in that which is to come.

He was in a better frame when he afterwards said—"All the days of my appointed time will I wait, till my change come." And he was standing on a loftier mount, and looking through a clearer medium, when, at a subsequent date, he saw salvation from afar, and, in the confidence of faith and hope, exclaimed—"I know that my Redeemer liveth, and that he shall stand, at the latter day, upon the earth: and though, after my skin, worms destroy this body, yet in my flesh shall I see God." When Elijah, fleeing from the wrath of Jezebel, sat down under a juniper-tree, and in utter despondency as to his ever being able to accomplish any more good in the world, requested God to take away his life, and give him admittance to that peaceful world where the wicked cease from troubling, and the weary are at rest, he acted in a manner that we can very well understand, and betrayed an impulse of which our own hearts may, at times, have been conscious; but though he was a good man, this was no part of his goodness. It was begotten of ignorance and unbelief. He little knew the service and the honour which awaited him. He was not to die of starvation, and leave his unburied bones to bleach in the wilderness. While he yet spake, angels were hovering over him with needed supplies. When, in the strength of that meat, he went forty days, and came to the Mount Horeb, voices of God and heavenly visions re-assured his fainting faith: and after he had cast his mantle on Elisha, instead of dying the common death of men, chariots and horses of fire were commissioned to bear him aloft, in visible glory, to the mansions of peace. "Salvation with eternal glory," is a thing to be hoped and waited for: and the experience of these holy men of old discovers a weak side of human nature, in reference even to a thing so Christian and so desirable as departing from the body to be present with the Lord. There is reason to believe that very few attain that admirable balance of the soul which Paul evinced, in that he did not know which to choose, being in a strait betwixt two, having a desire to depart and be with Christ, which is far better, yet perfectly and joyfully willing to abide in the flesh, suffering and toiling for the edification of the church, and the salvation of sinners. Even Whitefield, who at one time wished for a voice that might be heard from pole to pole, wherewith to proclaim the tidings of salvation, at another time was so depressed by the discouragement arising from small success, as to say his great consolation was, that in a short time his work would be done, when he should depart and be with Christ. The remark having been made in the presence of William Tennent, and his opinion on the subject demanded, he replied, with some degree of abruptness, that he had "no wish about" the time of his death. When further pressed by Whitefield, he added—"No, sir; it is no pleasure to me at all, and if you knew your duty, it would be none to you. I have nothing to do with death; my business is to live as long as I can, as well as I can, and to serve my Lord and Master as faithfully as I can, until he shall think proper to call me home."—(Log College, p. 140.)

While full and final salvation after death and in the resurrection, is thus an object of hope, giving rise to the duty of patient waiting, there are providential deliverances, which in Scripture are very often called salvation, and which, as we judge, are primarily intended in the text. When after his people had been groaning in bitter bondage for many years, God revealed his power and mercy, and with a high hand and an outstretched arm, led them forth to liberty and a rich inheritance, this was salvation, and under this name it was celebrated in that sublime song of triumph which Israel sang on the shore of the sea, while their enemies "sank like lead in the mighty waters." "The Lord is my strength and song: he is become my salvation." That too was a great salvation, which Israel experienced, when after sowing in tears by the rivers of Babylon, they gathered the remnant of the tribes, and with mingled tears and praises, laid the foundations of their temple, and restored the worship of their God. In the history of the church, during and since the age of miracles, there have been many salvations; interpositions of God, so necessary, so seasonable, so evident, that they were gratefully recognized as the operation of his hand. And in the life of individual believers, salvations are wrought, which though they may not attract the world's notice, are sweetly assured to his own heart, by the manner and time of their occurrence, and the divine consolation with which they are accompanied. It may have been an affliction grievous to bear; or a danger from which there appeared no way of escape: or a temptation which assailed the most vulnerable part of our nature, and excited the worst passions of the heart.

Under the pressure of these evils, our duty and our privilege is to hope and wait for the salvation of the Lord. This stands opposed on the one side, to the error of despondency; sinking to inactivity and despair, as if there were no salvation; and on the other, to the sin of presumption, which is unwilling to wait the time, and submit to the methods of God's providence and grace, and resorts to human devices and unauthorized means of deliverance. It is not the help of man we are to look for, but the salvation of the Lord. In all our personal straits and temptations; in all trials of the church; in all the perils and calamities of the country; and under the dark cloud of mystery which overhangs the world, the duty incumbent on us, as the rational creatures and believing children of God, is neither to sit down in sullen despair, as if nothing but ruin were before us; nor, trusting in our power of endurance, to wait till the evil has spent itself, and passed away; nor to put our trust in an arm of flesh—in the strength, the wisdom, the policy of men—but it is to look on high from whence cometh our help. In times of distress and great darkness, there is strong temptation to betake ourselves to unauthorized means of relief, which, besides the sin involved, plunge us into deeper difficulties. What promised to be a quicker method of deliverance, puts farther off the day of salvation. In his perplexity, and amid the clustering dangers which environed his path, Saul, instead of repairing to the Lord, went to the *witch of Endor*, only with the result of deepening his guilt and hastening his perdition. Leagues with Egypt and Assyria were made by Israel to their own hurt; they leaned on a broken reed which pierced the hand, when they might have grasped an Almighty arm. "The salvation of the Lord," stands opposed to all the human expedients, which spring from ignorance, unbelief, and presumption. In all personal and public trials and dangers, the only safe, and for many reasons, the best course to pursue, is this which is indicated in the text,—to hope and quietly wait for the salvation of the Lord.

II. And this brings us to the second general aspect of the subject, which is the *duty inculcated;* and in reference to this, two points in particular are set forth with prominence. One of these regards the manner, and the other the motive of the duty. The duty is to hope and wait for the salvation of the Lord: and the special aspect of the duty is the patience with which we should hope, and the quietness with which we should wait. The design is not to excite, but to repress certain activities of the soul. It is meant to keep down impatience, and that childlike eagerness which cannot endure delay, and takes no account of those great laws of nature and Providence which interpose time and space between the present trial and sorrow and the blessed deliverance in which it is destined to have its issue. Our impatience, besides being a sin against God, and a source of torment to our own hearts, is utterly vain, having no power to accelerate the unfolding of the Divine purposes. The more absolutely quiet we are, in the sense of the text, the better for ourselves: and this is an instruction which none but those who desire an excuse for spiritual apathy and irreligion will be likely to misunderstand. Patient hoping is not insensibility and indifference to the distant salvation, nor is quiet waiting the same with supine and fatalistic inactivity. The man who conforms to the direction of the text, and most fully exemplifies the character it describes, is keenly alive to the value of salvation, and unceasingly active in the performance of all labours, and the use of all means that tend to secure it, and which, by the ordination of God, are necessary antecedents to its bestowment. The Christian who can adopt the language of the Psalmist as descriptive of his own subdued and chastened state of mind, saying—"I have behaved and quieted myself as a child that is weaned of his mother: my soul is even as a weaned child"—is one who hungers and thirsts after righteousness, and desires complete redemption, and works out his own salvation with fear and trembling; and, as a good servant who waits for the coming of his Lord, he stands, with his loins girded about him, and his lamp burning.

He is not quiet in the sense of being asleep, or of neglecting his duty, but only in the respect that his heart is free from the unrest of discontent with his lot, and from all fretfulness under the burdens of life and the appointed conditions of salvation. His quietness is not the apathy that springs from unbelief, but the mental repose which is begotten of an abiding trust in God.

If not a showy trait, it is a very precious grace, and a very difficult attainment. There are elements and tendencies in our nature which draw us strongly in the opposite direction: and for one child of God who exhibits "the patience of hope," and quietly waits for his salvation, you will meet with many whose hearts are oppressed with needless anxieties, or chafed under the fetters of their outward condition, or deceiving themselves with the thought that they are yearning for heaven and immortality, when they are only quarrelling with the sort of probation through which they are appointed to enter the rest which remaineth for the people of God. It is just as much a Christian duty to wait as to labour, and a higher Christian achievement. It requires more self-control, and more thought; a wider view of God's methods in providence and grace, and a stronger confidence in their infallible wisdom and absolute certainty. In the genealogy of the graces, as traced by Paul, Hope is the daughter of Experience, and out of Hope ariseth waiting; "for if we hope for that we see not, then do we with patience wait for it."

Both hope and waiting have their germ in experience. It is so in the natural life of men. The middle-aged and the old, who have a long while been in contact with the laws of our condition and the realities of life, have acquired experience, and they have learned both to hope and wait for the temporal blessings which Providence gives to man; while children, who have no experience, are all impatience and impetuosity, and if their power were equal to their will, would overturn the order of the universe.

These quiet graces, whose very nature forbids their being demonstrative, are, therefore, commended by their intrinsic excellence; and this may be set down as first among the reasons why "it is GOOD both to hope and quietly to wait for the salvation of the Lord." It is morally good; good in the sight of God. It is an exercise and state of soul becoming our character and condition as dependent creatures; it accords and fits in with the principles and plan of salvation which gives the earnest of our inheritance now, reserving its fulness and perfection to a future day and another world—which plants the seed of grace in the heart, and nurtures it by the dews and rains of many summers, and gives it deeper root and inner life by the frosts and storms that come in the winter of our adversity. And as it respects that form of salvation which is given as a blessing on our labours and an answer to our prayers,—the conversion of sinners and the spread of Christ's kingdom,—it comes by little and little, not rapidly, but gradually, as the leaven permeates the meal, as the tree unfolds from the seed, and as the harvest is garnered long months after the seed-sowing. "Be patient, therefore, brethren, unto the coming of the Lord. Behold the husbandman waiteth for the precious fruits of the earth, and hath long patience for it till he receive the early and latter rain. Be ye also patient. Stablish your hearts, for the coming of the Lord draweth nigh." This law of the kingdom which requires time, and involves delay, lies at the foundation of hope and waiting, and exalts them to the value and dignity of moral virtues and Christian graces. It is, therefore, good to exercise them.

Among the special considerations which further show why it is good, and how good it is to exercise these graces, is the absolute certainty that those who hope and wait for the salvation of the Lord, shall not be disappointed. The more ardently we hope, and the longer we wait for an expected good, the more bitter our disappointment, if, at last, we miss the prize. And if, besides being long expected, it is intrinsically important, a blessing so great that to lose it, is to make shipwreck of happiness, and fail in the end and aim of life, the disappointment becomes intolerable, and crushes the spirit. There are men whose nature it has soured beyond the power of any earthly medicine to cure and sweeten. Judge then, how utterly insupportable would be the anguish of those who had gone through all the toils and sorrows and changes of time, hoping and waiting for immortality and eternal life, if these pictured glories should vanish into unsubstantial nothings, when expectation was at its highest pitch; or, retaining their reality and their splendour, should be withheld from us, and awarded to others who had run the heavenly race with more fidelity! That such disappointments will be suffered, we know, but not by those who commit the keeping of their souls to God in well-doing, and who, with humble faith, are hoping and waiting for his salvation. Their "hope maketh not ashamed." That which they have desired and looked for shall be received. Salvation, as a blessing on their labours, as a deliverance from their troubles, and as the complete redemption of their entire nature from sin, shall, in God's own good time, be given, and the only surprise occasioned will be, that it so far exceeds all that their eyes had seen, or their ears heard, or their hearts imagined of what the Lord would do for his people. To get the object desired, and then discover that it is a totally different thing from what we expected, is even a worse disappointment than to miss it entirely. In neither respect can the children of God fail to realize their hopes. "The hope of the righteous shall be gladness," both in the certainty and in the glory of its fulfilment. "Beloved, now are we the sons of God. And it doth not yet appear what we shall be; but we know that when He shall appear, we shall be like him. For we shall see him as he is." And, my hearers, if you would know whether the hope that is in you is destined to have this blissful fruition, the infallible criterion is given. "And every man that hath this hope in" Christ, "purifieth himself, even as he is pure."

In addition to this, we may say that hoping and waiting for the salvation of the Lord are good in their present influence. Besides being morally good as Christian graces; and good in respect to the perfect safety of trusting in God for the future blessing of eternal life, they are good in the sense of being immediately beneficial, both to ourselves and others. They are greatly promotive of our present happiness. The hope of future blessing and deliverance begets patience under the evils and difficulties of our lot, and gives such satisfying earnests of what is in reserve, that we are contented with the condition assigned us, and feel, at times, a peace which passeth understanding. And while this heavenly calm is diffused within, an influence is shed abroad in the whole sphere of the Christian's life and intercourse, which helps his brethren and honours religion. A believer who possesses his soul in patience in the midst of all earth's changes, and when men's hearts are failing for fear of the things which are coming on the world, who stands on the rock of God's eternal truth, and avows his unwavering confidence in the justice, the wisdom, and the mercy of the Divine providence; and exhibits a cheerful hope, while he quietly waits for the salvation of the Lord; is a tower of strength to his brethren—a living epistle of commendation to the religion he professes. Except it be the endurance of fiery trials in days of persecution, there is scarcely a more signal exhibition of its power. When unbelief and worldliness throw those who know not God into a commotion of anxiety and fear, and when perilous times do but stimulate their avaricious greed, and fire their restless ambition, let the children of the kingdom abide in peace; let them stand in their lot, and show that Christ in the heart, the hope of glory, contents and satisfies the needs and yearnings of an immortal soul. Wait with patience—work with hope, and suffer without complaint: and remember, the Lord is at hand. His salvation is nigh.

The time is short. And now "The God of all grace who hath called us unto his eternal glory by Christ Jesus, after that ye have suffered a while, make you perfect, stablish, strengthen, settle you. To him be glory and dominion for ever and ever. Amen."

SERMON X.

THE LOVE OF CHRIST, KNOWN, YET UNKNOWN.

Eph. iii. 19.—*And to know the love of Christ which passeth knowledge.*

It seems a contradiction to speak of knowing what cannot be known; but like some other of the apostle's sayings, the paradox is a precious truth.

The discrepancy is on the surface and in word; the harmony is profound and real. In one aspect, the love of Christ may be known; in another, it "passeth knowledge."

The subject concerning which these dissimilar statements are made, is the most important within the scope of human knowledge or thought. Christ is a being with whom, in one relation or another, we all have to do. It is in him and through him that God deals with our sinful world. By Christ we must be saved, if saved at all, and before his judgment-seat we are summoned to appear. In his character and his feelings we have a deep stake; and to men who are conscious of their spiritual necessities, no theme is so comforting as this of our text—the love of Christ—and just because it "passeth knowledge" it is ever new. It is the heart of the gospel. Christ is the manifested love of God. The good news from heaven is that God loves the world, and all Scripture centres in the person and grace of Jesus.

The subject thus belongs to the highest mysteries of redemption, and is purely spiritual. It can interest deeply none but a spiritual mind, or a soul which the Spirit of God is preparing, through the conviction of sin, to receive the offered salvation. It requires love to appreciate love.

The subject must feel, in some degree at least, what the object discloses, or there will be no perception of its qualities; and hence the apostle, desiring that these Ephesian Christians might know Christ's love, prayed that they might first be "rooted and grounded in love," as the precedent condition of acquiring this knowledge. If you are a lover of Jesus Christ, the subject will be pleasant to you; possibly it may melt your heart into tenderness, and fill you with joy unspeakable and full of glory. If you are a sinner, burdened with conscious guilt, you may be led by such an exhibition of truth to lay down your load at the cross. And whatever your state of mind, the theme cannot be inappropriate; for it is the core of that glorious gospel which is the power of God to salvation to every one that believeth. The love of Christ, as *known*, and yet *unknown*, and *unknowable*, is the form of truth which the text exhibits. We may find both interest and edification in developing the harmony of these ideas. Both statements present the love of Christ in the relation it sustains to our intelligence, the one having regard to our capacity of knowledge, and the other to the limitation of that capacity. The love of Christ is something which may be known, yet not completely and exhaustively known by finite minds. The infinitude of the Godhead belongs to it; and we can no more define it with the measuring-rod and the sounding-line of our finite faculties, than we can, "by searching, find out God, or know the Almighty to perfection."

Knowing God is one thing; knowing him to perfection is another and a different thing, possible only to himself. The gauge of an infinite nature is an infinite understanding; so the measure of infinite love is the infinite mind that feels it. Approaching the love of Christ from our point of view, and with our powers of apprehension, we find that it is something which may be known—that is, which may be discovered and certified to our souls as a divine reality—and yet that there is an amplitude and an immensity belonging to it which stretches far beyond our present vision; and, in this respect, it is unknown, and must for ever remain so. There are two familiar facts of experience which harmonize the seeming contradiction of the text. One is the distinction between partial and complete knowledge, in almost every department of human research. There are very few subjects, if any, of which our knowledge is perfect, including not only all that is known, but all there is to know.

We encounter impassable boundaries in every direction. We can tell the sensible qualities of a clod of unorganized matter, but while we know there is a substance which underlies those qualities and hides behind them, we cannot discern it, and much less describe it. We look on a blade of grass, perceive its colour, form, texture, and assign it to its place according to the classifications of botany, but that occult principle of vegetable life which determines its growth and species, eludes all scrutiny of microscope or metaphysics. In one sense it is known; in another it passes knowledge. We stand on the shore of the ocean, and its illimitable expanse stretches out to the point where sky and water seem to touch. We speak truly when we say we have seen the ocean; but our knowledge is almost nothing, compared with our ignorance. We have only gazed on its surface; we have not gone down in fancy even to its "dark, unfathomed caves," where the waters sleep in perpetual repose; and we have surveyed but a little patch of an area that is almost immense. The same disparity exists between our knowledge and our ignorance of all the works of God. They are all invested with the mystery which belongs to himself—the Infinite and the Eternal. Of Creation, Providence, and Redemption, it is alike true—"we know in part." It is because we are finite, and God is infinite. The love of Christ is referable to the same law. We know it, and yet we know it not. Where the difference between the known and the unknown is so great, it frequently happens that subsequent discoveries greatly modify previous views; and sometimes what we had called and considered knowledge "vanishes away" in the clearer light to which we have attained: and the question arises, whether what we know, or think we know of Christ and his redeeming love, may not be subject to the like mutations, and be displaced by future disclosures. Seeing through a glass darkly, perhaps, it is but shadows and illusions we behold. Looking with childish eyes, and thinking with a child's understanding, may we not hereafter, becoming men, put away as puerilities what now we dignify as knowledge?

In the world of philosophy and metaphysics, theory has chased theory like the flitting clouds of the sky: and even in the domain of natural science, the knowledge of one age has been proved to be ignorance by the next. Have we any guarantee in the matter of our salvation, that what we know of Christ and his love will not in like manner be dissipated by the clearer light of coming revelations? This suggests a second remark touching the difference between knowing anything experimentally, and knowing it comprehensively, or the difference between knowing its nature and reality, and knowing its extent or amount. In the former sense the love of Christ may be known: in the latter it passeth knowledge. Though, in a comparative view, it is but little of it that we know by experience, the knowledge thus acquired is of such a nature as to give perfect assurance to the mind. The evidence is like that of the senses: it is the touch and taste of the soul. If you quench your thirst at a spring which gurgles up at the foot of a mountain, you have as complete and certain knowledge of water, as though you could penetrate the hidden recesses from which that spring arose, or could follow it in all its meanderings, and observe its increase till it mingled in the great river, and finally is lost in the mighty ocean. You know, by that single draught of a cupful, the qualities of water, though you know not its extent—whence it comes and whither it goes. It is thus with the believer's knowledge of Christ's love. He tastes, and sees that the Lord is gracious; but as to comprehending the length, and breadth, and depth, and height of that whose reality and nature he is assured of, this is quite impossible. It will form an eternal study, and affords room for endless progress. But that progress will be in the line on which he has already started. It will be just knowing more and more of the extent of that love of which he already knows the nature by experience. All the witnesses or the philosophers in the world, or that ever will be in the world, could neither deepen nor destroy any man's conviction as to the adaptedness of water to quench thirst; experience is the highest and the last evidence that the case admits of, and this he has. The love of Christ is witnessed to the sense of the inner man in the same way. "He that believeth hath the witness in himself." "The water that I shall give him shall be in him a well of living water springing up into everlasting life."

It thus appears how the love of Christ in one view is known, and in another unknown, and what the security is that nothing

14 *

that shall be developed in time or eternity can essentially change the views and impressions of it, which the Christian now entertains. The only sense in which change is possible, is the better knowledge of what he already knows imperfectly; and the maturing of those experiences, the germs of which are already implanted: and this is a process which, for aught that appears, may go on for ever.

New aspects and exhibitions of the love of Christ may continue to be unfolded through immortal ages. Taking with us the twofold conception, the truth and harmony of which we have thus endeavoured to set forth, we may now come to the direct consideration of our Redeemer's love, in those qualities and manifestations of it which are revealed in Scripture, and ascertained by experience. In every view we can take of it, it will be found a "love that passeth knowledge."

We might trace its antiquity, and we should find its origin in the remoteness of a past eternity. It antedates the existence of man, and the foundation of the world. In the certain foreknowledge that the creature he had proposed to make would fall, "the Word who was in the beginning with God and was God," had thoughts of love to man, and the Counsel of Redemption was entered into between the Persons of the Godhead. "From everlasting, from the beginning, or ever the earth was," the wisdom, the Λογος, the Eternal Son of God existed, and his delights were with the sons of men. Yielding himself to the Father's will, in reference to the salvation of the fallen race, Christ was from everlasting "fore-ordained" to be the Redeemer of sinners.

Here is a mystery deep and awful as the interior nature and the relation of person in the triune God. That is a mysterious, an incomprehensible love, which anticipated our fall, our existence, the creation of the world in which we live, and provided for an emergency which was almost infinitely distinct. Nor was it a mere governmental plan, a politic calculation of what was best to be done in the case that was certain to arise. The Scriptures do not so represent the matter: but in the most express terms ascribe the whole scheme to the love and compassion of God. "Christ loved the church, and gave himself for it," and "God so loved the world that he gave his Son."

In its antiquity—its absolute eternity—the love of Christ is mysterious, and solemnly impressive.

It "passeth knowledge," in the sovereignty of its discriminations. If it is a wonder that he should love apostate creatures at all, it is even more a mystery that he should distinguish among creatures equally guilty and miserable: yet, that he has done so is a fact revealed in the word of God, and in the presence of which we can only say, as he himself said,—"Even so, Father, for so it seemed good in thy sight." Angels were a nobler race, earlier created, and sooner undone by sin. Their rebellion extinguished God's love for them; and thunderbolts of vengeance hurled them down to hell, where they are reserved in chains and darkness unto the judgment of the great day. From their exalted nature it is probable that they suffer beyond anything that men can suffer. They need redemption therefore, and it would be a bold, if not presumptuous assertion, to say they are for any reason incapable of being redeemed. We do not know that it was impossible to Almighty power and infinite wisdom. We only know the fact that it was not done—a fact not only mentioned in Scripture, but brought in for the purpose of illustrating the rich and sovereign grace which redeems sinners of mankind: "Christ took not on him the nature of angels; but he took on him the seed of Abraham."

Creatures who once had shone as seraphs near the throne of

God, were passed by and left without a Saviour, and without hope, while to us, who, among rational creatures, are at the bottom of the scale, Christ came to seek and save the lost.

Can you solve the mystery of this sovereign discrimination? And is not this very mystery an element in the moral power of the love that saves us? Kindred to this in nature and in mystery is the sovereign freeness of Christ's love to individual sinners of our race.

It is a glorious truth that the love and redemption of Christ have relations to all mankind. The nature which Jesus assumed into unity with his eternal divinity, is that borne by every individual of the race which God hath made of "one blood, to dwell on all the face of the earth." The atoning virtue of the blood he shed on Calvary, is such as justifies the offer of salvation to "every creature under heaven," and warrants the faith of every one who is willing to receive it. To this extent and in this sense, God loves the world, and there is no difference between the Jew and the Greek, or between one man and another. But in point of fact, how wide the difference which by his providence he puts between the nations of the earth, and between individuals in the same community? As it respects the means of grace and the offer of salvation, some have them, and others have them not, and this difference, in a multitude of instances, is linked with salvation, and in all cases, sustains an important relation to it.

Furthermore: within the circle of those who live under the light of the gospel, there is "an election of grace," composed of actual believers. Many of those before me this morning, have an humble trust that they are of the number. To such I propound the inquiry—How came you to be a believer in Jesus, while so many around you live and die in impenitence? Is it because you were by nature, better than they? No, in no wise. You were the child of wrath and the servant of sin, even as others. The Scriptures ascribe the cause of the difference to the special love and special grace of the Lord Jesus Christ, who by the effectual working of his Spirit applies the redemption which he purchased by his blood; and all true believers confess the fact when their Christian heart finds utterance in devotion.

They thank God for providing redemption, but more, if possible, for applying it. That is a form of love more tender, special, and personal. It brings our individual soul under the eye of Omniscience, and the thought that the heart of Jesus flowed forth to us, is quite overwhelming. When you behold him, the babe of Bethlehem, you wonder and adore, and are ready to lay at his feet the costliest oblations of earth; gazing at him on the cross, you mourn for him, and weep for your sins; but when he comes to you yourself, with garments died on Calvary, the good Shepherd following his wandering sheep in the wilderness, and bearing it back to the fold in safety and in triumph, your inmost soul is melted, and you break forth in that song which is the prelude of heaven's eternal anthem, to Him that loved us and washed us in his own blood:—

> "Jesus sought me when a stranger,
> Wandering from the fold of God."

"By the grace of God, I am what I am." "God who is rich in mercy, for the great love wherewith he loved me, even when I was dead in sins, hath quickened me together with Christ."

The love of Christ to the individual heirs of salvation is its most precious and potent element: but certainly also, the most mysterious. You have often asked the reason why, only to answer with adoring wonder and thankful tears.

Unsearchable in its sovereign freeness to individuals, the love of Christ "passeth knowledge" in the nature and extent of its sacrifices. The accepted standard and measure of love is the amount of what it will do, give, and suffer, for its object. Human love is tested thus, and sometimes is proved to be very small, though sometimes as deep as that which a person feels for himself. The profession of love, if unsupported by substantial and visible fruits in act and service, is justly suspected of insincerity: if it have these seals, it needs no verbal declaration. That man is our best and most devoted friend who sacrifices and suffers most on our behalf.

Pleasant words, courteous acts, and all the gentle charities of life, are not without their value, but it requires a heart of warm and deep affection to suffer for us. A parent will do it for the child that is bone of his bone, and flesh of his flesh, but outside the circle of nearest and dearest kindred this style of love is seldom seen. The love of Christ is peculiarly and pre-eminently a suffering love. As a Redeemer, his pathway lay through the midst of mighty sorrows and mysterious sufferings: but he "loved the church," and therefore gave himself for it, to all the humiliation and the grief involved in its salvation.

From the time he left his glorious throne, to the hour he returned to it, he was a sufferer, either in the sense of deprivation or of positive pain: and his sufferings were, for many reasons, incomprehensible and mysterious. It is an accepted article of theology, that the Godhead is impassible, or incapable of suffering, yet the only form in which we can think of the Incarnation, is that of an obscuration of his glory, a laying aside somewhat which made the act a sacrifice, and the assumption of somewhat which involved humiliation in the second Person of the Trinity. The Scriptures so present the subject, and we need not fear to follow where they lead us. "Ye know the grace of our Lord Jesus Christ, that though he was rich, yet for your sakes he became poor."

When we behold him on earth, the Godman, the Christ, there is no difficulty felt, when we think of him as a sufferer; and from first to last we see him, "A man of sorrows and acquainted with grief." He suffered, being tempted "in all points like as we are, yet without sin."

He suffered in his body, and in his soul; from men, from devils; and from the stern justice of Heaven: and all for the love he bore to perishing sinners. If his sufferings pass knowledge, so also his love, and the one as much as the other: and it were a fit study for us to-day, to make one of these the gauge of the other. Though both are mysteriously intense and deep, the one is visible, the other inward and spiritual; from that which is seen, we may estimate what is unseen. The tears he shed over Jerusalem, the deep sigh that he heaved at the grave of Lazarus, the "strong crying and tears" with which he prayed in the garden of Gethsemane; the bloody sweat that appeared as he lay prostrate on the ground, being in "an agony," and "his soul exceeding sorrowful even unto death," the thorns that pierced his sacred brow, and the barbed arrow that entered his soul when Peter denied him; and all those clustering woes and heavy loads which, by the agency of man and the permission of God, oppressed him on the cross, till sinking beneath their overwhelming pressure, he bowed his head and gave up the ghost,—these, and such as these, are the visible exponents of a sorrow, and so the visible demonstrations of a love, which no articulate speech can utter, or finite understanding grasp.

How wondrous was the burning zeal,
Which filled the Master's breast,

When all his sufferings full in view,
  To Salem's towers he pressed?
Dear Lord, no tongue can duly tell,
  Thy love's prevailing might,
No thought can comprehend its length,
  And breadth, and depth, and height.

"Greater love hath no man than this, that a man lay down his life for his friends. But God commendeth his love towards us, in that while we were yet sinners, Christ died for us."

"Passing knowledge" in its sacrifices, the love of Christ is alike incomprehensible in its benefits. That which results to us from the love and sorrow of Jesus, is in general salvation! We know it, and yet we know it not. In one sense we have it, in another, we have it not; but we wait till Christ shall come the second time without sin unto salvation. In both respects it "passeth knowledge," but in the one more than the other. What the love of Christ gives us now, is pardon and peace, and hope, and "joy unspeakable and full of glory." We painfully feel that the redemption of our souls is but in its incipient stages; temptation without, and corruption within, is a serious and constant drawback to our happiness; yet would we not exchange for thrones and sceptres, what Christ gives us even now, in the grace that helps us, and the love that comforts us, and the sweet communion that unites our sympathetic souls together, and the honour he puts upon us as co-workers with himself in achieving the redemption of men. The experiences of grace below, are worth more than all worlds to us, and are so accounted by the true believer. He has feelings at times which he cannot express—which he, perhaps, does not try to express, unless to God. Tears of penitence, gratitude, adoration, betray them. They are mixed, it may be, with "groanings which cannot be uttered,'' but taken in their complexity of light and shade, of joy and sadness, they are a sacred treasure which the Christian lays away in the innermost shrine of his soul. He would rather die than surrender it.

If this be true, and no exaggeration, what shall we say or think of the benefits which Christ's love reserves for us in a future life and a better world? If the ''joy of salvation'' is unspeakable, what will be the joy of heavenly and eternal glory? Though it ''doth not yet appear what we shall be,'' we know something of that wondrous destiny, and have the data for a sort of spiritual arithmetic by which the relation and the ratio of grace to glory and earth to heaven may be determined. It is but an approximation, yet it is substantially true.

Grace is an earnest of glory; a little of it in advance, to teach us its nature, and assure us of its future possession. The difference is that between a taste which provokes the appetite and a full meal which satisfies hunger. Grace is the ''first-fruits of the harvest,'' and no more in comparison with eternal glory, than a handful of stalks to an ample barn filled in every part with sheaves.

Under another figure, grace is the childhood of the believer, when he thinks as a child and speaks as a child: the state of glory is his perfect manhood when, ceasing ''to know in part, he shall know even as also he is known.''

The Christian's earthly state is the night of his ignorance; heaven ''is the perfect day'' of bright illumination, which will scatter all clouds from his sky, and all darkness from his heart, and make him acquainted with the interior nature of mysteries of which on earth he did not know the existence. In every element of our personal character and relations that state will be ''far better,'' than the present, and the ''love of Christ'' will discover itself in new and glorious forms throughout eternal ages. The prophets who, with but half-knowledge of their predictions, foretold "the sufferings of Christ, and the glory that should follow;" the apostles who, with the Holy Ghost sent down from heaven, proclaimed the redemption which is through his blood; and the angels, who with holy eagerness desire to look into the mysteries of Jesus' grace to guilty man, are pursuing still the sublime study in the realms of light, and the declaration of the text is as true to them as it is to us—the "love of Christ which passeth knowledge." If we know this love in the remission of our sins and the purification of our hearts, we shall presently join that "innumerable company" of glorified students, and as fresh revelations break on our enraptured gaze, the "new song"—for ever new—will burst from our lips, and "Worthy the Lamb that was slain, to receive power and riches, and wisdom and strength, and honour and glory and blessing," will resound through all the plains of paradise.

The experience of earth, in its great essential feature, will be transferred to heaven—the love of Christ, known by a blessed experience, and yet in its divine and infinite fulness, "passing the knowledge" of human souls and finite natures. If it could be comprehended, its transcendent charm would vanish, and heaven would lose one of its most peculiar joys.

On a theme so high and holy, our words and thoughts and comparisons are poor and beggarly; yet must we thus speak, or not speak at all. As we could, we have set before you that love whose chief expression we this day commemorate in the Holy Supper.

It is mysterious and infinite as the Godhead of Him in whom it dwells. It "passeth knowledge" in its eternity, its sovereignty, its freeness, its sacrifices, and its benefits. And now I lay it on your heart as the balm of its wounds, and the very power of God for your inward and eternal redemption.

His blood paid the price of your release from the curse of the law; his love loosens the "bond of iniquity," and attracts the ransomed soul to a willing and loyal service. If his love to you "passes knowledge," yours to him should exceed all other loves that sway your heart. For his infinite love, give him your sincere and supreme affection—all that the weak vessel of a finite and sinful heart can contain. By the response you make to this appeal, your spiritual character and condition will be tested. With the blood-stained pledge of love in his hands, he comes to you this day, as to Peter by the sea of Galilee, mildly but solemnly asking the question—"Lovest thou me?" It is as much as to say—"I love you—I have loved you with an everlasting love—I have died for you—I am living to make intercession for you—I am ready to crown you with glory and honour, and give you eternal life,—Lovest thou me?"

The secret answers which are made to this question he hears. One in the profound consciousness of a true heart, may be, says, with Peter—"Lord, thou knowest all things: thou knowest that I love thee."

Others—a goodly company—can say, perhaps, with Paul—"The love of Christ constraineth us, because we thus judge, that if one died for all, then were all dead: and that he died for all, that they which live should not henceforth live unto themselves, but unto him which died for them, and rose again."

A self-distrusting heart, melting into tenderness, exclaims—

"Lord, it is my chief complaint,
That my love is weak and faint:
Yet I love thee and adore,
Oh! for grace to love thee more."

Another, drawn hither and thither by the opposing forces of grace and sin, and bewildered by contradictory proofs, will sigh, with Newton—

> "Let me love thee more and more,
> If I love at all, I pray;
> If I have not loved before,
> Help me to begin to-day."

Below this, love is non-existent, and many, by their silence, confess that, unto them, Christ is "a root out of a dry ground, having no form nor comeliness." To these let me say, in his name, Christ this day, now and here, makes you the tender of his love and salvation. "I love them that love me, and those that seek me early shall find me. If a man love me, he will keep my words: and my Father will love him, and we will come unto him, and make our abode with him."

SERMON XI.

THE DISPENSATION OF THE SPIRIT.

JOHN vii. 39.—*But this spake he of the Spirit, which they that believe on him should receive: for the Holy Ghost was not yet given, because that Jesus was not yet glorified.*

IN its most general aspect, this passage suggests the idea that God, in saving men, works according to a plan. There is order, sequence, dependence in his working. He does one thing, rather than another; and at a certain time, rather than before or after. In his own infinite and eternal mind, there is no such thing as the succession of ideas, or the discovery of truth by logical processes; but when the thoughts of God come forth in revelation and accomplishment, in the experience of man and the salvation of the church, there is observed a logical relation of the parts, and a successive development, in time, of the Divine Mind, which show that the whole work of redemption proceeds according to a perfect and eternal plan. "The History of Redemption," as President Edwards names the actual unfolding of this plan, in the calling, gathering, and sanctification of the church, is as much more orderly, and—so to speak—more profoundly philosophical, than any other history, as the church is the object of God's more special care and immediate control—in fact, the workmanship of his own hands.

That such a plan exists, binding all Divine acts and human events connected with the salvation of men in one great economy, and requiring them to occur in a certain consecutive order, is indicated in the clearest manner by the two Testaments, the Old and the New, which reveal the will of God, and record the gradual accomplishment of his purpose. The Old naturally and necessarily precedes the New: the New is required to fulfil and develop the Old. The one is the primary school-book, which the church studied in its childhood, under tutors and governors. It contained "the rudiments" of Divine knowledge, milk for babes: the New unfolds the higher mysteries of the kingdom of heaven, and carries its disciples "on to perfection."

This settled plan appears also in the different, successive, and improving dispensations under which the covenant of grace has been administered. The *patriarchal*, with its scanty revelations, and simple worship, and pilgrim life, was, at the Exodus, and in Canaan, merged in the *Jewish*, which was characterized by a complete, and even cumbrous system of rites and laws, "imposed until the time of reformation," when Christ came, fulfilling the law, bringing in a "better covenant," and setting up the *Christian dispensation*, under which the kingdom of God is to exist, and grow, and be purified, until the church militant shall be swallowed up in the church triumphant, and all means of grace and ordinances of worship shall be displaced and made unnecessary by the presence of Jesus, and the fulness of an "eternal redemption."

Another remarkable indication of the Divine plan, of which the history of the church is the visible evolution, is the manner in which the Persons of the Godhead come forward on the scene of revelation and of action. Under the Old Testament, the mystery of the holy Trinity was but obscurely revealed, while the unity of the Godhead is set forth in great prominence: and as, in the economy of redemption, the Father represents and acts for the Godhead, we may regard the Old Testament as in some sense the dispensation of the Father. It was long, obscure, preparatory. At its close, the Son became incarnate, and the period of his earthly sojourn was the dispensation of the second Person of the adorable Godhead. It was very short, but the greatest events of the world's history were crowded into it. The atoning death of Jesus Christ was the culminating point of all previous history, and the point of departure for all that is yet to come. In the thirty-three years of his humiliation, Jesus did more for the world's salvation than had been achieved in the four thousand that preceded—much as that was, and of indispensable necessity. What the period lacked in mere chronological duration, is more than compensated by the magnitude of its events, and the rapidity with which the scheme of grace advanced towards its consummation. Having done all that was assigned him,—all that in his humiliation it was possible for him to do, the Son returned to his glory, and the Spirit is revealed in the Divine personality of his nature and the abundant grace of his mission. How long his "ministration" will continue is unknown to men. All that is revealed is, that it will continue till the mystery of God is finished, and the purchased redemption applied to all the saved. In exhibiting the work of the Spirit in its connexion with that of the Son, and the Father, and as having an appointed place in the order of events and of time, in the progress of human salvation, the text gives us a theme of meditation both interesting and practical, and in every respect of the highest importance.

The form of truth it presents, is the previous withholding and the present bestowment of the Holy Spirit. "But this spake he of the Spirit, which they that believe on him should receive; for the Holy Ghost was not yet given; because that Jesus was not yet glorified."

1. The statement that "The Holy Ghost was not yet given," covers the whole period of the Old Testament dispensation, and the earthly ministry of Jesus Christ, even up to the very hour of his ascension. In determining the sense of this statement, it is obvious, on the slightest inspection of Scripture, that it does not and cannot mean a total and absolute withholding of the Spirit. It does not mean either that the Spirit was not revealed or that he did not operate on the minds of men before Christ entered into his glory. He was revealed, and he did work as a spirit of inspiration in the prophets, who "spake as they were moved by the Holy Ghost," and as a spirit of holiness in the hearts of believers. He went further: he strove as a Spirit of conviction with the antediluvian sinners of Noah's time, and with unbelievers in Israel, who "rebelled" against Jehovah, and "vexed his Holy Spirit."

In both miraculous operations and saving influences, the Spirit did things of the same kind that he did after the ascension of Christ, and that he does now.

The difference is one of degree: and when it is said he "was not then given," the meaning must be that he was not bestowed in the same manner and amount as now. If he had not been given at all—the world would have lain in absolute darkness and death. Not one soul would have been converted and sanctified. The existence of such men as Abel and Enoch before the flood; of Abraham, Isaac, and Jacob, in the age of the patriarchs; of Moses, Joshua, and David, Samuel and Isaiah, and others of whom time would fail to tell, in the periods of the Judges under the theocracy, proves that the Spirit of God wrought in the souls of men with mighty power. As there is a sense in which Christ was in the world before his incarnation, appearing in the form of a man, in those momentary theophanies which patriarchs and prophets beheld; so there is a sense in which the Spirit was in the world before he was "given" by the ascended and glorified Saviour.

But this was in a measure so small that, generally and popularly speaking, it might be said, the Spirit was not yet given. With this announcement of fact, the Evangelist with equal explicitness assigns the reason for it. "The Holy Ghost was not yet given, because that Jesus was not yet glorified." The previous withholding of the Spirit was not an arbitrary restraint imposed on the love and grace of this Divine person and mighty agent, but had a ground in the great economy of salvation which the wisdom of God devised. A certain lapse of time, and progress of events, and performance of Divine acts, must take place before the Spirit can properly, and with the best effect, be given in this particular manner and in such copious effusion. And in particular, it must needs be that Jesus first suffer and enter into his glory. On this hinged the descent of the Spirit. On the strength of the Saviour's promised coming, the Spirit had been given in a small degree; sin had been pardoned, and the glad news of salvation published within a limited circle; but it required the accomplished facts of his incarnation, life, death, resurrection, and ascension to glory, to prepare the way for the Spirit's mission, and to supply the materials requisite to its rapid and complete performance: and with such light as the Scriptures afford, we may find it a profitable study to trace the connexion between the glorification of the Son and the gift of the Spirit.

On earth, the glory of Christ was veiled by the likeness of

human flesh and the form of a servant which he assumed, and especially by the shame of his death on the cross. When he burst the bars of the grave, the cloud began to pass off; and during the forty days which intervened before he ascended, the radiant Divinity which his sacred body enshrined shone forth with brightening lustre, until from Olivet he disappeared from mortal eyes, and entered into the glory he had with the Father before the world was. Much as this is, it is not the whole of what is implied in the glorifying of Jesus Christ. Besides resuming the throne, the sceptre, and the glory which he had relinquished, when "for our sakes he became poor," he was "crowned with glory and honour" as the mediatorial king of the world and head of the church. Because "he made himself of no reputation, and took upon him the form of a servant, and became obedient unto death, even the death of the cross, God hath highly exalted him, and given him a name which is above every name, that at the name of Jesus every knee should bow, and every tongue confess that Jesus Christ is Lord." Such is his glory, and first of all we connect the gift of the Spirit with his regal office and universal dominion. The Spirit is a donation worthy of heaven's king. When he ascended up on high, he "received gifts for men," chief and first of all of which is the bestowment of the Comforter. Standing amid the scenes of that wondrous "day of Pentecost," Peter referred them to the glorified Saviour, whom the cavilling Jews around him had crucified and slain: "by the right hand of God exalted, and having received of the Father the promise of the Holy Ghost, he hath shed forth this, which ye now see and hear." This passage, while it connects the bestowment of the Spirit with the princely exaltation of Christ, suggests the further idea of its dependence on a covenant-engagement between the Father and the Son.

The Spirit was promised to Jesus, in trust, as it were, for the church and the world, on condition that he would die for men, and, by his atonement, remove all moral and legal obstructions out of the way of their being renewed and sanctified. His resurrection from the dead and entrance into glory was the proof that he had fulfilled the condition of the promise, and now not only the mercy, but the righteousness and truth of God concurred in sending forth the Spirit.

Underlying these facts, and even more deeply imbedded in the economy of grace, there is another reason why the mission of the Spirit should be deferred till after the sacrifice and ascension of the Son, and when these had taken place, should be no longer delayed. The purchase of redemption was the act of the Son; its application is the work of the Spirit. Naturally, the purchase precedes the application, and there appears no reason, when the one had been made, why the other should not immediately proceed. The sovereign balm of atoning blood was prepared, and the world is perishing in its sin; why should the Spirit longer tarry?

The lever which is to raise mankind from the horrible pit and the miry clay of their spiritual ruin, is furnished in the cross, and in the facts and doctrines of the gospel which reveal it, and there is no longer any fitness of things, nor economic necessity, nor reason of any sort, why this Divine and mighty instrument of regeneration and life should not be applied to elevate, redeem, and save the lost. Jesus is glorified in heaven; now let him be glorified on earth by the revelation of his grace, and the application of his blood to those who sit in darkness and lie in the embraces of spiritual death. As before he was glorified the Spirit was not given, now that he is crowned with light and invested with universal and supreme dominion, enlisting his providence in aid of his grace, let the Spirit of love and power come down in the plenitude of his gifts and influences, and abide with the church, and breathe his quickening breath upon the world!

II. Having thus found a vital connexion existing between the mediatorial glory with which the risen Saviour is crowned, and the ministration of the Spirit which follows it—a connexion so close and necessary, that before one of these events had taken place the other could not occur, and could not be longer delayed after its appointed antecedent had become a fact of history—we have remaining the most directly practical portion of our subject, in tracing the characteristics of this last dispensation of the covenant of grace, which has for its grand peculiarity and crowning glory the mission of the Holy Ghost.

It is fully implied in all that has gone before in this discourse, that the church is thereby placed in an advanced position. If any one thinks that the visible glory of the pillar of cloud and fire, the celestial voices, the angels' visits, the inspired prophets, and miraculous deliverances which were the salient points and distinguishing features of the Old Covenant, were better than this calm, quiet, spiritual kingdom, of which you cannot say "Lo, here, or lo, there," this is but to confess that in our individual progress we have not kept pace with that of the Divine plan; and it is to run against the express decision of an inspired apostle, who describes the former as "the ministration of death," and asks, in the face of all its outward and material splendour—"How shall not the ministration of the Spirit be rather glorious?"—2 Cor. iii. 8.

If you fancy that the golden age of the church must surely have been enjoyed when the incarnate God dwelt among men, and they beheld his glory, and bowed at his feet, and reposed on his breast, I acknowledge it is hard, on general grounds, to show that such a thought is mistaken, and would not venture, in an authoritative manner, to pronounce it so, if he himself had not declared it "expedient that he should go away, that the Comforter might come." A glorified Redeemer, revealed by the Spirit, and seen by faith, is more to the soul than Jesus was to Mary Magdalene, when in that well-known voice he pronounced her name, and she fell at his feet to worship him; or to Thomas, when gazing upon his pierced hands and wounded side, he cried —"My Lord, and my God."

Gather up all the tender and holy memories which these Gospel Histories record; group all the scenes of which Incarnate Love was the luminous centre, Bethlehem and Nazareth, the temple and the garden, the upper-room at Jerusalem, and the house of Mary and Martha,—view him with every ray of light which the recorded facts of his life and the colouring of a sanctified imagination cast upon him, and yet I must assure you that this view of Jesus is dim and distant, compared with that direct spiritual vision of his grace and glory which the illumination of the Spirit affords to the believing heart. "Thomas," said he, "because thou hast seen me, thou hast believed: blessed are they that have not seen, and yet have believed."

The Spirit "glorifies" the Son by revealing him to faith; and when thus apprehended, the vision inspires joy unspeakable and full of glory. Our first lesson, therefore, is to appreciate the wondrous privilege we enjoy, occupying a higher position, and, under the teaching of the Spirit, having more knowledge of Christ and salvation than patriarchs, prophets, or apostles, up to the day of Pentecost. And on this subject no didactic statement or proof-text of Scripture will so commend the truth to our convictions, as the inspired narrative of facts which occurred at Jerusalem on the fiftieth day after the Saviour's resurrection, and the tenth from his ascension. The event which then took place was the subject of many Old Testament predictions, and of the Saviour's recent and specific promise. "This is that," said Peter, "which was spoken by the prophet Joel: And it shall come to pass in the last days, saith God, I will pour out of my Spirit upon all flesh: and your sons and your daughters shall prophesy, and your young men shall see visions, and your old men shall dream dreams; and on my servants and on my handmaidens I will pour out in those days of my Spirit." And Jesus, in the hour of his ascension, commanded the apostles not to depart from Jerusalem, but to wait for the promise of the Father, "which," saith he, "ye have heard of me: for John truly baptized with water, but ye shall be baptized with the Holy Ghost not many days hence."

Excited and inspired by such promises, the church waited and prayed through the intervening days. When the day of Pentecost was fully come, the ministration of the Spirit was inaugurated with an unprecedented and glorious outpouring of miraculous gifts and converting grace.

Two things are specially observable. One is the instantaneous and wonderful progress which the apostles themselves made in the knowledge of Christ, and the nature of his kingdom and salvation. After all he had taught them on this subject, both before and after his resurrection, they surprise us, in the moment of his ascension with the question,—"Wilt thou, at this time, restore again the kingdom to Israel?" Showing that the veil of carnal hopes and Jewish prejudices was still upon their hearts. He gave them no satisfaction, but told them to "wait for the Spirit." After he was come, they did not need to inquire. A flood of spiritual illumination fell upon the Old Testament, on the facts of the Saviour's life and death, and upon all his doctrines, and for the first time, they comprehended the glorious truth that the kingdom and salvation of Jesus Christ were spiritual: and they never needed to learn that lesson over again. The "anointing" they received, was once for all; it remained with them, leading them into all truth, and bringing all things to their remembrance. Dear and precious as is the name of "Comforter," by which our translators render the original title of Paraclete (παράκλητος), which Jesus applies to the Spirit, it seems to narrow the sense of the term. Comfort, "joy in the Holy Ghost," which, of course, we greatly desire and highly appreciate are much, but there are other effects of his presence and power, which are not less important to the growth of the renewed man, the upbuilding of the church, and the conversion of the world. Prominent among these, and comprehensive of most, is the teaching office of the Spirit. He is both the inspirer and the interpreter of Scripture. Having taught prophets and apostles to write it, he now teaches the church to understand it. In this double sense, he is "the Spirit of truth." The "Comforter, which is the Holy Ghost, whom the Father will send in my name, he shall teach you all things, and bring all things to your remembrance, whatsoever I have said unto you." His illumination relates primarily to Jesus Christ, the sun of the spiritual world; and since all Scripture, with more or less directness, points to him, the Spirit opens our eyes to discern its doctrine, touching all divine and heavenly things. When he is come, "He shall testify of me," said Jesus. "He shall take of mine, and shall show it unto you," and by this testimony and manifestation, "he shall glorify me." While Christ is thus revealed and glorified in the church, and in the view of the believing heart, there is required a revelation of the sinner to himself, that his need of this glorious Redeemer may be felt, and his salvation embraced: and accordingly the "mission of the Comforter," is to "the world, convincing of sin, of righteousness, and of judgment." Without the Spirit, the sinner is blind, not only to the grace and glory of Jesus Christ, but to the fact of his own guilt and ruin: and would perish in eternal darkness, if this holy and blessed agent should withdraw his influence. We may, therefore, say, in brief, that the sanctification of the believer, the preservation of the church, and the salvation of the world, depend immediately on the power of that Divine Spirit whom the glorified Saviour sheds forth on men.

While, in our thoughts and doxologies, we adore the Father, and love the Son, we should with equal fervour of gratitude and affection, worship and bless the Spirit!

Our relations to him, under this last economy which is the prelude to heaven, are most peculiar. The "Father Almighty," is the "Invisible God," "whom no man hath seen, or can see." The Son, after a transient manifestation on earth, has returned to heaven, and is hid from view. The Spirit is given in his room; he is already given, and broods like an all-embracing atmosphere over the world. He "abideth for ever," and is not like a wayfaring man that tarrieth for a night. The relation we are placed in to the Spirit may be expressed by the attitude and act of the risen Saviour, when suddenly appearing in the midst of the apostles, he "breathed on them and said, Receive ye the Holy Ghost."

Say not in your heart, who shall ascend into heaven, to bring the Spirit down? He has already descended, and is pressing on every avenue that leads to the inner sanctuary of the soul, to enshrine himself there, the Spirit of light, and power, and holiness, and joy: and the command of the glorified Redeemer to each of us this day is—"Be filled with the Spirit."

The freeness with which the Spirit is given, and the abundant measure in which his influences may be enjoyed, are points of instruction very clearly implied in the text, and of the deepest interest to us all.

He is spoken of as a gift, and in the immediate context is compared to water, which, of all natural elements and temporal blessings, is one of the freest and most abundant. From "him that believeth on me, as the Scripture hath said, shall flow rivers of living water: but this spoke he of the Spirit of which they that believe on him should receive." Water is had for the asking, and our Father in heaven is infinitely willing to "give the Holy Spirit to them that ask him." The dew that distils in silence while men sleep, and the rain that falls in copious showers, irrigating the fields, swelling the streams, and purifying the air, are natural symbols of the absolute freeness, the overflowing fulness, and the beneficent effects of the Spirit's influences. Predicting these "last days" of the Spirit's ministration, Jehovah declared by the mouth of Isaiah—"I will pour water on him that is thirsty, and floods upon the dry ground. I will pour my Spirit on thy seed, and my blessing on thine offspring. And they shall spring up as among the grass, and as willows by the water courses."

Freely given, acceptable to all, and fully adequate to every want of the individual, and the world, the Holy Ghost, in his Divine personality, his official character, and his special relation to men in this last earthly form of the kingdom of God, demands the peculiar and devout consideration of the church: and I present to you, my brethren, the doctrine of the Spirit, in hope, that we may attain to a better appreciation of our privilege, and that by coming into line in thought and action, with the plan of God, we may enjoy and improve the gift which is brought so near

A practical reflection, which naturally arises, is, that if Christians and the church do not possess the Spirit in the plenitude of his sanctifying and comforting influences, it is because they place obstructions in the way of his entrance to their hearts.

This is a necessary inference from the doctrine which we have enlarged upon and proved from Scripture, that the Spirit is already given by the glorified Saviour, and is an abiding presence in the world. If the Spirit is not in our heart, it is not because God withholds him, but because we are not in sympathy with him. If there is no light in our dwellings when the sun is shining in the heavens, it is because the windows are darkened and the doors are shut. Remove the obstructions, and his beams will fill every chamber. This which we draw as an inference from the Divine plan which assigns the Spirit to this last dispensation, is fully implied in a multitude of texts which exhibit our duties towards the Spirit. These nearly all imply his presence, his readiness, his urgency.

The exhortation not to resist him, implies that the hand of his gracious power is already laid upon us; the warning not to "grieve" him, imports that his loving embrace already enfolds us, and the command—"Quench not the Spirit," were meaningless, if the Divine spark were not already fanned by his holy breath. The precept that bids us "be filled with the Spirit," resembles a command to inhale full inspirations of vital air. "Receive ye the Holy Ghost," is the Saviour's salutation to his people. If we have not the Spirit, in sanctifying and converting power, it must be, because we obstruct his entrance to our souls, or drive him out by sin. Neglected duties, secret sins, unholy passions, and conformity to the world, "quench the Spirit," and leave us in darkness and death, when the light of the Spirit is shining all around us, and whilst his quickening power is brooding over a perishing world, as it brooded upon "the face of the deep" at first. It is our sin not to have the Spirit. There is not the shadow of an excuse for it. I pray you, think of this longer than you sit in these seats. When you read your Bible, or kneel in your closet, or pray with your children, or walk the street, or transact your business, open your heart to the Spirit of God. "Walk after the Spirit." "Walk in the Spirit." "To be spiritually-minded is life and peace."

If the stinted measure in which Christians and the church possess the Spirit is to be referred to the hinderances which they interpose, the continued impenitence of sinners has the same explanation. It is not because God has denied, but because you have resisted the Spirit, that you are still unconverted, and without part or lot in his salvation. The Spirit has often reproved you of sin and warned you of danger. At times he has urged you strongly in the direction of duty and the cross. You trifled with the opportunity—you knew not the time of your visitation—you turned to folly, to business, to sin, and are now approaching death without pardon and preparation for heaven. I beseech you, sin no more against the Holy Ghost. He will "not always strive." If you suffer him not to seal your soul to the day of redemption, you must be sealed unto the day of wrath.

SERMON XII.

THE BLADE, THE EAR, AND THE FULL CORN.

MARK iv. 26–29.—*And he said, So is the kingdom of God, as if a man should cast seed into the ground, and should sleep, and rise night and day, and the seed should spring and grow up, he knoweth not how. For the earth bringeth forth fruit of herself, first the blade, then the ear, after that, the full corn in the ear. But when the fruit is brought forth, immediately he putteth in the sickle, because the harvest is come.*

IT is in Scripture as in nature. When we look out on the material universe, some objects are so great, so prominent, so universally present, that none can overlook them. The earth, with its mountains and rivers, the sky, with its sun, moon, and stars, are as open to the view, and as familiar to the thoughts of children as of men, and, if not so well understood, yet as clearly seen by the unlettered peasant as by the erudite philosopher. What all thus see in nature, is, of course, most important to be seen: but we know it is little more than the mere surface of things, beneath which lie concealed ten thousand marvels of creative skill and power, which science in its endless progress brings to light. Analogous to this, there are in the Scriptures great doctrines and salient facts which rise like mountains on the plain of revelation, so bold and obtrusive that the most inattentive reader cannot fail to observe, and, in some degree, comprehend them: and beauties so obvious that it requires almost nothing beyond our natural taste and sensibility to discover and enjoy. Again, there are truths and beauties which disclose themselves only to the observant, the studious, the devout, but which, when discovered, are felt to be as real as those that are better known, and come to us with the added charm of a fresh acquisition.

Of the truth of these remarks, we have thought this beautiful simile of the Saviour, which only Mark records, might afford an illustration. What it has in common with other parables is familiar: what is peculiar to itself, and is its chief lesson, may have specially arrested the attention of very few: and it is possible that the general resemblance of its imagery to that in the parable of the sower, which in this gospel precedes, and to that of the "mustard-seed" which follows it, may have led, in a degree, to the oversight of the point in which it differs. With the seed and the field, the growing grain and the time of harvest, and the incidental lessons which are clustered around the central law of vegetation, we are well acquainted. There is, perhaps, no natural fact which is made the image and vehicle of so many spiritual truths; but it is possible that some—perhaps many of us—have not particularly studied, or clearly grasped the truth which the Saviour meant to convey when he represented the spiritual husbandman as leaving the seed to itself, after having cast it into the soil, and, free from anxiety, if not with carelessness concerning it, giving his attention to other matters. Certainly this is a phase of "the kingdom of God," which we are less in the habit of considering than some others: we do not say that it is more important, but would only suggest that it is necessary to the completeness of our views and the best development of our Christian experience.

The passage under consideration presents three or four related truths to which we ask your attention, and first and chiefly to that just now adverted to. It gives character and form to the parable, and stands at its beginning. "So is the kingdom of God, as if a man should cast seed into the ground, and should sleep, and rise night and day, and the seed should spring and grow up, he knoweth not how, for the earth bringeth forth fruit of herself."

The rising night and day, if the expression stood alone, might be supposed to imply even an excess of anxious care for the seed which had been sown; but in this connexion it plainly means the very opposite of this, and simply denotes the state of feeling and manner of life led by one who had discharged a piece of business—had done either all that was in his power, or all that the matter in hand required in order to its completion and success. The natural fact which gives us the expression of this spiritual and divine truth, affords a perfect illustration of its sense and its limitations. When a farmer has deposited his seed-wheat in a well-prepared field, his part and agency in the production of the crop is absolutely at an end. He can proceed no further, and there is nothing more for human power to do. He has come to the boundary which no man can pass over, on one side of which is the sphere of human labour, and on the other the sphere of Divine efficiency. If he chooses to put himself about what belongs not to him, and forebode, as many do, excessive rains, parching droughts, and untimely frosts, he may do so, but he will not thereby hasten or retard the processes of nature, or change the course of things in the slightest degree, or in the least particular. The "taking thought" which our Lord declares cannot add one cubit to our stature, or make one hair white or black, is equally fruitless when expended on the seed which we have committed to the care of God, by casting it into the earth. A pious trust in a benignant Providence, and the ancient promise of summer and winter, seed-time and harvest, should relieve the husbandman of anxious care; and, piety and providence out of the question, experience and common sense should teach him that his anxiety, however intense and tormenting, does no good, and may well be dispensed with. Nevertheless, it is important to mark the point up to which human labour and pains are of use, and of such indispensable necessity that, in their absence, all the self-acting powers of the earth to which the parable refers, and the subtle agency of the invisible God, will never produce so much as a handful or a grain of wheat. The husbandman of the parable did not resign himself to ease, or go to other occupations, till he had "cast his seed into the ground." This implies more than it expresses. It suggests a careful preparation of the soil, to make it a fit receptacle of the seed, and shows that the part allotted to man in natural husbandry, though humble, is necessary, and in amount quite sufficient to occupy his time and exhaust his powers.

The sense of the figure being thus plain and unmistakable, we inquire for its counterpart in the high realities of the spiritual world. And here we meet a question of vital importance to the interpretation of the parable. Is the man who casts the seed into the ground and leaves it the Lord Jesus Christ, or does this represent the ministers of the word, who publish his doctrines and become the instruments of salvation to their fellow-men? If we refer the language to Him, there is the difficulty of its attributing to him what seems unworthy of him;—inattention and sleep, and even ignorance, which might appear to go beyond what is warranted by the fact of his having withdrawn from the world and "gone into heaven," leaving his truth and his church to work their way on earth without his bodily presence.

But the language need not be pressed in its literal breadth, and, all things considered, we incline to the view which regards Jesus himself as being, though not exclusively, yet primarily intended by the sower in this, as in the like parable of the tares in the field.

This representation agrees also with that in the parables of the talents and of the pounds, which speak of him as going into a far country, and remaining away for a long time, leaving his servants meanwhile to act on their own responsibility, and in accordance with their own free will. Applying this description to the actual facts of history and experience, it has a twofold verification in the church and in the soul. Coming to the earth by his incarnation and visible ministry, Jesus planted the seed of his immortal and life-giving doctrine in the field of the world; and then, as if in the assured confidence that the seed would grow, and yield a plentiful and glorious harvest, he returned to heaven to await with patience the maturing of the crop. That he gives no attention to the growing grain, and leaves it without the fostering care of his quickening Spirit, is certainly not true, and is not of necessity implied in the terms of the text: the thing intended is the fact of his personal and bodily absence, and the inherent life and certain growth of his truth and grace as a deposit in the church and in the world. In the conditions which surround it, the seed of evangelical truth is as sure to live, and grow, and fructify, as is the grain which the farmer sows in the alluvial soil of his well tilled fields. The vitality of seeds is wonderful. It is said that a grain of wheat which was found in the hand of an Egyptian mummy, where it had lain for perhaps three thousand years, germinated, and according to the primeval law, brought forth seed after its kind. The word of God, planted in the field of humanity, is such a deathless germ.

> "Though it lie buried long in dust,
> It shan't deceive our hope."

Scattered from a Divine hand, it shall be like the rain and the snow that come down from heaven and return not thither, but water the earth, making it bring forth and bud, that it may give seed to the sower and bread to the eater.

The ordinance of the day and the night, and the law of the seasons, and the nature of all material things shall sooner change than this Divine seed shall return to the Giver of it void, or fail to prosper in the thing to which he sent it. The harvest of a regenerated world and of a glorified church is therefore certain. If we withdraw our view from the relations of Christ and his truth to the world, and regard his dealings with the individual heart, there is even here a sense in which, after the seed of a regenerate nature is given by the Saviour's first and special coming to convert the soul, he in a manner withdraws, and deals with it no more in this marvellous and powerful way, till it is ripe for the heavenly garner, when he comes the second time, and gathers the matured grain. The word of God, implanted by the Spirit and received by faith, is the seed of the new life in gracious souls. Once rooted in the spiritual nature, it never dies. Moral hinderances within and without, corresponding to drought, and cold, and shade, in the natural world, may retard its growth and impair its vigour, but it is a germ of immortality, breaking at length through all fetters, creeping forth to the sunlight of divine love, in which it delights, and yielding the fruit of perfect sanctification. "Immortal principles forbid the sons of God to sin." "He that is born of God sinneth not; for his seed remaineth in him, and he cannot sin, because he is born of God."

The word of God is the *seminal principle*, the divine germ from which the new life of the soul arises, and out of which "the new creature in Christ Jesus is unfolded:" and that is a beautiful commentary on this view of the text which we have from Peter, who describes the Christian as "born not of corruptible seed, but of incorruptible, by the word of God, which liveth and abideth for ever." When it takes root in the heart, its own immortality is the pledge of life eternal to the soul with which it is united, and such an interposition of Jesus Christ is never again required till the work of grace is done, and He who sowed the field returns to reap the grain.

But we need not, and indeed cannot, with consistency, regard Christ as the *exclusive sower of the seed.* In the work of saving sinners and recovering the world to God, there are many things in which we can have no participation with Christ, and in reference to which it may be said, that "of the people there was none with him." Such an exclusive Divine act was the atonement, and, in general, all that pertains to the mediation which reconciles men to God.

In other respects, believers are taken into union and fellowship with Christ; becoming members of a body of which he is the head, animated with his life, controlled by his Spirit, and co-working with him, as the instruments of his power, and the channels of his grace to the world. In a lower sphere, and in a limited sense, they do the same things that he doeth, becoming, through their prayers and labours, the instrumental saviours of those of whom he is the only and efficient Redeemer. If he above all others is the sower, who with effectual power sows the seed of truth and grace in the heart, his inferior ministers and servants are sowers too, who scatter the precious seed of the word in the broad field of our lapsed humanity: and for these, there is a lesson of peculiar interest. It is aimed against one of our *mistakes*, to call it by the softest name, and is designed to cultivate a grace which is alike honourable to God and promotive of our own happiness. The state of mind which it condemns, is a distrustful and anxious care about the results of our labour; the feeling it describes and approves, is a peaceful and confident hope that the same God who in nature gives the increase, will in due time crown our labours with the success which is meet, and bring to maturity every work of grace which we are instrumental in beginning. It requires a little discrimination to see precisely what it is which on the one side is condemned, and on the other is commended by the image of a man casting seed into the ground and dismissing it from his thoughts, and giving himself with a light heart to other occupations. It does not discourage labour and pains, but is meant to confine them to their own sphere, and show how and where they are to be applied.

We stand in no sort of need of being warned against excessive industry in seeking a spiritual harvest, or against having too eager and longing desires for the success of our efforts in the conversion of souls. Our danger lies all in the other direction. Both as it respects labours and desires, we constantly fall very far below the measure of our duty and opportunities, and there is nothing here or elsewhere in Scripture, which is calculated to restrain our exertions or lessen our ardour. We cannot possibly do too much in the wise and prudent use of means and endeavours to bring men to the knowledge of salvation. As in natural husbandry, the more pains that are taken to prepare the soil and put it in the best condition, the greater the prospect for an abundant yield of choice grain, so it is in the department of our spiritual toil.

In these preliminary acts, and in this humble sphere of feeble instrumentality, we can neither do nor feel too much, and the assurance that he shall come again, bringing his sheaves with him, is given only to him that goeth forth and "weepeth, bearing precious seed." But having done this, our duty ceases with our power. Duty is ours; events are God's. Having exhausted our strength and pains on means and labours, it is both our duty and our privilege to commit the case to the Lord, in cheerful hope that the result will in its season appear, and be such as will redound to the glory of God, and our own happiness and reward. This is not indifference about the result, not caring whether it come soon or come at all, neither is it inconsistent with prayer that it may be both speedy and glorious, but the precise thing it bids us put away is an unbelieving and useless anxiety about the result of our labours; a carefulness which springs from the want of perfect confidence in the promises and gracious designs of God, and only makes us uneasy and unhappy, without furthering, in the remotest manner or slightest degree, the object on which it is vainly spent.

And this suggests a principal reason for cultivating the believing, hopeful, happy temper, and frame of mind which the parable recommends. Corroding care even for spiritual results renders us miserable, and does no good. Therefore, let it be dismissed, and let the apostolic exhortation which bids us "be careful for nothing," be followed in its widest scope, and in all its applications. But the greatest reason of all is, that a confident and joyful hope in those who sow the divine seed of God's word by their sanctified labours, honours and pleases him, and thus silently tends to secure the blessings which unbelieving fears and forebodings hinder rather than help. Those whose toils in the work of human salvation God has most largely blest, have commonly been not only men of abundant labours, but of strong faith and cheerful hope: men who believed that God would do as he said, and that the gospel was verily the power of God unto salvation. Faith, and hope, and patience are as vitally related to the harvest of redeemed souls as are the pains and efforts of spiritual industry. "Behold, the husbandman waiteth for the precious fruit of the earth, and hath long patience for it, until he receive the early and latter rain." "Be ye also patient: stablish your hearts, for the coming of the Lord draweth nigh." Doing our part, we may rest assured that God will do his. "The earth bringeth forth fruit of herself," when once the seed has been cast into her bosom, and just so soon as any word of truth has been uttered, or spiritual service has been rendered, or holy influence has gone forth from us, it passes into the region over which God presides, and is taken under his care, and combined with the invisible and mighty agencies of his providence and Holy Spirit!

In the moral world there is, under the mediation of Jesus Christ, a "good ground" and a prepared soil, into which, when the seed of the word is cast, it brings forth fruit of itself, without human care, and under conditions which the grace of God has ordained. God's efficient care dispenses with our fruitless anxieties, and lays a good foundation for peaceful trust and patient waiting.

It is possible that some of you may be tempted to regard this frame of mind, now brought forward in the light of a virtue and grace, as of suspicious and doubtful character: and it must be acknowledged that it bears a superficial resemblance to a state of feeling which meets unqualified disapprobation in the Scriptures: nevertheless, the difference is as wide as the poles between the Laodicean indifference which does nothing, as well as cares for nothing, and the quietness and rest of those who, having done their duty, look with confidence for the promised blessing. And just here, it is in place to note the fact that a right dividing of the Divine word does not give the same truth to all persons. There is milk for babes, and strong meat for men, and a portion in due season for every phase of character, and for every condition of religious experience. And it is easy to see that the peculiar form of truth on which we have been dwelling, is not needed by a certain class of persons, and perhaps we ought, in truth, to say a certain class of Christians.

Individuals who are "at ease in Zion," neither feeling anxious about results, nor expending labour and pains on the instrumentalities which are designed to build up the kingdom of God and to save the souls of men, are certainly not in danger of running into an excess of anxiety, and need no caution against it. They would only be injured by the thought; and if such are here, I forewarn them that this part of Scripture truth is not for them. But to such as are labouring hard in the Lord's field, and ardently longing for the visible fruits of their toil, and yet are laying upon their souls a burden of care, which the Divine Husbandman himself has been pleased to assume, the lesson is neither dangerous nor useless, but altogether salutary and beneficial.

Relieved of distracting and distressing anxieties, we are enabled to pursue the labour which belongs to us with a lighter heart, doing it in larger measure and with greater efficiency.

In seeking to unfold and illustrate this, the principal and characteristic lesson of the parable, we have left but little space for noticing its subordinate teachings, which are yet of much importance. Two or three points may be touched in a few words.

1. In saying that the seed groweth up we "know not how," the mysterious nature and working of grace is hinted at. It is not regulated by natural laws, though they afford many illustrative analogies. It cannot be reduced to a science, like agriculture or mechanics. There is no philosophy of the Holy Ghost. Regeneration is not the result of any forces which human reason defines and gauges, much less controls: and the divine life which is breathed into the soul by the mysterious visitation of the Spirit, blowing like the wind, of which we cannot tell whence it cometh and whither it goeth, is afterwards maintained by supernatural supplies from the same invisible source, and is "hid with Christ in God." The processes and the instrumentalities by which it is advanced, are often such as reason would reject; and the subject of grace himself murmurs at and accounts them, at first, instruments of destruction, rather than of edification. And the very experiences which mark the Christian's forward movement are oftentimes to himself the most painful mysteries, viewed rather as evidences of backsliding, than as victorious struggles with corruption, or temporary defeats, which are necessary to prepare him for a final triumph.

In retrospect, the way that God has led us is very wonderful, and the secret history of the heart is not less marvellous than the events and the course of the outward journey. As the seed grows secretly, and no science can explain the mystery of vegetable life, so the life of God in the soul of man—the growth of that immortal seed of truth and grace which the Spirit plants—is a mystery which eludes all rational criticism, and is to be accepted simply as a truth of revelation, and as a fact of experience.

Asserting its mysteriousness, the imagery of the text gives us a beautiful expression of its progress, through successive stages, to its destined maturity:—"First the blade, then the ear, after that, the full corn in the ear." In the wondrous transformation of the soul thus typified, there is, in the very beginning of it, a secret process hid from mortal observation, resembling that swelling and germinating of the seed beneath the surface of the ground; anxious thoughts, deep convictions, and silent prayers, which precede and accompany the birth of the soul, into the kingdom of heaven, and, for a time, a shrinking disposition which conceals the new and strange experience. When the crisis is past, and the soul emerges into the light and joy of forgiveness and the hope of salvation, religion becomes more positive and outspoken, and the tender "blade" of the new life appears. It is joy, and peace, and love, delight in the ordinances of Divine worship, and the communion of saints. Or, under another figure which the Scriptures use to describe the same thing, it is the simplicity and confidence, and docility and new-born joys of childhood introduced into a world of novelty and beauty, and glory.

By insensible and slow degrees, this incipient condition of grace advances, till the simple and tender "blade" assumes the rounded development of the "ear," or head of grain, which may stand for the outline of a definite Christian character. It is strength, and stature, and symmetry added to the joyous experiences of the soul's "earliest love:" and while there may be less of sensible delight, there is more of the substantial and enduring qualities of Christian character. The advancement measured by the difference between the blade and the ear, is just the process indicated by the apostle, of "adding" to the "faith" which first embraced Jesus Christ for salvation, the graces of "virtue, knowledge, godliness, charity," and all the rest which form and beautify the Christian life. And as in nature there is a progress beyond the formation of the ear, to the "full corn in the ear," so in the growth of grace, there is a mellow ripeness of piety observable in many Christians, which rests like a crown of beauty on their heads. It is not so much the glow of the heart's first love which marks the infancy of grace, or the vigorous activities which characterize the zeal of its manhood, as it is a deeper acquaintance with God and with ourselves: inspiring profound humility, patience in tribulations, deadness to the world, and more of charity in our judgments. It is the case of those who being "planted in the house of the Lord, are fat and flourishing, still bringing forth fruit in old age."

The uses of this feature of a gracious life are two. It should teach us not to "despise the day of small things," in others or in ourselves; and, it should incite us to unwearied struggles after higher Christian attainments. The modest little blade which presses up through the parting earth, is not the ear nor the full corn in the ear, but it is that from which they grow, and without which they could never be.

Have charity and patience for these faint uprisings of grace in others; tread them not rudely down, but cherish them as buds of promise and germs of salvation: and if you find nothing more in yourself, destroy them not by unbelief, despondency, or neglect. Yet be not satisfied therewith. "Go on to perfection." Court the sunshine, inhale the air, drink in the rain of heavenly visitation: and shrink not from the chilling blasts and beating storms which "root and ground" the soul in the knowledge and love of God. By slow and sure advances, you will thus reach the maturity which Christ has appointed for you, and then will come another crisis of surpassing interest. He who sows the seed and waits for its growth and ripeness, does not leave the grain to perish where it grew. But "when the fruit is brought forth, immediately he putteth in the sickle, because the harvest is come." It is transferred from the field to the granary! By this pleasing image, the Saviour describes an event from which nature recoils.

As it is no damage to the grain to reap it, and gather it into the barn, but only that which takes place in the course of nature; so to the Christian, in whom the ripe fruits of grace are produced, it does no harm, but only completes and secures for ever the work of his redemption."

The "Reaper who in our gardens gathers flowers, transplants them in the Paradise above, and the sickle which so rudely cuts the yellow grain of ripened piety, gathers it to its predestined place under brighter skies, and starts it upon a new and higher development to which eternity sets no bounds."

Why then should the children of the kingdom be afraid of death? Unnatural to us as creatures, and infinitely to be feared by unpardoned sinners, it is the appointed and desired issue of our course as Christians.

It is but a removal—a transplantation—a saying to those who occupy the lowest room, "Come up higher." "For the believer who comes to his grave in a full age, like as a shock of corn cometh in his season," there is no reason to weep: and, if in ourselves, the inward man is renewed day by day, we need not lament the decay of our natural faculties. It predicts a glory soon to dawn.

SERMON XIII.

GOD'S WITNESSES.

ISA. xliii. 10.—*Ye are my witnesses, saith the Lord.*

ALL creatures that God has made, and all the operations of his hands, are his "witnesses." In different forms and varying degrees, they testify somewhat concerning the invisible God, whom no man hath seen or can see. The sun, the moon, the stars, bear witness to "the Father of lights," who kindled these celestial lamps, and hung them out in the visible heavens as the symbols of himself.

All that has been given to them they impart, declaring the "eternal power and Godhead" of Him who dwells above them in the insufferable light of the "third heavens." And not these mighty orbs alone, but all creatures, down to the blade of grass and the lily, which divine art has painted, fulfil the same great office. Whatever of divinity is impressed upon them, that they show to all beholders, and thus render the tribute of their testimony to Him who "made them all." And not the creatures in themselves, but their order, their relations one to another, and their movements,—in a word, *Providence*. as well as *Creation*,—brings its offering of testimony to the Being and Character of Him who rules the worlds.

Even in the absence of a direct and verbal revelation, "He

hath not left himself without witness, in that he giveth us rain from heaven, and fruitful seasons, filling our hearts with food and gladness."

And while all outward and material things give concurrent evidence of His existence, power, wisdom, and goodness, a testimony comes up from the depths of the human soul to his character as a *moral Governor*, the lover of righteousness, and the avenger of sin. "When the (heathen), which have not the law, do by nature the things contained in the law, these having not the law are a law unto themselves, who show the work of the law written in their hearts, their conscience also bearing witness, and their thoughts the meanwhile accusing, or else excusing one another."

The testimony which is obtained in these different forms from nature, is fundamentally important: without it there could be no religion; yet it alone is not sufficient to lead men to the saving knowledge of God. The testimony is true, but it is not adequate.

Neither creation, nor providence, nor conscience, nor all of them together, make known the whole character of God. The view presented is correct as far as it goes, but it is partial and incomplete; and being taken from the stand-point of sinners, it is obscured and distorted by the blindness of their hearts. If, therefore, it is the will and pleasure of God that men should come to the true and saving knowledge of himself,—as from the very perfection of his character we are warranted to believe,—a further testimony is necessary. He gives it in the revelations of his word, wherein all things which pertain to life and godliness are sufficiently made known; and above all, in the mission and ministry of his Son, whose coming and kingdom, Messiahship and Godhead, were "witnessed beforehand by the law and the prophets," and at the time of his appearing were attested by signs in heaven and wonders on earth. To prepare his way and point him out, was the peculiar office of John the Baptist, of whom it is said that he "came for a witness, to bear witness of the light, that all men through him might believe."

Of himself, Jesus declared—"To this end was I born, and for this cause came I into the world, that I should bear witness unto the truth."

After he had accomplished the work which his Father gave him to do, and had returned to his glory, "the word" which had begun to be spoken by "the Lord" was "confirmed unto men by them that heard him, God also bearing them witness, both with signs and wonders, and with divers miracles and gifts of the Holy Ghost, according to his own will."

In view of all this, it might seem reasonable to ask—"Is not the gospel sufficiently attested? What further need have we of witnesses?"

The gospel and its Divine Author have already received greater witness than that of men, and as when Jesus was on earth, so now there is a sense in which he "receives not testimony from man." His own mighty deeds were the credentials which accredited him as God's ambassador to the world, and now it is his own omnipotent grace that "confirms the word with signs following" its ministration in souls redeemed from iniquity. Without this direct testimony of Jesus to his own gospel, it would quickly vanish from the faith of the world.

But this, so far from displacing and rendering all inferior testimony needless, prepares the way for it—in fact, creates it: and he now says to his church, and to every company of believers—"Ye are my witnesses." It is a position of the highest honour and most solemn responsibility. Witnesses for God, his character, his honour, and the interests of his kingdom on earth, depend on the testimony we bear. The image of the text represents him as in some sort on trial before the jury of an unbelieving world.

In civil courts the verdict turns on the testimony rendered, and when the property or reputation, the liberty or life of a fellow-citizen is imperilled, every one who is possessed either of honour or conscience, feels deeply the solemnities of an oath, and weighs well the testimony he utters. The judgment which the world pronounces on the gospel, the cause, and the salvation of Jesus Christ, has a very intimate dependence on the testimony borne concerning it by the professed friends and followers of Christ. They are the only living and visible witnesses he has in the world. I do not say that any testimony they can bear, will certainly carry conviction to the minds of all men. A person who enters the jury-box with a rooted prejudice, or a dishonest purpose, will not be convinced by any amount of evidence which may be submitted. There were men who with the character and life, the doctrine and miracles of Jesus full in view, did not believe on him. They had prejudged his claims, and their hatred of his doctrines blinded them to the clear proofs of his divinity. None are so blind as those who will not see, nor so skeptical as those who are unwilling to believe. We are therefore, not to conclude that the unbelief of the world results entirely from the defectiveness of the church's and the Christian's testimony—much less, that it is thereby justified.

But though conviction may not be forced, nor effectually secured in all cases, it is certain that the testimony which professing Christians bear to Christ and his gospel, is closely and vitally connected with the success of his cause and the salvation of men.

I. And we may assume as a first and fundamental position, that it is needed. It requires no proof that the world around us remains in unbelief, and turns with indifference or scorn from the overtures of the gospel. Unbelievers are in much the same case as those idolaters whom the prophet describes in the context: "Blind people that have eyes, and the deaf that have ears" They are rational, intelligent, accountable, and in every other direction employ their faculties as reasonable creatures might be expected to do. They desire knowledge, they go in quest of light, they put themselves to expense and pains, to acquire information which may be turned to account in forwarding their temporal interests.

If they felt and acted in the same way with respect to religion, the necessity for the personal testimony of Christians would not be so urgent as it is. They might find everything which they need to know, fully and clearly stated in the Scriptures; they might, if they would, hear the doctrines of salvation proclaimed and expounded in the sanctuary. They might see in the life of Jesus the faultless model of that character which it is their duty to copy.

In this manner, a far more complete and perfect exhibition of Divine truth might be obtained than it is possible to get from the character and life even of those who most closely copy those of Christ, and afford the fullest exemplification of the gospel precepts, in their walk and conversation. But there are many who use none of these means of acquainting themselves with the truth. For strong, but very bad reasons, they "come not to the light." If they are ever to behold it, it must be carried to them. The only Bible they read is that which is printed in the character and conduct of those Christians with whom the intercourse and business of life bring them into contact. And even in the case of those who are in the habit of reading the Scriptures, and frequenting the house of God, the superadded testimony of Christ's living witnesses is greatly needed. If not required to impart knowledge—and much less to give revelations additional to those contained in the Scriptures, it is greatly necessary for the purpose of arresting attention, and producing conviction, and for this, it is, as we may see, admirably adapted. The tendency and purpose of testimony is to produce belief and conviction, and the Christian, as a witness for God, is like the books of a circulating library which pass from hand to hand, and house to house. So far as he bears the image and breathes the spirit of his divine Master, he is a "living epistle known and read of all men." In the absence of Jesus, he represents him. Since those lips which once spoke on earth have become silent, he speaks for him, though it be with a stammering tongue; and though the light in which he shines is a borrowed radiance, and but a dim reflection of the Sun of righteousness, he stands forth amid surrounding darkness, holding up the taper of his testimony for a Saviour whom men neglect or revile. It is because of this relationship to Christ as witnesses for him, that the same things are affirmed of him and of his followers.

Speaking of himself, and directing benighted sinners to the true source of salvation, we hear him say, "I am the light of the world:" addressing his disciples, and teaching them at once, the height of their privileges and their obligations, he says,—"Ye are the light of the world." He is the source; they the reflectors of light. He the sun, they the moons of the system, and as the moon shines most brilliantly and fulfils the purpose for which it was "ordained," when the sun is absent, so these upon whom the light of their departed Lord yet lingers, illuminate the night of the world.

Considering the attitude which unbelieving men occupy toward Christ as he is revealed in the Scriptures, and held forth in the ordinances of his church, it is evident that there is not only room for the peculiar instrumentality referred to in the text, but that there is an imperative necessity demanding it. The economy of salvation involves it as a prominent feature.

II. Its adaptation to the end in view will appear from considering, in the second place, the qualifications of believers to be witnesses for God. The character and position ascribed to them take for granted that they *know* something concerning God which others do not know, or at least which they do not believe or duly consider: and further, that what they know of God may be certified to others by their testimony. Our mental constitution and experience lead us to rely on testimony, and the most of all that we know or believe is taken upon the report and authority of others. The sphere of our personal knowledge, experience, and investigation, is very limited, and the sum of our information would be small indeed, if nothing were admitted or received beyond what falls within the range of our own immediate cognizance. But if we accept what others know and testify, the field of our knowledge is immensely enlarged: and this we do in reference to every department of human science, and every interest of man.

Testimony holds an important place in religion. Not to believe any testimony, is more preposterous and absurd than the simple credulity which "believeth every word." In weighing the testimony of witnesses, we inquire, in the first place, into their integrity and veracity, and at the threshold decide the question of their credibility. Are they worthy of belief? If there is good reason to question their truthfulness, we do not give them credit, however positive and explicit their statements. Subjected to this criterion, are Christians credible witnesses when they speak on God's behalf? All that is necessary to entitle them to credit, is that they should be as truthful as other men are—persons whose word would be unhesitatingly believed if they gave testimony before an earthly tribunal. That, as a class, the people of God are such, is a point which does not require argument. Even the world relies upon a person's Christian profession as a guaranty for his veracity—such is the result of experience and observation. It is not, therefore, pretended that Christians are unworthy of confidence when they give testimony in behalf of the religion they profess, and of the God whom they serve. The attack is made, not upon their credibility, but their competency as witnesses. It is admitted that they mean to speak the truth, and that they think they are doing so; but then, it is urged, they are ignorant, mistaken, deluded; and hence, notwithstanding their honesty of intention, their testimony cannot be relied on. This method of neutralizing its power is by far the most plausible which the world and infidelity employ; yet a little consideration is sufficient, as I think, to show that the objection is without validity.

Consider what it is that renders any person a competent witness. It is not his general information, nor his learning, nor the extent of his experience. These may, in particular cases, add something to the strength of his statements, but the validity of testimony does not rest on any such foundation. The most illiterate person in the community, a youth, a child even, may bear witness to a fact which has fallen under his own observation, and prove it with the same irresistible conviction in the minds of others, as if it were sworn to by the most learned judges who preside in our courts. Whether a Christian be gifted with much or little of mental power and cultivation, he is perfectly competent to testify to that which has fallen within the range of his own observation and experience. If other men declare that they have never had any such experience, this is mere negative testimony, and is of no more importance than that of a hundred witnesses who were not present when an event happened, or an action was performed, if brought to discredit the evidence of one man who was present and did see it.

Consider also what it is to which the people of God give testimony, and their competency as witnesses will be still further apparent. It is not to the truth of an opinion, nor to the correctness of an argument, nor, in general, to the Divine origin of the Christian religion, nor yet to the fact that the Bible is the word of God. This they assuredly believe, and confidently affirm; and, as logical deductions from what they do testify, these propositions may follow as necessary consequences; but it is freely conceded that Christians are not competent to prove, by direct testimony, the abstract truth of the gospel: that it is not an object of their immediate knowledge and experience.

Witnesses are not called to prove the correctness of opinions and the truth of doctrines, but the state of facts. And Christians, as the witnesses of God, certify nothing but the facts of their own knowledge and experience. This is distinctly indicated in the words which follow the text as the subject-matter of their testimony: "Ye are my witnesses, saith the Lord, and my servant whom I have chosen, that ye may know and believe me, and understand that I am he." "I have declared, and have saved, and I have showed when there was no strange god among you; therefore ye are my witnesses, saith the Lord, that I am God." The dealings of God with their own souls is the matter of fact to which believers witness: and who can say, with any show of reason, that they are incompetent to prove a thing of this nature? That a man is possessed of certain views, feelings, and principles of action, is just as susceptible of proof by his own testimony, as are the outward doings of his life. Apply this principle to the great fundamental fact of Christian experience, and one of the greatest stumbling-blocks to an unbelieving world—the fact of the soul's regeneration by the Spirit of God. Is it not of such a nature that it may be proved by testimony? And is not the person who has experienced it a competent witness? He knows, by infallible evidences in his own heart, that, in a moral and spiritual view, he is not the man he once was. In the time past of his life, as he remembers well, he lived "without God in the world"—he restrained prayer—he sought his chief joy in gratifying "the lust of the flesh, the lust of the eye, and the pride of life," and had no sort of relish, but, on the contrary, an unconquerable aversion for all spiritual pleasures and employments. Now, all this is changed. He not only leads a different life, but is conscious of different affections, motives, and sources of enjoyment. "Old things are passed away: behold, all things are become new."

Spiritually, "he is a new creature:" of this fact there is no doubt: but a question remains. How has the change been effected? Is he as certain that it has been wrought by the Spirit of God, as he is of its being wrought at all? He did not see this Divine Agent descending upon him, nor consciously feel the hand of omnipotent grace laid on his heart. It is admitted, the author of regeneration is invisible, and his action on the soul, mysterious. "The wind bloweth where it listeth, and thou hearest the sound thereof, but canst not tell whence it cometh, and whither it goeth: so is every one that is born of the Spirit."

How then can the converted sinner be assured that his heart

has been the subject of a supernatural, Divine influence? He knows it from the nature of the effect wrought upon him. Its greatness proves that it sprang from a power immeasurably above his own, and its spirituality and holiness connect it immediately with the "Father of lights, from whom cometh every good gift, and every perfect gift."

He is profoundly conscious that the natural bias of his heart was not in the direction of such a change; so far from this, he remembers well that he positively repelled the outward agencies and inward convictions which looked toward it, and is deeply persuaded that if he had had his own way, he never would have been different from what he was by nature, a child of "disobedience and of wrath." He is therefore just as certain that God is the author of the change, as that the change has taken place. Having "the witness in himself," both of its reality and divinity, he is competent to bear witness of it to others.

This testimony is indefinitely strengthened by the multitude of those who unite in it. In every age, thousands and millions have uttered it, and all around us are those who testify that God has renewed their hearts.

If in the mouth of two or three witnesses, every word shall be established, much more shall this great fact of regeneration by the Spirit of God be confirmed by the consenting testimony of millions. And when proved, it draws along with it the whole of Christianity. The chain of gospel doctrine and of God's redemptive purposes, which extends from a past to a coming eternity, at this point comes into direct and sensible contact with men, and fastens one of its golden links in the experience of every regenerate soul. The link draws after it the chain, and grasping this, we make sure of all. Or, stating the argument in the fewest and simplest words,—if regeneration is a fact, the gospel is true. Though the Christian, therefore, is not competent to bear witness to the truth of the Christian religion, he is in every way competent to prove a fact on the existence of which the truth of that religion hinges.

Another point in reference to which the testimony of Christian experience is peculiarly clear and strong, and the unbelief of the world is peculiarly stubborn, is the fact of God's hearing prayer, and faithfully fulfilling his promises to those who call upon him. Like the former, it is obviously a fact—if sufficiently proved—of vital connexion with the whole doctrinal system of the gospel. If it is a fact that God hears prayer, then all that the Scriptures teach respecting the mercy-seat, the throne of grace, the sacrifice and intercession of Jesus Christ, is true doctrine. Can the fact then, be established, without quoting proof-texts from the Scriptures, and upon the ground of human testimony? On this subject there is an accumulation of proofs—a mass of testimony—recorded not only in the pages of the Bible, but in volumes of religious biography, and witnessed by living men, which, if brought to bear upon the determination of any other question of fact, would settle it for ever, beyond the possibility of cavil or doubt.

By a wider induction of individual facts and experiences than was ever brought to prove a natural law or a scientific principle, it is established that Jehovah is a prayer-hearing and a prayer-answering God. Thousands of the best men on earth not only believe but testify that their own prayers have been answered. The previous prayer and the subsequent blessing stand in such a marked relation, the one to the other, that they recognize the latter as God's answer to the former, and devoutly cry with the Psalmist—"I love the Lord, because he hath heard my voice and my supplications."

Other applications of the principle under review might be made, but time does not allow, and our purpose does not require it. These are sufficient to show that believers are both credible and competent "witnesses" for God, establishing by their testimony facts of Christian experience and life which draw after them, by inevitable sequence, the whole system of revealed truth.

III. When God, by the mouth of the prophet, said to Israel —"Ye are my witnesses," it seemed to be his purpose to summon them to the performance of the function implied in the character: and we may now bestow a brief consideration on the forms in which this duty may be most effectually discharged.

To the first place among these must be assigned, as I imagine, the silent testimony of a holy life. This is by far the most convincing. A regenerated and holy man sustains the same relation to the grace of God which the material universe sustains to his power, and wisdom, and skill. The world witnesses to its Creator, and in like manner the saved sinner witnesses to his Redeemer. He is a piece of Divine workmanship —a "new creation in Christ Jesus." He is more: he is such a visible image of the invisible God, that men "take knowledge of him" as bearing the similitude of the heavenly and divine, and like the primitive Christians, in the case of the converted Saul, "they glorify God in him." Such is the nature of this silent testimony. The degree of its power depends on the clearness and completeness with which the Divine likeness is delineated on the heart, and held forth in the life. Some portraits are such exact copies, as to be immediately recognized by those who have seen the original. Some Christians are such miniature images of Him who hath renewed them after his own likeness. In others, the images of the earthly and the heavenly are so blended, that it is difficult to decide which predominates; and the effect on our minds resembles that produced by discrepancies and contradictions in the testimony of a witness. Its power is neutralized by its inconsistency.

And as one ascertained falsehood casts suspicion on all the evidence that is rendered, and prevents even that portion of it which may be true from gaining credit, so with regard to the testimony we bear on behalf of God. Our faults and follies are not judged of by themselves, and referred to the unsubdued corruption of the heart: but they are allowed to vitiate the virtue and piety with which they are connected, and they do, in fact, throw a cloud over all the better aspects of our character.

In my opinion, there are few subjects which Christians have more need to ponder with devout and faithful self-examination than the question, how far their testimony for God is nullified by the blemishes of their character, and by the practical contradictions of their life. It is probable that none of us is aware how much we do ourselves to destroy our influence. We see the faults of others, and are blind to our own. With a zeal not according to knowledge, we set ourselves to pull the mote out of a brother's eye, unconscious of the beam that fills our own. While labouring under such a hallucination as this, we are but sorry witnesses for God. Let us all, my brethren, cultivate the habit of looking at home—of practising severity in the judgment of ourselves, and charity in judging others—and let us make it our daily study to bear a uniform and consistent testimony to that gospel which we profess. A man who breathes a Christian spirit, and exhibits a Christian deportment; who lives and moves in the atmosphere of that charity which "thinketh no evil, seeketh not her own, and is not puffed up"—whose animating principle is that "wisdom that cometh from above, and is first pure, then peaceable, gentle, and easy to be entreated, full of mercy and good fruits, without partiality, and without hypocrisy,"—such a man bears a testimony to the gospel and grace of God, which the world can neither "gainsay nor resist." Such a character is just as evidently the fruit of Divine grace, as the light that shines around us is an emanation from the sun. Light is self-revealing. It needs no one to bear witness to its existence and its nature. We open our eyes and behold it. In like manner, holiness in the characters and lives of men is a beam from the "Father of lights:" its divinity is self-revealing: and the more brightly it shines, the more convincing is the witness it gives to the being and character of God. By the appointment of the Lord Jesus Christ, and in the degree of their actual sanctification, believers are "the light of the world." Having announced the fact and the doctrine, Jesus turned it into an exhortation; and what he said to the disciples, I now address to you: "Let your light so shine before men, that they may see your good works, and glorify your Father which is in heaven."

That passage from the sermon on the mount exhibits completely the argument we are considering. Personal holiness—the "good works" of Christ's disciples—are the effect of Divine grace, and are so recognized by those who observe them, and their natural tendency is to lead men to "glorify God." If, through the obstinacy and blindness of unbelief, this result should not be in fact produced, they may at least "stop the mouths of gainsayers," and "put to silence the ignorance of foolish men."

While this silent testimony of a blameless life is by far the most efficacious form of witness-bearing on God's behalf, it is not the only method.

A holy life will secure attention and credit for any verbal testimony we may have opportunity and strength to utter. The power of words depends largely on the known character of the man who speaks them. An unchristian life neutralizes completely the most pious exhortations. But "how forcible are right words" when "spoken in season," and proceeding from one whose character and life assure you that they come forth from the heart, and are uttered in deep sincerity.

Live so, that you may be able consistently, and without a blush, to speak for God: and when occasion offers open your lips, and "declare what the Lord hath done for your soul."

Be not "ashamed of the gospel of Christ." Be a firm and fearless witness for him who loved you and gave himself for you, and he may put on you the honour of "converting" sinners from "the error of their ways, and of saving souls from death." And if you bear witness to him in a world where his name is dishonoured and despised, he will bear witness to you in the presence of his Father and the holy angels. The martyrs were so named because they were witnesses for Christ. A multitude of them which no man can number, have gone up in chariots of fire to the throne of God. Follow them. "Seeing you are compassed about with so great a cloud of witnesses, lay aside every weight, and the sin which doth so easily beset you, and run with patience the race that is set before you, looking unto Jesus the author and finisher of our faith." Above all, look up to him who "witnessed a good profession before many witnesses," and now from his glorious seat, cries down to you, "Be thou faithful unto death, and I will give thee a crown of life." "Ye are my witnesses, saith the Lord, and my servant whom I have chosen: that ye may know and believe me, and understand that I am he: before me there was no God formed, neither shall there be after me. I, even I, am the Lord; and beside me there is no Saviour. I have declared, and have saved, and I have shewed, when there was no strange god among you: therefore ye are my witnesses, saith the Lord, that I am God."

What testimony, my brethren, shall I bear on your behalf, to these our friends who are yet strangers to the grace of God? May I tell them from you, as well as from God, that there is salvation in Christ for perishing sinners? With your consent, then, I give this testimony, and say to them, "We have found the Messias." "That which we have seen and heard declare we unto you, that ye also may have fellowship with us: and truly our fellowship is with the Father, and with his Son Jesus Christ."

We testify unto you that God hears prayer, that he pardons sin, that he imparts a peace which passeth all understanding, and inspires the hope of everlasting life. "We are journeying unto the place of which the Lord said, I will give it to you: come thou with us, and we will do thee good: for the Lord hath spoken good concerning Israel." Will you receive our witness? If not, will you believe the eternal God under oath? Hearken to his testimony: "As I live, saith the Lord God, I have no pleasure in the death of the wicked; but that the wicked turn from his way and live: turn ye, turn ye from your evil ways; for why will ye die, O house of Israel?"

SERMON XIV.

INCREASE OUR FAITH.

LUKE xvii. 5.—*And the apostles said unto the Lord, Increase our faith.*

THIS prayer of the apostles for an increase of faith, stands in immediate connexion with a lesson which the Saviour had addressed to them, on the duty of forgiving injuries. It would seem as if his doctrine on this subject had made a deep impression, and that the idea of forgiving those who trespass against us, indefinitely and without end, was quite in advance of their present attainments. Without, however, questioning the obligation of the duty, they confess their insufficiency for its performance. It required more grace than they yet possessed, to forgive an offender seven times in a day. It needed faith to do what they had already done, in leaving all to follow Christ, but here is something more difficult. To our unholy natures revenge is sweet, and when prudence or principle restrains us from inflicting evil on those who injure us, the temptation is strong, to cherish in the heart feelings of resentment, and, at least to punish men with our indignation and contempt.

The natural man yields to this temptation, and it is one of the noblest triumphs of grace in a regenerate soul, to forgive men their trespasses even as we hope for and need the forgiveness of God. If the divine life within us is feeble and languid, we shall be in the same measure, vindictive and unforgiving, and any who will not from his heart forgive an offending fellow-mortal proves himself to be under the condemnation of God. And while this request of the apostles confesses their unpreparedness for so arduous a duty, it shows a just appreciation of the true source of a Christian's strength.

Persons less instructed in the nature of experimental and practical religion, and looking superficially at the subject, might have prayed for an increase of meekness, or patience, or humility, that when offences came, they might be met with a calm and unruffled temper. These are excellent graces, of which we have immediate need when exposed to provocation or injury; but they are dependent upon and nurtured by a more radical principle of the Christian character.

Faith underlies, precedes, produces them. Praying for the increase of faith, is in effect to pray for their increase; and thus tends to keep down unholy resentments. And more than this, faith itself operates directly and powerfully on the duty and act of forgiving injuries. In fact, there is nothing but faith in God as the Judge of men, at whose bar we all must stand, and on whose pardoning mercy we depend for salvation, that can subdue the vindictive spirit which delights to do to others as they have done to us. Forgive one another, as God for Christ's sake hath forgiven you: this is the irresistible argument, and it is faith alone that brings it down and makes it influential as a motive amidst the temptations and duties of every-day life. The light which the connexion thus throws upon the text, is that an increase of faith is the grand preparation for performing the most difficult duties, and meeting successfully the trials to which we are all exposed. The subject is in the highest degree practical, and of universal application. Let us give it earnest heed. It is the increase of faith: and nothing would just now be more in place, than for us to breathe the prayer of the apostles: "Lord, increase our faith:" and inasmuch as faith cometh by hearing, let us meditate devoutly on what the Scriptures teach concerning this important subject.

That for the increase of which we pray is *faith:* and it is natural, and not unnecessary to begin with some consideration of ITS NATURE.

How often the word occurs in Scripture, and how large a place is held, and how vital an office is performed by faith in the salvation of the soul, you need not be informed.

In a sense not true of any other act of the soul, or of any other grace of the Spirit, we are saved by faith. We are justified by faith; we stand by faith; we walk by faith: and the life we now live in the flesh, we live by the faith of the Son of God. So radical is it in religious character, and so pervading in the acts and life of the Christian, that he is named therefrom a *believer.* What, then, is faith? In one aspect it is very simple. As an exercise of the soul, it is only to believe: and there is nothing more mysterious in the faith which saves us, than in the belief and trust we repose in men in the social and commercial intercourse of life. If it be considered with respect to the objects on which it rests, and the fruits which it yields, and the circumstances under which it is exercised, it presents an almost endless variety of phases, and is linked with every doctrine of the gospel, every form of Christian experience, and every condition of life. A careful study of the Scriptures will bring us, I think, to the conclusion that the two great characteristics of Christian and saving faith regard the grounds on which it rests, and the objects at which it looks. It is unlike all merely human faith, in that it rests on the authority of God, testifying to men in the Scriptures in reference to what they could not otherwise know.

This appears to be the sense of the apostle where he says—"we walk by faith, not by sight," and in that other and notable text which defines faith as being "the substance of things hoped for, and the evidence of things not seen." These passages assert what the religious history of men demonstrates, that certain and accurate knowledge of the spiritual and eternal world is obtained only by revelation from God. Neither sense nor reason can pierce the veil that hides the awful and grand realities which are about and beyond us; the wisest and purest of the ancient sages attained to nothing better than plausible conjectures and uncertain hopes. The "hidden wisdom which none of the princes of this world knew," is made known in Scripture: "as it is written, Eye hath not seen, nor ear heard, neither have entered into the heart of man, the things which God hath prepared for them that love him: but God hath revealed them unto us by his Spirit." Faith is the firm belief of these Divine revelations: it rests on the testimony of God; it believes the Scriptures "for the authority of God speaking therein," and is thus a supernatural and divine principle, believing on the ground of God's veracity, and is wrought in the soul by his power. It does not, therefore, "stand in the wisdom of men, but in the power of God," who first reveals the truth in the Scriptures, and then discloses it to the heart by the inward teaching of his Spirit. This, then, is the first element of faith: it receives and relies on Divine testimony in regard to things otherwise unknown and unknowable. Its second great characteristic regards the objects to which it looks. The testimony of God reveals truths, and discovers objects: and faith embraces the truth, and looks at the things which this testimony discovers. An illustration from nature may render this distinction clear. The spiritual world, the Scriptures, and faith, have their several types in the material universe, the light of the sun, and the human eye.

The earth, without the light of the sun, is wrapt in darkness; and when the light shines, there is no perception of the form and beauty of the world without the eye; as, "in the beginning," God first made the earth, then the light, and, last of all, brought man upon the scene to behold and admire his workmanship. Thus, also, in things divine and supernatural. There is the spiritual world, but hidden from mortal sight till God pours upon it the light of revelation; and even after this is done, there is no discernment of the grand and glorious objects with which it is filled, till the eyes of the understanding are opened, and the new organ of faith is exercised.

The effect of this on the soul resembles that of the sun on our bodily senses and actions. It imparts knowledge, awakens feeling," and determines conduct. Opening our eyes upon the natural world, we see in one direction a beautiful landscape, to be admired; in another, a frightful danger to be avoided; here a treasure to be secured, there a labour to be performed, and in yet another direction, a path to be trodden. So, when a man is translated from the darkness of unbelief into the marvellous light of faith in the revelations of the gospel, "old things pass away," like shadows of the night and chimeras of a disordered fancy, and all things become new. New ideas, new emotions, new pleasures, "newness of life," and a "new creature," is the certain and happy result. Every truth of the gospel and all the things of the spiritual world, are included in the object of faith, and just so far as they are known and present to the view of the mind, they produce an effect suitable to their nature.

Faith in the promises of God imparts peace and joy; faith in his threatenings, awakens godly fear; faith in the doctrine of immortality and the retributions of a future state, moves us to earnest preparation for death and eternity; and our daily life is governed by the "powers of the world to come." If we believe in God; even that he is, and that he is a rewarder of them that seek him; if we believe in the attributes of his glorious nature; in the strictness of his law, the power of his providence, the freeness of his gospel, and the infinite love he reveals and exercises towards men; through the mediation of the Lord Jesus Christ; it is evident that a faith like this must penetrate our inmost being, must rule in the heart, must mould the character, must shape the life; that it must stir profounder emotions and maintain a grasp on the soul as much more firm than anything else, as its objects are more glorious, great, and enduring than all the things which address themselves to reason and sense.

Thus we see the nature and power of faith. It is the soul's living contact with and sensibility to the truths and facts of revelation. Its every single act is, as it were, a glance of the eye at these impressive and solemn verities; and as it grows in strength and steadiness, it becomes the habit of "looking not at the things which are seen and are temporal, but at those which are unseen and are eternal." Such, in its nature, is that "precious faith" which all the children of God have "obtained:" but while, in its nature, it is alike in all the disciples of Christ, it differs greatly in its degree, and is susceptible of increase; and this brings us more exactly to the point of our text, and the subject of our discourse: the increase of faith. It may be very weak even where it is true and saving: and there are times in the experience of strong believers, when their faith is feeble, and they greatly feel the need of its increase.

In common, Peter was not specially deficient in this vital principle of the Christian character, but when walking on the water to go to Jesus, he saw the wind boisterous, and was afraid, he began to sink, and received along with the timely succour of Jesus Christ, the gentle rebuke,—"O thou of little faith, wherefore didst thou doubt?" And in that night of preternatural darkness and temptation when Satan desired to have him that he might sift him as wheat, though his gracious Lord prayed for him that his faith might not fail, it is certain that little more than the slenderest thread could have remained to unite him to the Saviour whom he denied. Thomas, more than the rest, it would seem, was staggered by the death of his Divine Master, and was so fixed in unbelief as to discredit the testimony of those who had seen their risen Lord, and was only recovered when the evidence which he had unreasonably required, was granted: but along with the condescending grace of Jesus, there was given a pointed rebuke—"Be not faithless, but believing."

These diversities which appeared among the immediate disciples of Christ are found among all Christians. In some of them, faith is very weak; in others, strong; in all it is capable of increase. It may increase—it ought to increase. We are as much commanded to believe with a strong faith as we are to believe at all. The warrant for faith is the veracity of God, and if he who believeth not God, hath made him a liar, and is guilty of a heinous crime, is there not an element of this sin, in the weakness of our faith, which begets doubts whether God will do as he has said, and which fears that he may not? Our reason for believing in God and his revelations at all, is a reason for the most absolute and unquestioning faith. And while the *ground* of faith—which, as we have seen, is the Divine testimony—not only warrants, but requires perfect and implicit confidence, and brings guilt not only on those who have no faith at all, but on those whose faith is weak; the same thing appears from considering the immediate and actual causes of this weakness of faith. One of them is ignorance of, and inattention to the word of God. The Scriptures are God's testimony: and how can we believe, any farther than we know and consider it? It is the word of God which begets, and supports, and nourishes faith: and in order to this, it must be devoutly read and listened to. Neglect of the Scriptures and ignorance of their contents are the food of unbelief; and a man who is mighty in the Scriptures is certain to be "strong in faith." The doubt and distress into which the disciples were thrown by the crucifixion of Christ, was the direct and obvious result of unacquaintance with the word of God. They trusted that Jesus was the Messiah, till he was put to death; and when that happened, they knew not what to think; whereas, if they had known the Scriptures and the power of God, they would have seen in his death the fulfilment of prophecy, and so would have found a fresh support of their faith. Their ignorance was culpable, and of course the unbelief which sprang from it was equally so: and while the risen Redeemer condescended to remove it, he pointed out and rebuked its guilty cause:—"O fools, and slow of heart to believe all that the prophets have spoken—and beginning at Moses and all the prophets, he expounded unto them in all the Scriptures the things concerning himself"—and while he spake, their hearts burned within them, their eyes were opened to know him, and faith grew up to a strength and stature which it had never reached before. If the unbelief which rejects Christ and salvation is condemned and punished as an aggravated sin, certainly the unbelief which lingers in the heart of a believer, and which might be expelled by a better knowledge and a more devout study of the Scriptures, is not innocent. It dishonours God, and paralyzes our own strength. Another and special impediment to faith, is the want of a good conscience. The apostle exhorts to "hold the mystery of the faith in a pure conscience:" in nothing else can it be held. Guilt is the natural extinguisher of faith, as much so as water is of fire. A guilty conscience—a conscience which is ever unquiet by reason of neglected duties and doubtful practices—is wholly incompatible with "confidence toward God," and "boldness" at the throne of grace. Destroying faith, it quenches the spirit of prayer, and renders impossible that pleading earnestness which prevails with God. Careless, unstable, unreliable, worldly-minded Christians have little faith. Their inconsistent life is at once the evidence of its weakness, and the cause of its continually becoming more so. For these and like reasons, we must proceed on the assumption that the weakness of faith is a fault to be repented of, not less than a want to be supplied. The prayer for more, is a virtual confession of our sin in having so little; nevertheless, it is a hopeful symptom. Is it the desire of our hearts? Is it your prayer to God, now and always—"Increase my faith?" If so, the methods and means of its increase will be of interest. On this point, we shall attempt but a few brief suggestions. In the text, the apostles asked of the Saviour, as a direct bestowment, that he would increase their faith; and this suggests that *prayer* is a means of increasing faith. It possesses, indeed, an admirable adaptation to this end. Faith is the gift of God, and therefore it is to be sought in prayer, as are all other divine blessings. If we have a little faith, and pray for more, God will give it to us by the inspirations of his Holy Spirit, helping our unbelief, and increasing our faith: while prayer thus obtains faith as a divine gift, and so adds to its strength, it exercises it as a grace, and according to a law of both natural and spirituul life, increases its vigour and activity. Prayer to the invisible God, in the name of the Lord Jesus Christ, for spiritual and eternal mercies, is purely an act of faith. Prayer is faith in exercise. If not identical, they are intimately related. They act and react on one another continually. Faith prompts to prayer, and prayer increases faith. It does so both in the nature of the act, and in the method of its answer. If the answer came always in the moment of asking, faith would not be nourished so much as sense would be indulged. The Syro-Phenician mother had strong faith when she began to cry to Jesus in behalf of her daughter; but when, after repeated and distressing repulses, she pressed her suit and triumphed, her faith mightily increased, and would have removed mountains; and from the lips of the Son of God, she received the precious commendation and assurance—"O woman, great is thy faith!"

The Christian who thus cries to God in his closet, and kneels with his family at the mercy-seat, and forsakes not the place where social prayer is wont to be made—will experience a steady increase of his faith. It grows by its exercise in prayer, by the grace which God gives in answer to prayer, by the very method of the answer, and by the fact of getting answer at all. Every instance of answered prayer establishes faith in Jehovah as a prayer-hearing and a prayer-answering God. Another means of its increase, entirely within our reach, is active employment in the service of God. If you wish to find a professor of religion who is "fearful and unbelieving," imagining difficulties and dangers in every direction; afraid to attempt anything for fear it will fail, and living without the joys and consolations of religion, go to one who does the least service in the church: and who habitually shrinks from or refuses to perform a large part

20

of Christian duties. Such a course of behaviour violates the fundamental conditions of the life of faith, and if the divine principle be in him at all, it can only drag out a sickly existence, with fewer and fainter pulsations. The law of its life and the condition of its increase is activity. It "worketh by love;" and this its native tendency must be complied with, in order to its growth. It may and must be nurtured by the word of God, and by the influences of grace, bestowed in answer to prayer, but these alone do not bring it up to a full and healthy development. It needs work.

Faith and works, though theological opposites in the matter of our justification, which cannot be mingled, are friendly allies and energetic co-labourers in our sanctification. In Abraham, the father of believers, faith wrought with his works, and by works was faith made perfect: its genuineness was evinced and its strength increased. Every act of sincere obedience to God that you perform, will increase your faith, and especially every act of self-denying service will have this effect. Try the experiment, and you will bear witness to its efficacy.

With reference to the means and methods of increasing faith. I only add further, that God has this end in view in all the dealings of his providence. It is of the very essence of our probation, that we are required and taught to live by faith: and the whole scheme of providence and grace is adjusted for developing and strengthening this habit of the soul. For this end the blessing on our labours is concealed or delayed; impediments are left or even placed in our path; the providential way of Jehovah is through the sea and in the deep waters; and the unfolding of his mighty plans and holy purposes is so slow that the forward movement in the life-time of a generation is scarcely perceptible to those who stand amid the world's confusions.

Sense and reason cannot pierce the clouds and darkness which surround him, and we are "shut up to the faith," which assures us that "justice and judgment are the habitation of his throne," and whether we can see it or not, "all things do work together for good, to them that love God;" and for the furtherance of that kingdom which is "righteousness and peace, and joy in the Holy Ghost." Thus, when sense is blind and reason baffled, are we schooled to the exercise of faith, and by the exercise, faith is increased. And oftentimes, the purpose designed by the Christian's afflictions is not so much the punishment of his sins, as it is the proof of his faith. Like gold from the furnace, it emerges from the fiery trial, approved, purified, perfected, and is found unto praise, and honour, and glory, at the appearing of Jesus Christ.

By such methods and processes, God answers our prayer for the increase of faith, and in so doing confers upon us the greatest blessing we can receive in the present world.

"Faith" is the great law, condition, and characteristic of our life on earth, as "sight" is the grand peculiarity and excellence of the believer's estate in heaven.

Faith is the radical grace and principle of Christian character; its increase is the virtual increase of all other attributes and principles. It works by love; it begets joy, peace, hope, and all the beautiful train of graces which adorn the character and bless the soul. It is the root from which they grow, and as, in material husbandry and horticulture, the only method of obtaining fruit and flowers is the planting of seeds, so, in this garden of the Lord, the virtues and graces which beautify the character and life of a Christian spring up from the germ of faith, and most abound where that divine principle is the strongest. In the increase of faith, sanctification, in all its elements and principles, is carried forward. Faith "purifies the heart." It is a principle of antagonism to all evil, and will not rest till every corruption is mortified and destroyed.

It is indispensable in the performance of our duties. If we depend on mere feelings for the impulsive power which shall urge and uphold us in the service of God, feeling may fluctuate, joy may decline, and darkness may surround us. We need, to keep us firm, and patient, and faithful, a principle which never suspends its operation; which grasps the changeless and glorious things of the spiritual world and the eternal future, and brings down from heaven motives and powers, when all within is comfortless, and all around discouraging! Faith is this bond of union and channel of communication between earth and heaven, between the soul and God.

Whatever of motive power there is for doing and enduring the Divine will, in the thought of God's all-seeing eye, in the solemnities of the judgment-bar, in the hope of everlasting life, and in the danger of eternal banishment from the presence of the Lord, and the glory of his power,—all this is by faith brought to bear as an incentive to fidelity in the duties of our earthly lot: and not the power of motives only, but the direct power of almighty grace, "helping our infirmities," feeding our hidden life with spiritual supplies, is conveyed by faith from its heavenly source. Faith is union with God in Christ; the fellowship of human weakness with Divine strength. Man's impotence obtains the aid of God's almightiness, and the believer is able to do what mere mortal power could never achieve.

Strong in the Lord and in the power of his might, the Christian performs duties which are painful to his natural sensibilities; and resists temptations before which others fall. With "the shield of faith," he quenches all the fiery darts of the wicked, and when the world and all its attractions are offered as the bribe of his fidelity and the price of his soul, faith looks away to the crowns, and palms, and treasures of a better country, and spurns the worthless baubles of earth. "This is the victory that overcometh the world, even our faith."

Have you this precious faith, my brethren? Bless God for its bestowment, and pray for its increase, till it shall hold the undivided ascendency of your heart, and govern your life. "Walk by faith," and you will walk safely, steadily, joyfully; and in the end of your pilgrimage, will reach the glorious objects which have been the pole-star of your earthly wanderings. "For now we see through a glass, darkly; but then face to face: now we know in part; but then shall we know even as also we are known." The church needs the increase of faith, and the sinner needs its first implantation.

Ye that have no faith, consider that your want of it is sin. Your unbelief is not owing to any intellectual inability, nor to any want of evidence. It is due to the indisposition and unwillingness of the heart. "He that believeth not God, hath made him a liar, because he believeth not the record that God gave of his Son. He that believeth on him, is not condemned: but he that believeth not, is condemned already, because he hath not believed in the name of the only begotten Son of God. This is his commandment: That we should believe on the name of his Son Jesus Christ, and love one another, as he gave us commandment."

SERMON XV.

THE SPIRIT AN UNCTION, A SEAL, AND AN EARNEST.

2 Cor. i. 21, 22.—*Now he which hath anointed us is God, who hath also sealed us, and given the earnest of the Spirit in our hearts.*

Some expositors would restrict the application of these statements to the apostles and other ministers of the word, who were endowed with peculiar gifts and graces of the Holy Ghost.

This does not, however, appear to be required by the context, and has nothing to support it in the general teachings of Scripture. In the confirmation which is named in connexion with the particulars here recited, the apostle expressly joins the Corinthian Christians with himself, as the subjects of it, and then proceeds, without any change of construction, to say that the same God who had "established" him with them in Christ, had anointed, and sealed, and given the earnest of the Spirit in their hearts. And while the structure of the passage favours, and even seems to demand this comprehension of all believers, the members, not less than the ministry of the church, as recipients of the grace described, our minds may be relieved of all doubt, by the fact that every one of these forms of spiritual influence is spoken of in other places, and some of them very often, as Christian characteristics and Christian privileges—an honour put on "all the saints," a blessing bestowed on the heirs of salvation.

A true minister of Jesus Christ, while he firmly maintains the order of God's house, is not so jealous of his official prerogatives as to envy the gifts and graces of the laity, or to grieve over good accomplished by other than apostolical and ministerial hands. If devils are cast out in the name of Jesus, by those who follow not with him, or are not invested with official robes, he will say with the Master—"Forbid them not," and with Moses, when one told him that, contrary to usage and order, Eldad and Medad were prophesying "in the camp," and not with the rest of the elders "round about the tabernacle"—"Enviest thou for my sake? Would God that all the Lord's people were prophets, and that the Lord would put his Spirit upon them!" What "Moses, the man of God," desired for the Israel of his day, is the devout prayer of all who have more zeal for the glory of Christ than for their own influence and distinction. In this description of the Christian's character and relation to God, there is a harmonious blending of dignity, and duty, and privilege; and the unity of the text consists in the common relation which all these particulars sustain to God as their author, to the Holy Spirit as their instrument, and to the soul of the believer as the subject in which they meet and blend: and the topic we have for consideration is the Holy Ghost, viewed in the threefold relation of an *unction*, a *seal*, and an *earnest*. "Now he which hath anointed us is God, who hath also sealed us, and given the earnest of the Spirit in our hearts."

I. We are, in the first place, to consider Christians as the subjects of a *Divine unction*—as God's anointed ones; and in the outset, let me warn you against the mistake of emptying this language of its high and precious significance, by regarding it as a figure of speech. The thing declared is an experimental fact, and a Divine reality—far more so than if, as in former ages, a holy ointment, with form and ceremony, were poured upon the head. The meaning of the language, however, can only be obtained by reference to this ancient usage.

The call and investiture of prophets, priests, and kings, was accompanied and symbolized by anointing them with oil. Thus Samuel anointed Saul and afterwards, the son of Jesse, to be king of Israel. In the ritual of the Jews, which prescribed the method of ordaining Aaron and his sons to the priesthood, we read of a "holy anointing oil," compounded with rare and costly spices; which was poured on the head of the priests, "to sanctify" them, as it is said. The meaning of the ceremony was obviously that of *consecration* to a particular office or function. It carried with it authority and obligation to serve God, and men as well, in a manner expressly indicated. Kings, priests, and prophets thus set apart, were spoken of as "the Lord's anointed," and on this account were treated with respect and veneration. In Jesus Christ, all the prophetic, regal, and priestly functions, which before had been divided amongst different persons, were united, and he, above all the sons of men, is the Lord's Anointed. Most of you, perhaps, well know that his name of Christ means one that is anointed. The Hebrew Messiah of the Old Testament, is the Greek Christ of the New; and the title is suggestive of the consecration he received to the mighty work of human salvation, in the triple character of prophet, priest, and king. A priest on his throne "after the order of Melchisedek." He received his ordination immediately from the hands of God, and was "anointed with the oil of gladness above his fellows," when the Holy Ghost without measure was poured upon him.

The oil of Aaron's consecration was but the symbol of an inward and effectual unction of God's Spirit, which both authorized and qualified Jesus, "to preach good tidings unto the meek."

Descending and remaining upon him, it prepared him for the ministry of labour and suffering to which he was appointed, and thus fulfilled the prophecy, that "the Spirit of the Lord should rest upon him, the Spirit of wisdom and understanding, the Spirit of counsel and might, the Spirit of knowledge and of the fear of the Lord." After he had run his earthly course and returned to his glory, the author of the book of Acts records it as a matter of simple history, that "God" had "anointed Jesus of Nazareth with the Holy Ghost." In the light of these remarks, we may see the nature of that anointing which the apostle attributes to believers.

As from Christ, they have their new life and new character, so from him they have their "new name" of Christians, or, Anointed ones. And their anointing, like that of the apostle and high priest of their profession, is by the Holy Ghost.

That they have the Spirit is a truth which shines throughout the Scriptures. He dwells in them, consecrating their bodies and souls as the living temple of his perpetual residence; but the peculiar truth which is here announced is, that they have the Spirit in the nature of an "unction," calling them to a special work and a holy vocation; separating them from the outlying and common world of mankind, and appointing them to stand, like Israel of old, in a sacred relation to God—a "peculiar people, a kingdom of priests." In our lowly sphere, and at an infinite remove from the glorious Head from whom we have our spiritual nature, name, and mission, it is nevertheless true, that Christians are actually and visibly conformed to the image of Him who is the first-born among them all, and in a modified sense, perform the same functions and do the same works. Like him they execute the office of a prophet, declaring to men the will of God for their salvation.

If he proclaims himself "the light of the world" did he not say to them, "Ye are the light of the world?"—"As the Father hath sent me into the world, so send I you." If in his priestly character, he draws nigh to God, and offers before the throne his intercessions for men, and by the merit of his sacrifice, secures the acceptance of their services and persons, are they not also intercessors; "a holy priesthood to offer up spiritual sacrifices, acceptable to God?" Paul, on the ground of his agency in the conversion of the Gentiles, represents himself as performing a priestly service in presenting them as an offering to God. And if it be difficult in the present condition and character of Christians to see the evidences and attributes of kingly dignity and power, it is to be remembered that the believer's "glory," like that of Jesus, is to be enjoyed in heaven and not on earth. It is the subject of a promise and the object of hope, waited for with "earnest expectation." For the present, we have a more direct and practical concern with the prophetic office of teaching and the priestly duty of praying for men, and this, we take to be the essential idea and main purpose of that anointing which God bestows on all his people. It separates them to his service in all the sacred duties of religion, and in all those good works and holy charities which tend to the salvation of souls and the improvement of the world. If the hands of some man of God, like Moses, had been laid upon you, as they were on Joshua; or if a Divine voice like that which startled the child Samuel on his bed, had fallen on your ear; or, if the Son of God, revealed in dazzling brightness, had appeared to you, as he did to Saul of Tarsus, your call to a special service would have been no more distinct, nor would have carried with it any higher authority than that which came to you in "the still small voice," with the soft breathing, and effective anointing of the Holy Spirit, when he opened your eyes to see, and your ears to hear, and your heart to embrace "the glorious gospel of the blessed God." In every form of external call and ordination, by which men are set apart to the special service of God, there is the possibility of mistake; and, in point of fact, many receive the imposition of human hands, who bear no credentials from Heaven. The unction of the Spirit has this grand peculiarity, that it qualifies as well as authorizes those who receive it, to serve God as prophets and priests in his holy and gracious kingdom. It enlightens, and sanctifies, and strengthens, and imparts courage, and endows even babes in Christ with a deeper discernment than "the wise and prudent" "disputers of this world" possess. The apostle John ascribes it to those whom he calls, "little children," and speaks in most emphatic terms of its effect on the mind and heart. If others apostatized, and were led away with the error of the wicked, he was sure *they* would not, "for," said he, "ye have an unction from the Holy One, and ye know all things," and "the anointing which ye have received of him abideth in you, and ye need not that any man teach you; but as the same anointing teacheth you of all things, and is truth, and is no lie, and even as it hath taught you, ye shall abide in him." As with respect to worldly vocations, the question whether an individual has a call to pursue any particular trade, or business, or profession, is determined mainly by his aptitude, his genius, or his taste for it. So in the department of those high spiritual relations and duties to which the followers of Christ are called. The nature of the qualification imparted, indicates that of the service to which they are appointed. With eyes enlightened to see the glory of Christ, and with hearts renewed after his likeness, and filled with the sweet sense of his love and the joy of his salvation, their mission to be the instrumental saviours of those who are yet in sin, is written in the work of the Spirit in their own souls, and is sure to be sought and found by those who feel the power of this most blessed unction. And this suggests, that the manner of life we lead, and the place which the salvation of men and the honour of Christ's kingdom hold in our thoughts and labours, is the criterion by which the question of our ever having received the anointing of the Spirit, is to be decided. If we allow the Spirit to lead us in paths of righteousness, and of holy benevolence, and of self-denying labours, we have the highest evidence possible, of that "holy calling," which, coming from God, leads to God, and is unto salvation. If we "walk after the flesh," and love the world, and are profoundly indifferent to the conversion of sinners, and the spread of vital religion and the gracious kingdom of the Lord Jesus Christ, we are "sensual," and "have not the Spirit;" and "if any man have not the Spirit of Christ, he is none of his."

II. And this shows how close and vital the relation is between the Spirit as an *unction*, and the Spirit as a *seal*, which is the second form of truth presented in the text. If we have the Spirit in our souls as an effectual anointing that consecrates us in heart and life to the service of God, we have consciously stamped upon our inward being the seal of God. Though it is not so expressed in the text, we learn from other places of Scripture that believers are "sealed" by the Spirit. The apostle refers to it as an experimental fact in the case of the Ephesians, that "after they believed, they were sealed with the Holy Spirit of promise," and exhorts them not to "grieve the Holy Spirit of God, by whom they were sealed unto the day of redemption." The Spirit in the soul is therefore the seal with which God designates his people: and the question arises whether the reference is to any special and peculiar influence and effect of the Spirit, or to his whole work in the sanctification of believers. There is no reason that we are aware of for restricting the language to any single aspect of the Spirit's work; and by extending it to the whole of what he does within a regenerate heart, we avoid the danger of a fanatical dependence on sudden impulses and superficial emotions, which may or may not proceed from his saving and gracious operation.

Profoundly mysterious though it be, with respect to its manner, likened to the wind, of which we cannot tell whence it cometh or whither it goeth, its effect on the character is not at all mysterious, but an actual and real thing—an object of consciousness, and even of observation. The seal of the Spirit is the soul's sanctification; it is faith, and love, and joy, and peace; it is deadness to the world, and delight in God; it is the spirit of prayer, and self-denial, and consecration to the Lord Jesus Christ. It is that image of the invisible God which is stamped upon the spirit and reflected in the life of all true Christians. The Spirit is the die, the soul the metal, and the likeness of God the character and the inscription imparted: and this precisely is what the Scriptures mean when they speak of the Spirit's seal, in so far as its substance is concerned. The peculiar lesson of the subject lies in the reasons why this work of the Spirit should be named a seal. Among men, and in the relations of common life and the transactions of business, a seal is used for a variety of purposes, which, however, have a general resemblance. It indicates proprietorship, it authenticates as genuine and trustworthy the instrument to which it is attached, and it preserves safe and inviolate whatever it is appended to. Thus, in this last sense, we seal our letters; and, for a like purpose, the stone laid upon the sepulchre of Jesus was "sealed."

Every one of these ideas and uses is embraced in the sealing of Christians by the Spirit of God. It is the stamp by which he claims them as his; the sign manual which authenticates them to the world and to themselves as his true children; and the sacred defence which preserves them unto his kingdom and glory.

Such a comprehensive interpretation is fully sustained by a collation of the passages where the figure occurs. If nominal Christians fall away to perdition, those upon whom God hath set his mark shall not—for "the foundation of God standeth sure, having this seal; the Lord knoweth them that are his." In the visions of John, he saw an "angel having the seal of the living God," who was sent forth to "seal the servants of God in their foreheads," with an evident view to their preservation from the calamities which impended over the church and the world. The same idea is expressed when Christians are spoken of as "sealed unto the day of redemption." The Spirit in our souls, with all his fruits in heart and in life, is therefore God's mark, by which the claim of everlasting love and redeeming grace is asserted, and from which the world may know, and we may know, the relation existing between the God of mercy and ourselves. The writing of our names in the book of life is an act of God, not open for our inspection, nor possible to be known in any other way than as it is followed up by the impression of the Spirit's seal upon our hearts. "Because ye are sons, God hath sent forth the Spirit of his Son into your hearts, crying, Abba, Father."

This seal of God is possessed of a quality that does not belong to earthly and human seals, and in which its value essentially consists. It is incapable of being counterfeited, and is therefore infallible. However curious and elaborate the workmanship on a material plate or die may be, some ingenious counterfeiter will make a pattern of it so exact that common observers can perceive no difference between the genuine and the false, and even experts may be deceived. And so, in the sphere of morals and religion, there are acts and characteristics which may bear a close resemblance to that which is true, and saving, and divine, and yet be the offspring of an unsanctified heart, or even come of the working of Satan. The magicians of Egypt, in successive instances, mimicked the miracles of Moses, and seemed to have the seal of Heaven affixed to their performances: and Jesus forewarned his disciples that false Christs would arise, showing such signs and wonders that, "if it were possible, they would deceive the very elect." And in the region of inward experience and outward relations to the visible kingdom of God, there are deceptive tests of a gracious state and false grounds of confidence, but we may safely affirm that the seal of God's Spirit may be certainly distinguished from them all: and whoever has the Spirit, is in possession of the highest possible evidence of being an object of God's peculiar love.

A more rooted prejudice and error was never overcome by evidence, than that of the apostle Peter, in reference to the admission of Gentile converts directly into the Christian church. With all his brethren, Peter had thought that "sinners of the Gentiles" must make two steps or stages before they could reach a state of salvation; first becoming Jews, and then Christians.

He thought that a believing heathen, must, like Abraham of old, "receive the sign of circumcision, for a seal of the righteousness of faith," and could not think otherwise, till he saw that God himself gave the higher seal of the Holy Spirit. Then he yielded, saying—"What was I that I should withstand God," and not baptize them that "have received the Holy Ghost as well as we?" If this one fact be surely settled, that the Spirit of holiness has been given us, we need look no further for the proofs of our acceptance with God: but lacking this, it is a ruinous mistake to build on anything else. If we could speak with the tongues of men and angels, and understood all mysteries and all knowledge, and if in all social relations our character were adorned by every virtue and courtesy which unaided nature, in its most faultless development, ever attains; and though at the baptismal font we had received that sacramental washing which symbolizes and seals the Spirit's purifying grace, and at the table of the Lord had drunk of that cup which "is the new covenant in his blood;" these outward seals of a visible church would attest nothing at all in our favour, if the Spirit of God had never descended upon us as a baptism of fire, consuming the dross of our corruptions, and sanctifying our souls and bodies to the Lord. "Sealing ordinances," as the sacraments of the New Testament are sometimes called, do not seal the salvation of any but *believers*, and believers are they who have the Spirit. Without the indwelling Spirit of God as the sanctifier of our nature, it is a fatal error to rest our hope on any other foundation; with the Spirit, we need not concern ourselves about anything else, whether it be the mode of baptism, or the figment of apostolic succession, or those minute points of doctrine in reference to which Christians of equal enlightenment and piety may, and do, differ in opinion. Recognizing the

Spirit as the seal which God impresses upon his chosen and redeemed people, it is a matter of deepest interest to us all, to know whether it is consciously and really stamped upon ourselves. It is implied in the nature of a seal, that it is capable of being discerned. Visibility belongs to its very idea. Its impression may be less or more distinct and deep, and on the surface of our sinful hearts, like characters traced on the sands, continually obscured and effaced by the overflowings of evil. But certainly we cannot but know the fact, if the Spirit unvails to us at times the glory of Christ, and fills the heart with a sweet sense of his awe, and inspires intense hatred of sin and godly contrition for our offences; and with groanings which cannot be uttered, makes intercession for us at the mercy-seat. "What! know ye not that your body is the temple of the Holy Ghost, which is in you, which ye have of God, and ye are not your own?"

III. The Spirit dwells in all Christians anointing them to the service and sealing them to the salvation of God, and in so doing becomes "*an earnest*" of their future and eternal redemption. The same God who anointed them, and sealed them, hath given the "earnest of the Spirit in their hearts."

Of this again we may say that it does not describe any new or specifically different work of the Spirit, but only views his whole gracious influence and operation in a particular aspect. It asserts the connexion between what God does for his people on earth, and what he will do for them hereafter and in heaven. The Spirit of grace and holiness which he gives them now, is the earnest—the pledge, prophecy, and part of what he has purposed to give them when grace expands into glory, and the dim light of earth brightens into the effulgence of an eternal day. "Earnest-money" is the sum advanced to bind the contract, and to ensure full payment at the time appointed; the "first-fruits" which ensure, in due time, the ingathering and consecration of all the harvest. Such is the sense of the term—the meaning of the figure—such the precious doctrine it announces. The Spirit of God in our hearts is the beginning of salvation, and is given to be the earnest of its eternal fulness; or, as the apostle elsewhere expresses it, "the earnest of our inheritance until the redemption of the purchased possession." What this "possession" is, we gather from a comparison of Scriptures, and find it to be a blessed immortality, including the resurrection of the body, and the unspeakable and endless felicity and glory of our whole redeemed nature. Depicting "the house not made with hands," to which the freed spirit of the Christian goes at death, Paul calls the work of grace wrought of God in the heart, an earnest of that blessed life; and writing to the Romans, the same apostle says, that "we who have received the first-fruits of the Spirit, are waiting for the adoption, to wit, the redemption of our body." The resurrection of Christ from the dead is the pledge that all who are "Christ's at his coming" shall rise to glory, because of their union with him by the bond of his Spirit. "Now is Christ risen from the dead, and become the first-fruits of them that slept." "But if the Spirit of him that raised up Jesus from the dead dwell in you, he that raised up Christ from the dead shall also quicken your mortal bodies by his Spirit that dwelleth in you." Here is a well of consolation. As certainly as God has given you his Spirit as a Comforter who enlightens, helps, sanctifies, and leads you in paths of holiness and peace, so certain is it that he will take your ransomed spirit to his presence in death; and in the morning of the resurrection will give you a body spiritual, immortal, glorious, like that of Christ.

And while the Spirit within is thus "the pledge of joys to

come," it is, at the same time, the foretaste of them, and gives the truest conception of heaven that is possible to dwellers in the flesh. It is not a figure of speech, but the plain statement of a fact, to say that the "earnest of the Spirit" is "heaven begun below," for it is part of that same experience, service, and salvation, which will constitute the joy of "the spirits of just men made perfect," when they go to the presence of Jesus and the bosom of God. It is not the pearly gates, and golden streets, and crowns of gold, the river of life, and the trees of paradise, that tell us most of celestial bliss, but the adoring reverence, and grateful love, and the holy joy, and the delight in God which the Spirit inspires when we muse of Jesus over the memorials of his passion, looking back to his cross and up to his throne.

The gorgeous imagery of the Apocalypse may excite the imagination and move the sensibilities of those who never wept for their sins, and have no "meetness for the inheritance of the saints in light." The question is: Have you the earnest of the Spirit in his holy fruits of "love, joy, and peace?"

And there is this other consoling thought, that while the earnest foreshows with infallible certainty a future blessing, it belongs to the nature of the case, and the idea of the thing, that there is an immense disproportion between the two. An earnest is a little, given as the pledge of much. One is the dawn struggling with the darkness of the night: the other a glorious day, without a cloud, and without a decline. The one is a secret fountain of living waters opened in the heart: the other is the river of life proceeding from the throne of God, and irrigating "the wide extended plains" of the better country. Precious as the foretaste is, it is almost nothing to that which "remains for the people of God." "Now are we the sons of God," and we have the seal of his adoption in our hearts; "but it doth not yet appear what we shall be" in the day of our coming manifestation.

Thus, my brethren, I have endeavoured to set before you one of the great mysteries of experimental religion, in showing you the Spirit of God in the threefold character and relation of an *unction*, a *seal*, and an *earnest*. And the fitting close of our discourse is the apostolic exhortation—"Grieve not the Holy Spirit." "Quench not the Spirit." Welcome his visitation; seek his influence; follow his guidance. Walk in the Spirit. Be filled with the Holy Ghost. Come from the four winds, O breath; anoint, seal, and keep us to eternal life.

SERMON XVI.

DIVINE GUIDANCE AND DISCIPLINE.

DEUT. viii. 15, 16.—*Who led thee through that great and terrible wilderness, wherein were fiery serpents, and scorpions, and drought, where there was no water; who brought thee forth water out of the rock of flint; who fed thee in the wilderness with manna, which thy fathers knew not, that he might humble thee, and that he might prove thee, to do thee good at thy latter end.*

THIS passage throws light on a subject of deep and abiding interest to the people of God. The methods of his providential dealing with his children and his church are a form of Divine revelation which demands more of the spirit of faith and submission than is required by the most mysterious doctrines of the Bible.

Such sublime mysteries as the Incarnation, the Trinity, and the Atonement, lying as they do beyond the sphere of reason's discoveries, are to be accepted by an act of simple faith in God, who reveals them: and this only involves that kind and degree of humility which consists in acknowledging the inferiority of our feeble intelligence to his infinite understanding. But when we turn from the revelations of *Scripture* to the discoveries of

Providence; from doctrines which address themselves to the understanding, to providential dispensations which defeat our purposes, disappoint our expectations, and wound our sensibilities, the case is very different, and we find it exceedingly difficult to believe in the wisdom and bow to the sovereignty of Jehovah. The feelings and behaviour developed in such circumstances, are a test of character the most infallible.

Under the Providence which guides the way and determines the lot of individuals, and churches, and communities, a twofold revelation is ever going on: God is revealed to men, and men are revealed to themselves; and both for the most important ends. Let us, therefore, make the subject of his PROVIDENTIAL LEADING AND DISCIPLINE the theme of our present meditations.

The text exhibits it under the threefold aspect of its *characteristics*, its *present effects*, and its *final purpose.*

I. With regard to the peculiar *characteristics of the Divine guidance*, we may take the description of Israel's condition and pilgrimage through the desert as embodying the substantial truth of universal experience. Besides being a chapter in the general history of the world, their case has the remarkable peculiarity of being the model, or type, of the Divine method with all men, and through all time. Israel was a typical people, and all that befell them had a prophetic reference, and "happened," as the apostle says, "for our ensamples, and is written for our admonition upon whom the ends of the world are come." The grand difference between the Divine guidance then and now regards the miraculous element, and the material, visible forms which it assumed: in all its essential characteristics it is the same. It must needs be so: it is exercised by the same God, upon men of the same character, and for the self-same purposes. Every feature of God's dealing with the Jews has its spiritual antitype in the methods of his providence towards ourselves. It is interesting to note the particulars in which the parallel holds true.

The guidance is real and actual in both cases. It is said in the text, that God "led" Israel through the wilderness. They were not left to choose their own way: it was divinely ordered from beginning to end. They had Moses for a leader, but he was obedient to the commands of a higher Power: "Jehovah led Israel like a flock, by the hand of Moses and Aaron."

And what is remarkable, he did much more than indicate the general direction in which they were to journey. He marked the precise track; appointed every encampment; gave the signal for every march and every halt throughout their entire wanderings. God assumed to himself the whole conduct of their progress: nothing was left to their own choice. Their taste, their temper, not even their judgment was consulted; and all this was done not in the absoluteness of Divine sovereignty, but in the tenderness of Divine compassion. It was the act of a Father whose wisdom and strength supplement the ignorance and helplessness of the child which he leads by the hand. As of old, so now, God leads his people. It is actual and real. No pillar of cloud and of fire is seen, but the vanished symbol has not carried away the indwelling God. It is the glorious mark of the New Testament age, that God is nearer now than he was before: and we know that a Presence more precious than that majestic sign rests upon the habitations, and leads the way of Israel still. The whole sacramental host, in its sublime procession, and in each of its lowly members, has yet "the Lord going before them" for a Leader and Guide, and "the glory of the Lord" as a "wall of fire" for their "rear-ward."

Not one of us is left to choose our own way. Taste, sensibilities, affections, reason, have their uses, but they are not adequate to decide the condition or choose the way which shall best subserve the interests of the soul: "The way of man is not in himself; it is not in man that walketh to direct his steps." This Divine oracle is verified in the experience and history of us all. In old age, and even at middle life, we look back with astonishment at the way by which we have come; our doings and our experiences are wonderfully different from all that we had purposed and expected.

A thousand incidents and events over which we had no control, have, as it were, impinged against us, and turned us from the intended course; and the point we have now reached is manifestly the resultant of forces external to ourselves, and high above all human calculations.

The counsel and the hand of God shapes the lot of us all: and the very "steps" of the good man are ordered by the Lord. This is true in a manifold sense. As it respects the path of duty, God leads his people by his revealed will in the Scriptures, and by the gracious influences of his Spirit in their hearts: and as it regards their outward circumstances and condition, he leads them by providential dispensations, which directly and deeply affect them in their persons, their property, their friends, their reputation—in everything which goes to make up the sum of their prosperity or of their affliction. That our worldly lot is appointed of the Lord, is a clearly revealed truth of Scripture; and that it exerts a powerful influence in the development and formation of character, is an equally certain truth, taught both by Scripture and experience.

2dly. This Divine guidance is exceedingly different from anything we should expect or desire. That country through which the Israelites were led, was one of the most horrid and inhospitable regions of the globe: "a great and terrible wilderness, wherein were fiery serpents and scorpions, and drought, where there was no water." If there had been no other possible route by which the land of promise could be reached, we should not wonder that this was chosen: but there was another, more direct and more easily travelled along the coast of the Mediterranean. That, to be sure, was not without its difficulties; the Philistines would have waged war on the people, and for this reason, (we are told), they took a different direction, lest seeing war so soon after departing from Egypt, they should "repent" and return.

Comparing the whole difficulties of the two roads, it is certain that the one selected was by far the most painful and trying to flesh and sense, and one that would assuredly have been rejected by man's unaided reason. Yet it was chosen of God as best for the purpose which he had in view. If the bodily comfort and temporal convenience of Israel, had been his aim, his procedure would, doubtless, have been very different; but designing to improve their character, and to prepare them for a high mission and destiny, he led them through scenes of trial, and exposed them to hardships, which served as a discipline for the correction of their faults and the development of their virtues.

But while this was his purpose, their thoughts and expectations were different. Uppermost in their minds was the idea of getting possession of Canaan, that goodly land of wealth, and beauty, and luxury; foremost in the thoughts of God, was the determination to make them fit for it. Hence the record of cross-purposes which their history perpetuates. They were continually surprised, perplexed, and angered even by the doings of God. It seemed to them, at times, as if he had made the greatest possible mistakes, and the acts of his providence were in the most absolute contradiction to the word of his promise.

They grew impatient—"their soul was much discouraged because of the way;" they murmured, they broke out in open mutiny against his leadership. Their wishes were not at one with God's purposes, and this was the root of all their troubles. It is the same with ourselves. Two things conspire to make us think strange of God's providential dealings. One of these is our natural and selfish desire of ease and prosperity. We not only desire, but, setting out in life, we expect to pursue the even tenor of our way, enjoying a steady flow of success and happiness. When this delusive hope is dissipated by the rude blasts of adversity, we take it greatly to heart; and if we do not indulge hard thoughts of God, we wonder very much that he should do as he does; and instead of coming directly to the conclusion that our character requires the discipline of these severe providences, we look intently at the second causes—the agents and instrumentalities which have occasioned our suffering and disappointment, and vent on them our regrets or reproaches. If men have injured us, our indignation against them prevents the recognition of Him who hath, at least by his permissive decree, commissioned them as his instruments. Few of us, I fear, have the piety of David, who, when Shimei cursed, said "Let him alone, for it may be the Lord hath bidden him."

To our selfish love of ease and prosperity must be added the consideration of our ignorance. We know but little either of ourselves or of God. Our weaknesses, faults, dangers, are, in a great degree, hidden from our view. "Who can understand his errors?" Ignorant of what we are, we are equally so in reference to what we need, and, most of all, ignorant of the best and most effectual processes and means by which our character may be improved and our dangers escaped. Not only are our understandings limited, as those of creatures must needs be, but our minds are blinded by self-love, prejudice, and pride: and nothing is more certain than that if we were left to prescribe for our own case, and choose our own way, we would commit the most egregious and fatal blunders.

Looking down from above, the Omniscient Eye sees us just as we are; it beholds what is within, and around, and before us; and with infallible certainty it appoints the treatment and discipline which the case demands. Of course the appointments of Infinite Wisdom do not move in the same plane with the wishes and purposes of our darkened understandings and selfish hearts. His thoughts are not our thoughts, neither are his ways our ways: "I will bring," saith he, "the blind by a way that they knew not; I will lead them in paths that they have not known: I will make darkness light before them, and crooked things straight. These things will I do unto them, and not forsake them."

Informed of this beforehand, we ought not to be astonished at anything which befalls us in the unfoldings of providence: we should not think it strange concerning the fiery trial which tries us, as though some strange thing happened to us: yet we are continually doing so, and are thereby showing how ignorant we are of the plans and principles of that holy and gracious providence which God exercises over his children and his church.

3. A third characteristic of his guidance and discipline is *its severity*. It is distressing to the flesh; it wounds most painfully our sensibilities: it is often so contrived as to strike the most tender point; it smites down the object of our peculiar idolatry. The great and terrible wilderness, the drought, the fiery serpents, and the scorpions, have their several antitypes in the experience of believers still. Under its ordinary and invariable conditions, their life is one of severe and ceaseless disci-

pline. Its labours, temptations, difficulties, disappointments, are more than a school of instruction; they are a gymnasium for exercise and training, in which the members and faculties of the spiritual man are developed and strengthened by being stretched to their utmost tension. The daily marches of Israel over the hot sands of the desert were a weariness of the flesh: and like to this is the daily routine of our common duties and toils, dull through sameness, and tiresome in their ceaseless recurrence. The mechanic in his shop, the labourer in the field, the mother in her family, the teacher in the school-room, the worker in any form of industry, is subjected to a discipline which, while not without its attendant pleasures, is wearisome and painful to our frail natures. A more comfortless experience is symbolized by the long and tedious encampments of Israel in the wilderness, when they had nothing to do but wait for the motion of the cloudy pillar which bade them strike their tents and renew their march. It would seem that in many places they tarried for months. This was probably felt to be a greater trial than the fatigues of travel. Soldiers grow so weary of the monotony and tedium of camp life, as to desire the change even of a hurried march, or of a hostile conflict. A calm at sea is represented by voyagers as quite insupportable; a storm would almost be welcomed for variety. There is something like this in the life of a Christian. He is commanded to stand still, and wait patiently the Lord's time. To all appearance, the work of God in his own heart, in the church, in the world, is at a stand-still; the tribes of the Lord indolently repose in their tents. His ardent spirit grows impatient; he chafes under the restraint, and almost questions the wisdom of Him who, from his high and mighty throne, directs the movements of his people, and sees it as necessary that they should halt at one time, as that they should go forward at another. But if it was fatiguing for Israel to march, and even more trying to lie idly in their tents, they had a harsher and worse experience when fiery serpents stung them, and enemies attacked them, and all manner of positive evils befell them. These all are reproduced in the spiritual foes which assail the Christian, and in the providential afflictions which overtake him. If fiery flying serpents are no more seen, the "fiery darts" of an invisible foe are hurled at him, and principalities and powers of evil bring their malice and strategy to bear upon him. And when, in addition to all that he suffers at the hands of them that hate him, God lays upon him the burden of some temporal calamity, the anguish he endures is terrible, and a "fiery trial" it is, through which he is caused to pass. How such afflictions as his can proceed from love, or tend to his advantage, it is impossible to see, and not easy to believe; but in the light of Divine revelation, we know that such is the fact.

4. A fourth and last characteristic of the *Divine guidance and discipline* exercised over Israel, was the *supernatural method employed to supply their wants.* The country through which they journeyed produced neither bread nor water adequate to their necessities. To all human appearance, they were repeatedly on the point of perishing by famine, or of dying with thirst. If it was a necessary incident of travelling through such a country, it was none the less a part of God's plan that their wants should not be supplied in the natural and ordinary way, as though it were by human providence and from common sources, but in a manner wholly supernatural, and, up to this time, unheard of among men: "Who brought thee forth water out of the rock of flint, and fed thee in the wilderness with manna, which thy fathers knew not."

Herein was a deep and divine mystery. "They drank of that spiritual rock which followed them, and that rock was Christ." And with respect to the manna—the angels' food, of which man did eat—He whom it typified has declared—"Moses gave you not that bread from heaven, but my Father giveth you the true bread from heaven." Their supplies proceeded immediately—almost visibly—from the hand of God. While he thus made them know "that man doth not live by bread alone, but by every word that proceedeth out of the mouth of the Lord," it also taught, in a figure, that the believer's life is "hid with Christ in God," and is nourished by streams which gush from the "smitten Rock" of an atoning Saviour, and by a celestial manna that daily falls about his habitation.

When the Hebrews awoke in the morning, they looked around their dwellings for the miraculous and heaven-sent food, and so were kept in habitual contact with God: and thus he deals with believers still. He requires, and, by the methods of his providence and grace, compels the Christian to resort to him every day, and to lead a life of actual and conscious dependence upon him for heavenly succour and supplies. If infidelity scoffs, let it do so; if the world, grovelling amid carnal pleasures and sensible objects, hears it with scornful incredulity, we must endure it; but it is a fact, that the life which the Christian lives on earth involves an element of the supernatural, brings him into daily contact and communion with God, and is maintained by supports, influences, and aliment which do not flow in the common channels of human agency, nor proceed from fountains of man's creation. The life which he lives in the flesh, is a life of faith on the Son of God: and he comes to look as habitually to the Throne of Grace for the food and refreshment of the soul, as he does to his fields and gardens for "the meat that perisheth."

Such appear to be the principal features of that GUIDANCE AND DISCIPLINE which God exercises over his people. Being in its nature an actual and real interposition which directs their way and shapes their lot, it differs exceedingly from all their natural desires and expectations, while it bears severely on their feelings, and requires them to depend on God, and repair to him daily for the supports of their spiritual life.

II. Why this particular method is adopted is an inquiry which naturally arises, and to which we find a very interesting and satisfactory answer in the text. In the case of Israel, it was designed to produce an immediate effect on their character, and a future effect on their condition: "That he might humble thee, and that he might prove thee, to do thee good at thy latter end." With you and me, my brethren, God is dealing in the same manner, and for the same purpose. With respect to our character, the design and tendency of Divine discipline is to produce the twofold effect of humility and probation. Under the providence of God, all men are proved. If the spirit of faith and submission exists in their hearts, trial brings it to the surface, shows to themselves and others what manner of men they are, and at the same time strengthens the gracious principle which it displays. If the spirit of unbelief and rebellion lurk within, probation strips off the mask; and that which before was hidden comes forth in words of murmuring and blasphemy, and in acts of open disobedience and revolt. It does not make a man wicked, but only shows him to be what he actually is.

Nearly the entire multitude of those who came out of Egypt appear to have been of this character, and after they had, amidst a scene of unparalleled mercies and judgments, disclosed their unbelief and rebellion, they were solemnly excluded from Canaan, and doomed to drag out a wretched existence and leave their bones in the desert. On others, the discipline of the wilderness had a different effect, especially on those who were children at the time of the Exodus, and who had grown up to maturity under the influences and amid the scenes of that long and wondrous journey. With few exceptions, the nation was composed of these, at the time this address was made to Israel. They had been humbled as well as proved; their spirit was chastened and subdued. They were schooled to the habit of renouncing self and depending on God; and thus they were, in a measure, prepared for that release from the discipline of toil and sorrow, which awaited them in Canaan. The church of Christ, and each of its members, is now undergoing a similar process to its preparation for a like glorious deliverance. Through the valley of humiliation we journey to the mountains of the heavenly Zion humbled first, to be afterwards and for ever exalted.

We need to be humbled. We all need it more than we are willing to confess, or are consciously aware. Proud self-reliance is the besetting sin of apostate humanity. The desire to be "as gods" was the door through which temptation entered, and ever since men naturally wish and try to be independent of their Maker. They trust in their own hearts, in an arm of flesh, in the sagacity of human reason, in the efficiency of second causes, rather than in the wisdom, the power, the providence, the revelations of God. So far as this goes, it is atheism; it is the insane and wicked attempt of a fallen creature to be a god unto himself. It is pride in its most offensive shape. God abhors it. He sets himself, in the dispensations of his providence, by the influences of his grace, by the solemn commands of his word, to condemn, and mortify, and root it out of our hearts. This aim he steadily pursues from the hour he first begins to deal with any of us in a specially gracious way, till the pilgrimage of life is closed.

Humility is the sense of our dependence on God; and this we feel when under the discipline of his providence. In sickness, when flesh and heart fail us; in financial reverses, when our shrewdest calculations are proved to be great mistakes; in political convulsions, like that which is now sweeping over the land and threatening to remove "the foundations of many generations;" in the trying interval of waiting, which separates between the time of our spiritual seed-sowing and the season of ingathering, when it seems as if we had laboured in vain and spent our strength for naught,—we are made to feel our weakness, to confess our ignorance, and, in the sense of absolute dependence, to place our only trust in God. If we understood and remembered this better, we should not wonder and complain so much of his providences. What he designs is to humble us, and this requires severe processes, and in some more than in others.

It required a schooling of forty years in the case of the Jews: it may take an equal, or even longer term with us; but the lesson is so valuable, the attainment so high, that it is cheap at any cost. Precious in itself, it is even more so in reference to what comes after, and is made to depend upon it. This is so glorious, that it may reconcile us a thousand times to the toil and pain by which it is preceded and purchased. God "humbles" us now, that he "may do us good at our latter end."

Our trials and disappointments and sorrows are but the training of the school-boy which fits him for the dignified and useful employments of manhood; the education of the heir for the use and management of his estate. During the period of his minority he differs nothing from a servant, though he be lord of all, but is under tutors and governors till the time appointed of the Father.

When that arrives, he enters on his possessions and enjoys his hereditary rights. The method of grace is in line with these earthly analogies: and in drawing to a close, I would bring this delightful truth to bear as a motive power on the heart and life.

1. Use it as a key to the mystery of providence. If we did not know what God was aiming at in the dispensations of his providence, we should be hopelessly perplexed. Apart from the glorious immortality which awaits believers in another world, it would be impossible to explain his dealings with them in this. Informed that he is proving, humbling, and otherwise educating them on earth, with a view to exalt them to thrones of glory in heaven, we can see the adaptation of means to ends, and, in some degree at least, comprehend and justify the ways of God to man. And what we know not now, we shall know hereafter, when the end is reached, and the purposes of God are all accomplished. Till then we may cheerfully rest in his wisdom and love, assured that in one way or another, and sooner or later, "all things work together for good to them that love God, to them who are the called according to his purpose."

2. The hope of that good which God will do to us at our latter end should not only reconcile us to the trials of our pilgrimage, but fill our hearts with holy joy.

The language in its naked simplicity is most beautiful and attractive—"To do thee good."

It is good that shall be done to us, and it is God that will do it: it will therefore be certainly and effectually done. He will do good to the soul, in its perfect purity and immortal life; and to the body in its resurrection, in the likeness of its Redeemer's glorified flesh: to both in their eternal union with one another and with himself. He will do us good at our "latter end." The good he now does to us is not small; but comparatively, it is so little that all good is spoken of as future. Past good is pleasant in the remembrance; present good is sweet to experience: but infinitely more important than either, is the coming good which God will do at our latter end, in death, and to all eternity.

What in particular it is, doth not appear. That goodly land into which Israel entered with shouts and songs, was its type,—a land of shady bowers, of enchanting landscapes, of crystal fountains, and delicious fruits. That was a paradise; but this is a better country, that is, a heavenly, in which those who have come out from so severe a bondage "shall hunger no more, neither thirst any more; neither shall the sun light on them, nor any heat. For the Lamb which is in the midst of the throne shall feed them, and shall lead them unto living fountains of waters: and God shall wipe away all tears from their eyes."

SERMON XVII.

THE BANQUET AND THE BANNER.

SOLOMON'S SONG ii. 4.—*He brought me to the banqueting-house, and his banner over me was Love.*

A DEEPLY spiritual mind is the best interpreter of this Divine song. To the earthly and carnal, profoundly ignorant as they are of the holy delights of communion with Christ, its meaning is hid, and the drapery of natural relations and endearments in which it is clothed might even prove "a savour of death unto death," exciting unholy desire, instead of lifting the soul to fellowship with Heaven. The parabolic dress thrown around the doctrines and discourses of the Saviour attracted and impressed the teachable and the believing, while it concealed the mysteries of the kingdom of heaven from those of a different spirit. It may be that the images and expressions of human love, which, even in the exaggeration and profusion of Oriental poetry, abound in this singular song, have been abused to foster other emotions than those which the Spirit of inspiration intended: and we know that infidel objectors have sneered at the Volume which contains such a book. But if this were sufficient reason for displacing it from the canon of Scripture, no part of the Bible would be left, since, from Genesis to Revelation, it has been all assailed by the same parties, and for the like reasons. To neutralize such cavils, and to prove the real tendency and use of this part of Scripture, it is enough to know that men who lived in closest fellowship with God have not only received this Song of Songs as a portion of his revealed will, but have found in it the peculiar nourishment of their spiritual life. To them, as Hengstenberg expresses it, "all nature is, as it were, turned into spirit: Whoso has made the Song of Songs a part of his very flesh and blood, must look on nature with other eyes. Even the human body is glorified in this poem."*

No book of Scripture abounds so much in allusions to natural objects, or so constantly makes them the vehicle of spiritual truths. Walking amid its gardens of spices and flowers, where every image that greets the senses is most agreeable, it is like a return to the primitive Eden of the unfallen race, where every tree that was pleasant to the eyes and good for food surrounded the innocent and holy pair, and at set seasons God, their Maker, met and communed with them. Such it was to Samuel Rutherford in the dark days of Scottish persecutions; and to Jonathan Edwards, whose metaphysical acumen was fully equalled by the depth of his devotion; and to the seraphic McCheyne, who, as it is said, had scarce left himself a text of its good matter from which he had not preached. This is sufficiently accounted for by the fact that its general theme, according to all evangelical interpreters, is the intimate union and mutual love of Christ and the church.

Than this no subject is more tender and inspiring. The Solomon to whom its imagery applies is no earthly monarch, but that heavenly Prince of peace of whom the son and successor of David was an eminent type. The newly married husband

* P. 279.

whom he represents is the Bridegroom of the church, and the fair one in whom he sees no blemish, is she whom his everlasting love elected, his precious blood washed, and the robe of his righteousness and grace adorned. Of the sacred union thus established, and the tender endearments thence arising, the passage before us is one of the most beautiful and suggestive expressions. It is the grateful, admiring, and delighted language of the church proclaiming the goodness and grace of her kingly husband and Lord. "He brought me," &c.

Our meditations may take their form from the two principal terms and figures which give shape to the text. A banqueting-house and a banner, though seemingly without natural connection, are significant of facts and ideas which meet and harmonize in the spiritual mystery of "Christ and the church."

I. In the first place, the church *acknowledges the gracious and blessed estate in which she finds herself, and indicates the agency by which she was introduced to it. "He brought me to his banqueting-house."*

We would not found a doctrine on so slender a basis as a poetical figure, but we cannot fail to observe the accordance between the form of speech here used and the teaching of Scripture in reference to that efficacious grace of God, which translates the soul into the kingdom of his dear Son. The love of God is gloriously displayed in making the provision of salvation, erecting the banqueting-house, and spreading the table with all that delights the taste and satisfies the hunger of our immortal nature. This was much, but love took a farther step when God proclaimed a universal invitation to famishing sinners to come in, saying: "My oxen and my fatlings are killed, and all things are now ready; come to the feast."

Can love go farther? Human love cannot, but God's can.

His table must be furnished with guests, and when words fail he sends forth an effectual power which goes to the delaying and reluctant creatures, who, if left to themselves, would "perish in their sin," and "compels them to come in." The word is scriptural, and need not alarm us. The compulsion meant is not applied to the body, nor to the mind, in such a way as to impair its most perfect liberty of choice. The gracious influence which God exerts penetrates, if I may so speak, deeper into human nature than the will. It enlightens the eyes of the understanding and renews the heart, and then the will, according to the law of its action, follows the decisions of the judgment and the impulse of the affections. Thus drawn by gracious influence and cords of love we yet come freely. Made willing in the day of his power, we embrace the salvation of Christ and bow at his feet.

The mode of this divine operation is a mystery. The breathing of the Spirit is like the movement of the wind, of which we cannot tell whence it cometh and whither it goeth. No metaphysics can uncover the point of contact between the divine and the human spirit which issues in the soul's transition from its native condition of death to life and joy in Christ, but the blessed fact is certain, and is the form of love which, above others, melts the heart and fills it with adoring wonder. The element of its peculiar power is that it links the love of God with ourselves. We admire that love as providing salvation, and in the catholic regard it has to all the world; and it does not appear altogether marvellous that other persons should be the subjects of its converting power, but the mystery of love is, that we in our separate individuality, we, in all our demerit and our sin, should be called to the knowledge of Jesus and the embrace of salvation! This mystery which we can only refer to the sovereign good pleasure of God, is that which dissolves the heart in penitential tears and adoring thankfulness.

"Why was I made to hear thy voice,
And enter while there's room;
When thousands make a wretched choice,
And rather starve than come;"

is a question which many a wondering disciple has asked, and to which better answer was never found than that we have so often sung in the banqueting-house of our Saviour-King:

"'Twas the same love that spread the feast,
That sweetly forced us in:
Else we had still refused to taste,
And perished in our sin."

The fervour of these grateful emotions is further intensified by the happy state and blessed experiences to which the called of God are introduced. The symbol of these is the banqueting-house of the church's adorable Head and Husband. Of earthly delights the scene and circumstances which the figure suggests are, perhaps, the highest type. Rich attire, congenial associations, enchanting music, delicious viands, and the cordial welcome of an esteemed and distinguished host, present an attraction which the "lovers of pleasure" pronounce their "chief joy."

Haman esteemed himself the happiest of mortals, when, on successive days, the beautiful queen of Ahasuerus called him to the banquet of wine which she had prepared. But a nobler than Esther, a greater than Solomon is here. The King of glory spreads his table, and opens his door, and issues his invitations. The pagan divinities were fabled to feast on ambrosia, and to drink nectar; and Milton describes the pleasures of "divine philosophy" as a "perpetual feast of nectared sweets, where no crude surfeit reigns." But there is a diviner luxury. Beyond the pleasures of taste, more pure and satisfying than those of reason, are the joys of our spiritual being. The sweetest luxury and the fullest contentment is that of the soul, when it is "satisfied with the fatness of God's house, and drinks of the river of his pleasures." This, in very deed, is a "perpetual feast," in which satisfaction is not satiety, but that thirsting no more for other streams which Jesus promised to those who should drink the water of life.

As no man who has drunk old wine straightway desireth new, because the old is better, so with those who have been introduced into the gracious state of guests in the house of God. Worldly pleasures become insipid, and the "pleasures of sin" are disgusting; and the new nature craves and delights in the supplies which Christ affords.

If from generals we descend to particulars, these supplies consist in such sweet experiences as peace of conscience, communion with saints, the witnessing and sealing grace of the Comforter, responding in the heart to the fatherly relation and love of God, the hope of everlasting life, and under all these spiritual and heavenly joys the alleviation of earthly sorrows, and the lightening of life's burdens. When we go into the banqueting-house of Jesus he comes into our hearts with all the train of his gifts and graces, and that sweet figure which represents him as supping with us, and we with him, becomes a divine reality. Oh, brethren, you know there is a direct enjoying of Jesus Christ, a tasting and seeing that the Lord is gracious, in acts of faith, and prayer, and holy communion.

In a degree this is the habitual experience of those who have come to the saving knowledge of Christ; but many things in the imperfection of this probationary life tend to depress and diminish these holy enjoyments, and the presence and urgency of material things intercept the vision of him "who is altogether lovely."

To indemnify us for this loss, which in our present condition appears inevitable, Christ has appointed times and seasons at which he invites us to special and uninterrupted communion with himself, and has established ordinances of worship through which the special communications of his grace are made. These are resting-places in the weary journey of life; oases in the sandy desert, like that to which Israel came at Elim, where were twelve wells of water from which they slaked their thirst, and threescore and ten palm-trees beneath whose grateful shade they reposed. This delight enjoyed in sacramental ordinances, which represent, and seal, and give the blessing and joy of salvation, most exactly and fully realizes the description of the text. Then and there it is that the happy and thankful Christian exclaims: "I sat down under his shadow with great delight, and his fruit was sweet to my taste. He brought me to the banqueting-house, and his banner over me was love."

Bunyan, in that wondrous allegory which paints the Christian's progress in its successive stages and shifting scenes, describes his pilgrim as, at one time, introduced to a building which he names the "Palace Beautiful," in which he saw many wondrous sights, and was filled with new and joyous experiences.

His guides and entertainers were the fair sisters Prudence, Piety, and Charity. He sat at a table furnished with fat things, and wine that was well refined. At night he slept in the chamber of Peace, which opened toward the sun-rising: and when it was morning, being conducted to the top of the house, and the day being clear, he saw in the distance "a most pleasant mountainous country, beautified with woods, vineyards, fruits of all sorts, flowers also, with springs and fountains, very delectable to behold." When told that the name of the country was Immanuel's land, "he bethought himself of setting forward, and they were willing he should." In seasons of gracious nearness and merciful visitation,—and most of all in the Holy Supper—that feast of love,—these experiences of a present salvation and glimpses of the coming glory are most largely enjoyed. It is here the Beloved of our souls meets with us in peculiar manifestation, and utters those words of freest welcome—"I am come into my garden, my sister, my spouse; I have gathered my myrrh, with my spice: I have eaten my honey-comb with my honey: I have drunk my wine with my milk: eat, O friends; drink, yea, drink abundantly, O beloved."

II. Called and brought by his grace into this estate of peculiar privilege and high spiritual enjoyment, of which a banqueting-house is the symbol, a somewhat different relation to the Redeemer is expressed by the added declaration—"His banner over me was Love."

Christ has a banner as well as a table, and over all who sit down in his banqueting-house, this ensign waves. Like national emblems, it too has an inscription. It is but a *word*, but that is significant of all that we are concerned to know. "God is *love*," and "*love*" is written on the banner of Jesus. On the flags which our brave soldiers bear in their long marches, and amid the smoke, and fire, and blood of battle-fields, the motto of the Union and various patriotic legends are inscribed with curious needle-work or in letters of gold.

The inscription on Immanuel's banner may be conceived of as written with the blood which flowed from his veins on the cross. It is a blood-stained banner: but while it is the blood of crushed and conquered foes that "stains his raiment," it is the blood of the cross that writes *Love* on the banner that waves over his redeemed people. If we have bowed to his sovereignty and embraced his salvation, such is our happy condition: "His banner over us is Love." The use of banners is natural to mankind. They are no relic of barbarism; but the most civilized nations use them, and are most susceptible to their peculiar power. This resides in the fact of their being emblems. They are visible badges and expressions of great ideas and soul-thrilling sentiments. To the eye of a patriot, the flag of his country embodies its sovereignty and grandeur, and inspires enthusiastic devotion to its cause, and complete identification with its fortunes. As an emblem, it is more potent than cannon to overcome the foe, because it acts with moral power on a thousand hearts that wield the implements of death.

In a figurative sense, Christ has a banner—that is to say, there is that in his character, the nature of his cause, and the relations he sustains to the church and the world, which finds a fit expression in such an emblem. Isaiah speaks of Messiah as being himself an ensign of the nations in the latter days. "There shall be a root of Jesse, which shall stand for an ensign of the people: to it shall the Gentiles seek, and his rest shall be glorious. Elsewhere he is said to have given a banner to his people, and they are called upon to lift it up as a rallying-point to all his friends, and as an image of terror to his foes.

1st. In the more particular unfolding of its suggestions, I remark, first, That this banner of love is a pledge of protection to all who are found beneath it. Hitherto it has been the happiness and boast of American citizens, that wherever they wandered, even to the ends of the earth, and among half-civilized nations, the flag of their country was respected, and spread over them the ægis of its protection. It carried with it the power and sovereignty of a mighty nation; and they were safe beneath its folds. The banner of the cross symbolizes the sovereign rule, the almighty power and the universal dominion of the Son of God. To him all power in heaven and earth is given: things material and things spiritual; all the agencies and forces of nature are put under him, to protect his church; and heaven and earth shall sooner pass away than one hair of their head shall be touched without his permission: and come what may, no *fatal* harm shall befall them. If in fighting his battles they lose their life, they shall find it again in life eternal, and shall be recompensed with a martyr's crown of glory.

This assurance of protection in a world where so many visible dangers threaten, is a precious item in the inventory of a believer's inheritance. It guaranties the absolute safety of the soul, now and for ever. It assures us that no temptation shall overtake us above that we are able to bear, nor affliction overwhelm us with any sorrow which grace cannot assuage, and Heaven cannot heal. When we go down into the valley of the shadow of death, the Shepherd and Bishop of our souls will be there, with his *rod* and his *staff*, the one for a support, and the other for a banner of defence against all dangers, real or apprehended, which the departing spirit fears. Under the "ensign" of our Redeemer's almighty power and quenchless love, we need not stand in dread of anything which is to happen. Nothing present or to come shall separate us from its protection. In the discharge of duty, and in obedience to his will, we may go anywhere, do anything, run any risk, and the invisible arm of an Almighty Defender will be around us still. A thousand shall fall at thy side, and ten thousand at thy right hand; but deadly harm shall not come nigh thee.

"When troubles rise and storms appear,
There may his children hide;
God is a strong pavilion, where
He makes my soul abide."

Therefore, let not your heart be troubled, neither let it be afraid: especially do not permit groundless anxieties and unbelieving fears to hinder you in your Christian duties, or keep you back from daring or doing anything which tends to further the kingdom of your Lord, and redounds to his glory.

2d. In the second place, the banner of love which Jesus Christ uplifts before and over his people is the symbol of the aggressive warfare that he is waging against sin and Satan, for the liberation and redemption of an enslaved world.

National emblems have their greatest use in time of war. Carried at the head of an advancing host, as the soldier gazes upon the colours that image the nation's power and pride, his spirit kindles with patriotic fire, and his heart settles in fixed resolve that this banner of beauty and glory shall not trail in the dust, nor pass to the hand of a conquering foe. The divinest realization of these images exists in the "Holy War" which is waged by the "Captain of our salvation." "The Lord is a man of war." When, with a high hand and an outstretched arm, he led forth his chosen people from the house of their bondage, he went before them in a pillar of cloud and fire: and as the tribes were marshalled round the tabernacle in four grand divisions, a "standard" bearing the names and the insignia of each was carried before them. The display was imposing and sublime: even Balaam, though he came to curse, was transported thereby into a lofty strain of prophetic benedictions. The visible glory of the cloud and the material ensigns of the tribes have disappeared; but Jesus, the "Leader and Commander" of his people, is going before them still, and displaying to the eyes of their faith his banner of love. It is the emblem of an exterminating warfare against sin, and of untold blessings and everlasting mercy to those who enroll themselves as his followers. Jesus is he whom, in the far off visions of faith, the dying Jacob saw, when he said—"The sceptre shall not depart from Judah, nor a lawgiver from between his feet till Shiloh come: and unto him shall the gathering of the people be." And Isaiah, in those later prophecies which unveil so much of Zion's future glory, saw Messiah as a warrior coming from Edom, with dyed garments from Bozrah, glorious in his apparel, and travelling in the greatness of his strength." Mighty to save his friends, he is terrible in vengeance upon his foes.

Of that sovereign power and universal dominion with which the Father has by right invested him, his banner of love is the emblem and the pledge that his conquests shall go on till in fact as well as in covenant "the heathen are given to him for his inheritance, and the uttermost parts of the earth for his possession." Like the wars between Israel and their heathen foes, the native dwellers in Canaan, this is one of extermination. It admits of neither cessation nor compromise, but must go on till there shall come no more to Jerusalem, the uncircumcised and the unclean, and the Canaanite shall disappear from the inheritance of God. As it was between Amalek and Israel in the desert, so it is between Immanuel and his enemies. Not only were those Pagan foes chastised at the time, but "Moses built an altar and called the name of it Jehovah-nissi—the Lord my banner, because the Lord had sworn that the Lord would have war with Amalek from generation to generation." The banner under which we fight was never lowered to an enemy. It is in the hand of our mighty Leader, who has himself led captivity captive, and planted it in triumph on the strongest hold of the adversary. The subjugation of every foe, and the conquest of every foot of territory which rightfully belongs to the Son of God is simply a question of time. It is foreordained, it is in process of accomplishment, and these mighty throes of the nations do but herald and hasten its coming. The year of jubilee is approaching; the banner of love, already planted on the continents and the islands, shall receive the adhesion of every tongue, and kindred, and "all flesh shall see the salvation of our God."

3d. The third and last suggestion we offer regards the relation and duty of the church and of individual men to the banner which Christ lifts up in the sight of us all.

The kingly character and office of Jesus powerfully appeals to the sentiment of loyalty and love in the hearts of those who have already bowed to his rule and embraced his salvation. To them, in a very important sense, he entrusts his cause and his honour in the world. He puts the blood-stained banner of the cross into their hands, and bids them hold it high and bear it forward till all the earth shall own its sway. "Thou hast given a banner to them that fear thee, that it should be displayed because of the truth." Accepting the trust, let us respond with love and holy courage: "We will rejoice in thy salvation, and in the name of our God we will set up our banners." The appeal for sacrifice and service is made to all hearts that are loyal to King Jesus. You that are called, and pardoned, and dressed in the wedding-garment of his righteousness, and seated in the banqueting-house of his love, will you now take the oath of allegiance anew, and with a deeper consecration than ever maintain your place in the sacramental host that march to victory and glory? In the ranks of this army there is room, and service, and recompense for you all, without respect to age, or sex, or condition. A willing mind and a loyal heart is the only qualification. When the followers of Jesus, in solid phalanx and shining array, thus devote themselves to his service, the church will "look forth as the morning, fair as the moon, clear as the sun, and terrible as an army with banners."

When we fall, let it be with our armour on, in the high places of the field, and clinging to the standard of our King. It is related that a French soldier who fell at Waterloo had grasped the flag of his country so tightly in death that when it was sought to remove it its captor only succeeded by taking the man and the standard, colours and corpse together. Fit emblem this of the Christian hero's death. May the like be ours! From the throne of his glory Jesus cries: "Be thou faithful unto death, and I will give thee a crown of life." "To him that overcometh will I grant to sit with me in my throne, even as I also overcame, and am set down with my Father in his throne."

To those who as yet sustain a different relation to this "banner of love," I present it as an emblem of peace between God and men, and invite you "in Christ's stead" to enlist under it. With precious blood in crimson lines Love is written on its ample folds. By the infinite depth of love divine it pleads with you, gathering its tender memorials from the garden, the cross, and the tomb! By the pardon, peace, and protection which it gives and guaranties, by the assurance of deliverance from your dangers, victory over your enemies, and an abundant entrance into the honours and joys of an everlasting kingdom of glory, you are urged this day to forsake the standard of rebellion and rally to that of your Friend and Saviour—the Son of God's delight, the adored of all believers.

There is room for you! Room in the Saviour's heart, room in the church, room at the communion-table, room in heaven at the marriage-supper of the Lamb. "Come, for all things are now ready." "The Spirit and the Bride say, Come. And let him that heareth say, Come. And let him that is athirst come. And whosoever will, let him take the water of life freely."

If still you hesitate, let your halting mind be decided by considering that you are absolutely shut up to the alternative of voluntarily accepting Christ's "banner of love," or of being crushed by the iron rod of his power and wrath. "Kiss the Son, lest he be angry, and ye perish from the way, when his wrath is kindled but a little. Blessed are all they that put their trust in him."

SERMON XVIII.

FAITH, HOPE, AND CHARITY.

1 Cor. xiii. 13.—*And now abideth Faith, Hope, Charity, these three; but the greatest of these is Charity.*

The religion of the Lord Jesus Christ is essentially inward and spiritual. "The kingdom of God is not meat and drink, but righteousness, and peace, and joy in the Holy Ghost"—not the outward observances of worship, nor the outward acts of morality, but those internal principles and affections out of which "are the issues of life." Human character is not words and deeds, but the motives and spirit which prompt our speech, and are embodied in our acts. The same words may be spoken, and the same actions performed from different or opposite motives. While, therefore, the outward exhibition of himself which a person makes before the world is, in the main, a true exponent of what is in his heart, it is not an unerring criterion. Acts of devotion and deeds of philanthropy may be performed without love either to God or men, and we cannot certainly know whether the doer of them is or is not a Christian. *Character* consists in the *principles* which have their seat in the soul, and are the spring and source of conduct. They are the affections, desires, and purposes that govern us, and which cannot be traced to anything deeper in our nature than themselves. For this reason they are called principles—first elements and fundamental laws of character and life. The character of every man is determined by the principles, good or bad, that control him: and the Christian's character is decided by the graces implanted and nurtured in his soul by the Spirit of God. The infallible test which we should habitually apply to ourselves is the presence or absence of those secret affections and exercises which are revealed alone to consciousness and to the Searcher of hearts. Faith, hope, charity, and all the train of gracious traits, are not so much the evidence as the essence of Christian character; and it is simply impossible that any one should possess them and yet be a stranger to the saving grace of God. They are the image of God visibly stamped upon our moral being. In the text, three of these hidden roots of piety are grouped together, and assigned a pre-eminence above all others. After naming the graces of faith, hope, and charity, the apostle adds, with rhetorical beauty and significant emphasis, the limiting expression—"these three," intimating that no more and no other graces belonged to the same class, or deserved the like distinction.

In one aspect, he puts them all on a level; in another view, he exalts charity above her sisters, faith and hope.

And this suggests the general arrangement we propose to follow in this discourse. In the first place, the apostle declares that the principles or graces named, are alike and equal in their permanency. "Now abideth Faith, Hope, Charity."

In the second place, he asserts that of these three enduring elements of Christian experience and life, the crown of pre-eminent excellence belongs to the last: "The greatest of these is Charity."

1. Let us view them first with respect to the quality in which

all agree, that is to say, their permanency. In the broadest and most general view, this is a high commendation. That which is short-lived is of comparatively little value. Even an object of the magnitude and glory of the sun would be unimportant if it shone for a day and then went out in eternal darkness. One of the most effectual dissuasives which the Bible brings to bear against the love of the world, is derived from its transitory nature and the shortness of human life: and religion derives its mightiest enforcement from the immortality of the soul, and the eternity of its salvation. Any good thing is important in proportion as it abides, and that which endures for ever is infinitely important. It is therefore no mean commendation which the apostle bestows on faith, hope, and charity, when he tells us that they abide. Furthermore, that which endures is presumed to be excellent in its nature: in fact, endurance is in many cases the test of excellence. That which is unsubstantial, shadowy, worthless, is short-lived. It perishes with the using; it vanishes away. The dross disappears, and is merged in other substances: the pure gold is imperishable: the fleeting cloud is driven with the wind, and returns no more; the mountain whose summit it hid abides in everlasting majesty and strength, and the star whose radiance it for a moment obstructed, shines on through countless years. In like manner, this *triad* of moral virtues and Christian graces assert their superior excellence by enduring in the freshness of their vitality throughout all the stages of Christian experience, and dispensations of the church, and the changes of time.

In this connexion they are in contrast with the miraculous gifts and powers bestowed on the church in the apostolic age. Through the supernatural influence of the Spirit, ministers and members of the church were enabled to speak with other tongues, to prophesy, to heal the sick, and do many things of like nature. The use of these gifts was to secure for the new religion and the infant church a speedy and secure establishment in the world. They were of great importance for that time, and were, moreover, of a showy character, visible and impressive in their exercise. They might be, and in some instances—as that of Simon the sorcerer—*were* coveted for selfish ends. They did not enter deeply into the inherent constitution and essential life of the church; and though commonly exercised by Christians and Christian ministers, they were not an infallible index of piety. Paul puts the case as conceivable and possible that a person might "speak with tongue of men and of angels," and yet lack the more vital elements of Christian character. Being thus superficial in their relation to the church, and temporary in their use, they passed away: and now there is no man who speaks with other than his native tongue, except as he learns it, and no worker of miracles is found in the church. Already the time has come of which the apostle spoke: "Whether there be prophecies, they shall fail; whether there be tongues, they shall cease; whether there be knowledge, it shall vanish away." But the passing away of these leaves the deeper foundations of Christian experience undisturbed. "Now"—that these things are gone—"abideth faith, hope, charity." They enter into the vital essence of Christian character, and endure for ever.

We may also view the permanency of these gracious principles in contrast with the external ordinances of worship and institutions of the church which have undergone great changes already, and must needs be subject to yet further mutations, as the church advances to her final condition. The Old Testament ritual of worship, having fulfilled its purpose as a prophetic shadow of better things to come, has been annulled and displaced by the rites of our Christian worship. Like a dilapidated building or a faded garment, the Jewish forms "decayed and waxed old," and in the time of the apostle, were "ready to vanish away." They have now departed; but the radical principles and vital spirit of piety which were embodied in those forms, and afterwards, for freer action and wider expansion, were transferred to the light and spiritual worship of Christianity, still live. The temple, the altar, the victim, the priest, the offerings to God, and the gifts to man, which the law prescribed, are seen no more; but the faith which brought the sacrifice, and the hope that looked and longed for a coming Redeemer, and the charity that showed pity for the poor, in those early days of revelation, still abide, and will never fail while God has a dwelling on the earth. "Faith, Hope, Charity," these three graces may, like the Trinity of Persons in the Godhead, have had a progressive revelation in Scripture, and an advancing power in the church; but there never was a time in the past, as there never will be in the future, when piety could be cast in any other mould, or displayed in any other forms. To the end of time, and under all the changes of outward condition which the church may undergo, the people of God will *believe*, and *hope*, and *love;* and all the more so as the soul and the church approach the perfection of the heavenly state.

There is yet another contrast, which may, perhaps, be admitted in this connexion, between the graces named in the text, and some other forms and phases of Christian experience, which peculiarly belong to certain stages of the believer's progress, and are affected by his outward conditions. The babe in Christ, and the veteran soldier of the cross look on the Christian life from widely different points of view, and, in many respects, with different feelings. One is warm with the glow of a new experience, and happily ignorant of the deep tribulation through which the soul must enter the kingdom of God. Human imperfection mingles with and tinges not a little of the convert's first experiences, and thus necessitates a series of changes in views and feelings that are often wondered at and lamented as a departure from the soul's first love, when they are only its gradual settling down from trust in flitting frames and feelings upon the immovable foundations of "faith, hope, and charity." The aged and deeply-experienced Christian feels that he has both lost and gained in many respects. He has parted with both hopes and apprehensions that are incidental to the commencement of a new life; and he has gained in strength of religious principle and stability of experience. The faith whose first trembling exercise was the embrace of Jesus Christ for pardon and peace, has strengthened and grown to be "the substance of things hoped for, and the evidence of things not seen," taking into its wide survey the whole firmament of revelation. The hope which, at its first rising in the heart, had primary regard to the negative good of escape from wrath, has come to look for the positive blessings promised to the faithful, and to wait with patience for their enjoyment.

And love, if it has lost somewhat of its freshness, has gained in steadiness, and depth, and practical fruits. Beneath all the changes and disturbances that take place upon the surface of our natural feelings and religious sensibilities, these radical principles of the Christian life abide and gather strength. Even those storms of sorrow and temptation which sweep away our pleasant thoughts and feelings, root these principles the more firmly in our souls, and we are gaining ground even when in fear of losing every thing.

If we pass over that wider interval which separates the experience of earth from that of heaven, it is certain that much that now enters largely into our exercises will be left behind. All of religious experience that supposes "temptation without and corruption within," all that is peculiar to a state of probation, toil, and suffering, will disappear with its cause and occasion. In that blessed state from which pain, and death, and every form of evil are banished, the passive virtues of patience and long-suffering will not be in requisition. And where there is no sin there will be no penitence, and those who have no unsupplied wants will feel no need of prayer.

Yet piety, in its absolute essence, will be the same in heaven as it is on earth, and there is a sense in which not love only, but faith and hope will flourish in immortal strength. In this manifold sense do these graces abide, the life, adornment, and blessing of the soul, the seal of God's children, the mark of the true church, when dispensations of religion have changed, and miraculous gifts have disappeared, and the exercises of an immature experience have been displaced by the completeness of the perfect man in Jesus Christ. They are the safest as well as the best treasure a man can possess. All else we have may be irrecoverably lost. Our property may make to itself wings and fly away, our health may fail, our reputation may be tarnished, our friends may withdraw their affection or go to their long home in the grave. If our happiness is bound up in these things, we may in a moment be impoverished and undone. But if the Spirit of God dwell in us, and attest his presence by the precious fruits of faith, hope, and charity, nothing present or to come shall rob us of our portion.

Under every change of outward condition, amid social and political agitations which shake or subvert the "foundations of many generations," and even under the invasion and stroke of death which penetrates to the "dividing asunder of soul and spirit," these vital graces abide, inwrought with the moral nature and inseparable from it for ever.

Of which truth the obvious application is, that we should cultivate these imperishable virtues which of themselves can bless the soul, and of which nothing in life, death, or eternity can deprive us.

2. Exalting "these three," above all other graces, the apostle makes an election of one from among the rest, and puts the crown of supreme excellence on the head of charity. They all abide, and they are all great, but "the greatest of these is charity."

A parallel to this we have in the intercourse of our Lord with his twelve disciples. He loved them all, but bestowed special privileges and honours on "Peter, and James, and John." These three were with him when he raised the daughter of Jairus from the dead, in the glory of his transfiguration, and in the hour of his deepest agony in the garden. Yet in this inner and selectest circle was the one disciple "whom he loved," and whose head reposed on his bosom, in nearest intimacy and holiest affection. And it helps our parallel to remember that this favoured disciple was, above the rest and above other men, the apostle of love, the incarnation and pattern of that divine charity to which the apostle gives the pre-eminence. It is not for us to question this pronounced judgment of inspiration, and all we may properly do is to inquire into its grounds and reasons, so far as they may be gathered from the teachings of Scripture and the nature of the thing.

The whole chapter is in praise of charity, whose excellence the apostle exhibits by expatiating at length and in great beauty of language on its precious fruits, and by giving it the preference, not only over supernatural gifts and miraculous powers, but over other Christian graces. The climax of his encomium is reached when he assigns it a higher place than the noble graces of faith and hope. It is greater than these. He not only implies but affirms that these are great, and all Scripture bears witness to the same point.

In one place he groups them all together, describing each by its peculiar fruit, remembering without ceasing, and with gratitude to God "the work of faith, and labour of love, and patience of hope" which were seen in his Thessalonian converts. A great many very weighty and very delightful things are said of hope. Believers are "begotten" thereto by the resurrection of Jesus, and in the regeneration of their own souls. The "God of hope" first inspires this divine affection in their minds, and then employs it as an instrument of sanctification to fit them for dwelling with the Lord, which is the object of their hope. On this stormy sea of life, where they are buffeted by the waves of temptation and sorrow, Christians "are saved by hope," which is an anchor of the soul both sure and steadfast. It is a precious grace, but charity is greater. The apostle goes further, and gives it the preference even to faith, which performs an office so peculiar in the salvation of the soul, and of whose power and working the Scriptures have so much to say.

The followers of Christ are named believers from their faith. Faith receives Christ for justification, and is the radical grace which sets even love in motion. We believe before we love, and does not the apostle tell us that "faith worketh by love?"

Faith is the root principle of the Christian life, the hand by which we receive Christ for pardon, and the bond of union which keeps the soul in contact with the sanctifying power of the cross. We are justified by faith, we stand by faith, we walk by faith, and this is the victory that overcometh the world, even our faith. One of the longest chapters of the New Testament is an elaborate commendation of faith, based on the example of great believers in the ages past. The eleventh of Hebrews is longer than this thirteenth of Corinthians; yet, after all, and in express language, the apostle declares that love "is greater than faith." How and why this is, is an interesting and legitimate inquiry.

1st. The first consideration that tends to enlighten the subject is derived from the intrinsic nature of love as an affection of the mind. It contains more elements of moral and spiritual excellence than either faith or hope. It more directly and deeply involves the exercises of the heart than faith, and it is more disinterested than hope, which expects and desires future good. Faith believes what God reveals, and hope looks for what God promises. Each is a moral virtue, and well-pleasing to God, but neither nor both together contain so much of what is all acceptable to God, and like God, as love. In God there is neither faith nor hope. The one is incompatible with his knowledge, and the other with his infinite and perfect bliss. He does not believe: he knows. He does not hope for anything, for he possesses all things; but "God is love, and he that dwelleth in love dwelleth in God, and God in him." The completest image of divinity which the soul of man can receive is the inspiration of that love, which abides infinitely and for ever in the Godhead. Add to this that faith and hope are but organs of reception, hands we stretch out to take the blessings which come to us from above and from afar, while love flows forth in generous admiration of another's excellence, or in sympathetic ministries to his griefs and needs, or rises in spontaneous adoration of the uncreated and infinite holiness and beauty of the Lord. It would thus appear that in its inherent nature love is a more excellent attribute of character than either faith or hope.

2d. In the second place love is the greatest, because it is the germ and principle of all moral and religious duties. This cannot be said of faith and hope, or of any other virtue of Christian character or grace of the Spirit. They do not contain love, but love contains them, as the apostle intimates in saying that "Charity believeth and hopeth all things." Love nurtures every other grace, and prompts to the discharge of every duty we owe either to God or men. It is the genial atmosphere and sunshine in which the graces grow and flourish. A soul completely and absolutely subjected to the control of love would be impelled spontaneously to the performance of every act which the Divine law requires to be done to ourselves, to others, or to God. Love is the substance of both tables of the law. It comprehends all morality and all religion. There is not one particular belonging to each which has not its root in this divine affection, which restrains from all evil and prompts all goodness.

To the inquiring lawyer Jesus said, "Thou shalt love the Lord thy God with all thy heart, and with all thy soul, and with all thy mind. This is the first and great commandment. And the second is like unto it. Thou shalt love thy neighbour as thyself. On these two commandments hang all the law and the prophets." The entire revelations of God, in law, and prophecy, and gospel, by Moses and by Christ, in so far as they bear on human duty, are comprised and condensed into the single element of love. Eden, Sinai, Calvary utter the same voice. Supreme love to God, complacent love of the brethren, forgiving love of our enemies, and benevolent love to all our kind, is the "whole duty of man." To this grace of the Christian heart must therefore be assigned the crown of an unquestioned supremacy.

3d. In the third place, its right to this pre-eminence is established by the peculiar difficulties which its exercise involves. There are difficulties which impede the exercise of faith and depressing influences with which hope has to contend. But neither of them is beset with so many and so great impediments as love.

As directed towards God, there is, indeed, nothing to hinder its exercise but the native alienation of our hearts from what is good. God is infinitely worthy of our supreme and constant affection, and every act of his providence and gift of his grace heightens his claim to our love. But the case is different in that other and wide sphere of duty in which it is not God but men that claim our love. Its exercise is exceedingly difficult and continually obstructed by impediments without and within. Our own selfishness is an antagonistic force that tends to repress and quench love and to dry up the fountains of all active sympathy and friendship. It costs time, and thought, and trouble, and money, to give our love expression and make it effective in promoting the happiness of our neighbours and brethren. If it overcomes these opposing influences, its power is great and its excellence is demonstrated. And while the selfishness of our natures is ever a clogging weight on the wings of charity, there is much in our relations to others and our circumstances in life that tends to chill the ardour of our affection, and which, unless it be firmly resisted, will end in making us thoroughly selfish, and in shutting us up within the narrow sphere of our own personal interests. The persons who claim our love are imperfect; they may have glaring faults; they slight or seem to slight us. The multitude around us rush on in pursuit of their own objects, regardless of ours, and perhaps willing to sacrifice our interests to their own. In such circumstances I need not tell you it is hard to maintain love in vigorous and unabated activity and fervour. If it triumph over such impediments, and live in the midst of these chilling damps, its mighty power is proved, and its title to the throne among the graces is well established.

4th. This title has a further and fourth support in the fact that love, in its obligation and the sphere of its exercise, is less affected than other graces by the changing relations and condition of men. Love is the law alike of fallen and unfallen creatures, of sinners who are in process of redemption, and of "the spirits of just men made perfect." The same cannot be said of faith, or hope, or patience; certainly not, in the same unqualified sense. There is a time coming in the experience of the believer when faith will be changed to sight, and hope be lost in fruition, and so far both will cease. In heaven they will not be, as they are on earth, the characteristic attributes of the Christian's condition, while the only change in love will be its wider range, deeper intensity, and more perfect joy. Love is the law of angels, it was the law of Paradise; it is the law of the church militant, and will be that of the church triumphant,

> "Where faith and hope are known no more,
> But saints for ever love."

On such grounds as these the supremacy of love is claimed and justified. With two applications we leave the subject.

1. The first is in the form of inquiry, and for the purpose of self-examination. Has love the practical ascendency in our hearts which the apostle assigns to it in the ideal character which he depicts? Is this theory of the graces actually embodied in our lives? Is love the greatest of our graces? Is it "the bond of perfectness" that ties the robe of Christian virtues about us, and arrays the church in the "beautiful garments" of salvation? Does "brotherly love" continue? Does it "abound?" Does

it break down the barriers of a cold selfishness, and unchristian alienations, and wicked resentments? It is a possible thing, that instead of being the greatest, it may be about the least of our virtues. The amount of our love is the measure of our religion.

2. Our second application is that of the apostle: "Follow after charity." It is susceptible of increase, and needs cultivation. And because of its supreme excellence, we shall do wisely to concentrate our desires and efforts upon it. If it grows, every other grace and duty will flourish: and it will grow, if your life is one of communion with God, of imitation of Christ, and of active endeavours to do good. The grace of God in our redemption is the grand argument for the love of the brethren, and of all mankind. "Beloved, let us love one another, for love is of God. And every one that loveth is born of God, and knoweth God. He that loveth not, knoweth not God; for God is love."

XIX.

THE LAW OF HUMAN PROGRESS IN ITS RELATION TO THEOLOGY.

An Address before the Society of Inquiry of the Western Theological Seminary, delivered in the First Presbyterian Church of Allegheny, April 15, 1862.

To the student of theology and the minister of the gospel, no subject can be of equal importance with the absolute truth and certainty of the doctrines which are taught from the Professor's chair, and delivered from the pulpit; and no questions of our day are more keenly debated or more profoundly interesting than those which, in one relation or another, concern this fundamental position. Are the elements of theology fixed or fluctuating? Is it, like other departments of human knowledge, a progressive science?

Are the Scriptures the only infallible rule of faith and practice? If this be conceded, then has their sense been so far ascertained as to determine and for ever fix the essential and controlling articles of religious faith; or, in the progress of learning and enlightenment, are we to look for such an insight into their "hidden mysteries" as may require the modification, and even involve the subversion and relinquishment of existing doctrines and systems? Or, denying the sufficiency and supreme authority of Scripture, are its teachings to be supplemented and explained by the oracles of reason? and its plainest utterances to be accepted or condemned, according as they commend themselves or not to the judgment and moral nature of men? The vital importance of questions like these, and the zeal with which they are mooted in the religious world, have suggested as the particular topic of this address, *The law of human progress in its relation to theology.*

This law, like most others, has both its uses and abuses. By some, its announcement will be thought to savour of rationalism and heresy. In their view, theology is so completely supernatural, and so fixed and absolute in its form, as embodied in a divine revelation, that no law of human progress can reach it, or leave any trace upon it whatever. In these, the animus of theological conservatism is commendable, and close of kin to that holding fast "the form of sound words" which is commanded as a Christian duty; yet the danger is possible of sticking in the shell,—that is to say, in the human form and expression of a doctrine,—and of losing the kernel of truth. By another class, this law is hailed with delight. It breaks all fetters, is the solvent of all difficulties, and opens before the theological explorer an unlimited region, over which he can ramble at will, ever learning, and never able to come to the knowledge of positive and final truth. The acquisition of to-day is displaced by that of to-morrow, instead of serving as a foundation on which to rear a structure which shall never decay, nor require to be rebuilt or remodelled. We hope to make it appear both that the extreme fear and caution of theological conservatives on the one hand, and the rash confidence of radical progressives on the other, have no warrant in the law of human progress, when rightly understood and fairly applied to the subject of revealed theology.

Between a right and sound conservatism which holds fast that which is good, and the spirit of progress which, in its experimental efforts to increase the sum of human knowledge, "proves all things" by a candid examination, there is and can be no proper antagonism; they both are grounded in our intellectual and moral nature, and are alike and equally necessary to any real advancement in knowledge, or to any improvement in the condition of mankind. If the truth already ascertained be not adhered to, the mind is adrift on a sea of uncertainties, blown about by every wind of doctrine; and if there be no feeling after the unknown, nor tentative handling of the untried, the stock of human ideas will not be increased, and the intellect of successive generations will never get beyond the limits which the thinking of the past has established. It is only in their abuse and extravagance that the spirit of conservatism and that of progress come into collision, and are to be feared and resisted. The boasted advance of theological science in our times is one of the boldest and most seductive phases of unbelief. It is thoroughly radical and destructive; not building on foundations already laid and tested, and thus, in the sense of Paul, "going on to perfection," but tearing them up, placing them in new relations, or casting them aside, as seems good to the builders on the tower of modern infidelity. Some of them, in justification of an attempt which implies the ignorance and childhood of past ages, plead the uncertain and feeble hold which the most fundamental doctrines of Christianity now have on the minds of men. "The brave and honest men of the church," complacently assumes one of the exponents of liberal Christianity,* "are seekers after fixed truth,

* Dr. Bellows.

rather than possessors of it. . . . The theological mind of the world is actually, and by reason of a change in human circumstances, in an unsettled state." From his point of view, nothing is apparent but "the tremulous fluid into which the old theologies have dissolved." As, according to a certain theory of the physical universe, it has been evolved from a nebulous and vapoury substance by the action of natural laws, and has at length assumed consistency and definite shape, so it is expected that the fragmentary and fugitive elements into which the beliefs of the past have been dashed, in an age of free thought and advancing intelligence, will after a while crystallize in solid forms, and admit of a logical statement.

We might join issue with this writer and the whole school of progressives, on the question of fact as to the existing condition of religious belief, and show reason for thinking that the doubt and uncertainty they complain of is mainly confined to themselves. We might disclose to them a region where the sun shines in unclouded brightness, and no "eclipse," or even "suspense" of faith is occasioned by the mists and vapours which ascend from the pride of man's unsanctified heart, and from the arrogance of that reason which believes nothing on the mere testimony of God. But without urging that the case with the theological world is not by any means so bad as it is represented, we are constrained to dissent entirely from the assumption which underlies all these speculations. Admitting, as is done by the school to which reference is made, that the Bible contains a revelation from God to teach mankind the way of salvation, it appears to us incredible that its fundamental doctrines should still be unknown, or be so inadequately understood and stated, that future discoveries in the field of Scripture might require our present knowledge and beliefs, either to be discarded as falsehoods, or sloughed off as antiquated and useless notions whenever the church and the world shall emerge into a higher life and a clearer light.

The law of progress, on which so great reliance is placed for discrediting the old and catholic faith of the church, does not stand in exactly the same relation to theology as to other departments of knowledge, and the true analogies it suggests rather support than militate against the permanence and certainty of all the foundation truths of religion, as these are apprehended by common and candid readers of the Scriptures.

In every branch of science, whether physical, intellectual, or moral, there are fixed data, facts certified by the testimony of sense or consciousness, and truths which are self-evident. If these are primary lessons taught to children, they are also the most important. They are absolutely certain, they are immutable, and they are the basis and condition of all subsequent progress. The remotest and grandest results which Newton ever reached in applying the calculus to the problems of astronomy were immediately dependent on the fundamental rules of arithmetic which we teach in the primary department of our schools; and with respect to practical and general utility they are immeasurably more important than their most abstruse and distant applications.

The progressives, whom we have in mind, are fond of comparing the history and advancement of the world to the different stages of human life, and since, in their judgment, mankind have now reached their majority, it is time to put away the childish beliefs and crude conceptions of former ages. It is readily granted that the difference is great between the knowledge of a man and that of a child, and that in many respects experience and education correct and displace early impressions, but there are some impressions and ideas which are never lost or rejected. They are the very elements of knowledge, laws of thought, germs of all progress, and are so early and completely incorporated with the intellectual constitution, that they seem to be part of our nature. The material objects which first greet the opening senses of a child remain in view till its eyes are closed in death, and that belief in the objective reality of the material world, which only the folly of idealistic philosophy doubts, then takes root, and other elementary convictions are implanted which not only lay the foundation for future acquisitions, but determine their general nature and their shape. A thousand childish opinions and impressions may fade insensibly away in the light of an expanding intellect and an enlarged experience, but these rudimental ideas and early beliefs abide, and the analogy, when fairly interpreted, rather confirms than invalidates the position that the vital and controlling truths of theology are permanent and immutable, not only changeless and certain in themselves, but also as to their substance and general form in the faith of the church.

But there is nothing that bears with such decisive force on this question as the fact that the data of all Christian theology are furnished in a positive and supernatural revelation. "*Litera scripta manet*," (the written letter remains.) We have a BOOK written in the language of men, containing the verbal expression and orderly statement of truth. Claiming our faith in its teachings on the ground of its divine Authorship, it addresses itself to our understanding, and is to be explained in accordance with the established laws of human language. Much of it is given in the simplest form of composition, in biography and history, and, taking it together, the Bible is a plain book, and in point of fact is understood in the same way, on vital points, by an overwhelming majority of all its readers.

Considering the source from which it proceeds, and the purpose for which it is given, we might expect the truths necessary to salvation to underlie all its parts, to be often recurred to, and to be embodied in the most explicit announcements. And is not this the character of the word of God? That men of equal learning and honesty differ in their interpretation and views of particular doctrines, and that these differences are regarded as of sufficient magnitude to justify the division of the church into separate denominations, we know, but it only proves that on points of less importance the light of Scripture is not so full and clear as in reference to those which concern the essence of Christian doctrine and the very being of experimental and practical godliness; and we remember that equal diversities of opinion in view of the same premises and sources of knowledge exist in relation to every important subject of human thought. If liberal and progressive theologians contemplated no more than the advancement in divine knowledge which clears up Biblical obscurities, harmonizes the smaller differences of evangelical Christians, and enables all the servants of God to see eye to eye; or, if their idea of the way and measure in which the progress of physical science bears on theology, were that, in giving us a wider and truer view of the works of God, it gave us a juster conception of his word, as when the Copernican system of astronomy displaced the Ptolemaic, or the discoveries of geology revealed a stupendous series of creations before the coming in of man and earth, in their present relations,—if only these and like modifications of Christian belief were in the expectation and aim of any, there would be no controversy between us. To this extent we believe in progress, and Christianity has nothing to fear, but rather has much to hope from the deepest researches of true science and sound philosophy.

If the "advanced thinkers" who glory in their freedom from the shackles of dogmatism could go no further than this, we doubt, from the spirit they betray, whether they would feel zeal enough to go even thus far. The game they are in quest of is more important; and the keenness with which they investigate every lane and by-path of criticism, and history, and archæology, is prompted by inveterate opposition to those great cardinal truths on which the living church of God is founded. If only the dross and tin of human frailty, the "wood, hay, and stubble" which mistaken builders have placed on the Rock of Ages, were cast into the alembic of their destructive criticism, we should bid them God-speed; but when the truths which the church has ever clung to with the same faith and affection that she gave to her Divine and glorious Head are thus handled, and we are told that the doctrine of the Trinity, of the Godhead and sacrifice of Jesus Christ, of regeneration, and of a future and eternal recompense in another world are vanishing from the minds of men, and no longer able to hold their place in theology or Scripture, because, forsooth, the spirit of free inquiry is abroad in the world, and an unparalleled advance has taken place in secular knowledge and Biblical learning, we demur, and cannot persuade ourselves that "the foundations of many generations" are to be thus summarily swept away. It is more than we can credit, that the church, for eighteen hundred years after the canon of Scripture was complete, has been ignorant and misguided as to the fundamental articles of her creed, and that, upon such points as these, the apostles, and the fathers, and the reformers, and the martyrs, were destitute of a light which has been vouchsafed to the students and rhetoricians of the nineteenth century. That the Scriptures, like the material universe, are an inexhaustible study, and that every age may add something to the treasury of things new and old which are brought therefrom is true; but no more true than that the grand and characteristic doctrines of revealed religion strike the reader of the Scripture at first view, even as the salient and obtrusive features of the earth and heavens force themselves on the notice of all beholders. If the subject of predestination has been disputed without a satisfactory issue and general concord, and if the mystery of the Lord's Supper still divides the faithful, when was there a time, since the beginning of the gospel, in which the disciples of Jesus did not believe in the fact of sin, the grace of forgiveness, the need of holiness, the atonement of Christ, the work of the Spirit, and the life everlasting?

That these great and controlling doctrines of evangelical religion are in the Scriptures, and so manifestly there that all seekers of truth are sure to find them, is not more conclusively proved by the fact that the faith of the church has always embraced them, than by the nature of the means which their impugners employ to discredit and explode them. Professing to receive the Scriptures as a revelation from God, the legitimate and obvious method of deciding the question whether these doctrines *are* contained in the Book, would be to fight the battle out on the field of interpretation. The controversy is reduced within the narrow limits of this question of fact: What is written? Do the words of Scripture, explained in accordance with the laws of language, and the recognized rules of exegesis, teach these truths, or do they not? If with such lights and by such arguments it cannot be shown that no such doctrines are taught by the writers of Scripture, there is, in all fairness, an end of the dispute, and neither party has the shadow of a right to go outside of the record, and both are in honour bound to abide by its verdict.

Far different is the course pursued by a large and influential section of those who assail the fundamental principles of the Christian faith. They reject the arbiter by whose decision they had pledged themselves to abide. They impugn the infallibility of the sacred oracles, and thus confess that, in their obvious meaning, the Scriptures do teach the doctrines which a liberal and progressive Christianity discards. If they do not teach these doctrines, there would be no reason for appealing from them to another tribunal: and the very fact that such an appeal is taken, is one of the most satisfactory confessions ever made as to what the actual sense of the Scriptures is.

A witness is not impeached unless his testimony is likely to have a damaging effect. Those who in this manner dishonour and degrade Scripture, are men who in words profess that they reverence its authority, and find in its pages a divine communication. Many of them speak and write under the solemnity of ordination vows, which bind them to hold forth the unadulterated truth of God in their ministrations; and if any one should say they were teachers of infidelity, he would be accused by them with making an unfounded charge, and using offensive epithets; but it is quite impossible to resist the conviction that they are traitors in the camp, who, under the plausible disguise of rendering Christianity acceptable or less offensive to thinking men, are undermining its strongholds, and preparing to surrender the citadel of the faith to its foes. They appear to have infinitely more respect for the intelligence of the age,—for the cavils and skepticism of an unbelieving world,—than for the most sacred convictions of those who love and reverence the word of God; and they seem to experience high delight in exploding, as they think, those blessed truths in the faith of which men "of whom the world was not worthy" have lived and laboured, have suffered and died, since the day that Christ ascended to glory. And not the spirit only which is diffused through their writings, but the desperate methods to which they have recourse in dealing with the Bible, at once define their own position in the religious world, and prove that the truths of evangelical Christianity are so deeply imbedded in the sacred record, that even the most violent "wresting" of the Scriptures is insufficient to dislodge them. The resources of criticism, philology, and dialectic subtlety are used, not so much to bring out their sense, as to sap the foundations of their Divine authority; not so much to ascertain what they say, as to prove that when it is ascertained it cannot be certainly relied on as an oracle from God. The inspiration and infallibility of the Scriptures are assailed on a great variety of grounds, and from many standpoints; with respect to matters of criticism, history, science, and morals. Even, it is alleged that all that the Bible contains cannot be inspired. They say it contains contradictions and anachronisms, and manifold marks of human infirmity: and yet they acknowledge it as, in some sense, a communication from Heaven.

How to eliminate the human error so as to retain the Divine truth, presents a problem which to other men might be difficult, but to them it is easy of solution. Men themselves must judge of the Book, accepting what to them appears true and worthy of God, and rejecting all that does not. The highest authority to which they defer, is their own reason and moral nature,—the "verifying faculty,"—to whose ultimate judgment all that purports to be a message from God must be submitted, even though it were attended with the most stupendous miracles of knowledge and power. "It is no longer held sufficient," says one of them, "to rest doctrines on texts of Scripture, one, two, or more, which contain, or appear to contain, similar words or ideas.

They are connected more closely with our moral nature; extreme consequences are shunned, large allowances are made for the ignorance of mankind."* Such men are not partial to dogmatic theology; creeds and confessions which enunciate the truth so sharply as to preclude the possibility of misconstruction or equivocation incur their contempt. The Christianity which has its basis in verbal statements and logical propositions is too angular and definite for them, and they take refuge in that vague and indeterminate thing which they call "the life," and which is developed from within, instead of being inspired from above. "The never-changing truth of the Christian life" is the only permanent and immutable element of Christianity which they admit, and they seem in love with it, because it means nothing, and leaves every man to think and do what is right in his own eyes. The πρῶτον ψεῦδος, the first lie, of this phase of modern unbelief is no novelty. It is the old controversy which has been waged from the beginning between faith in a supernatural revelation, and a proud reliance on the dictates of nature and the discoveries of reason. It is the natural preference of an unsanctified heart for a human philosophy, rather than for a revealed religion. Its advocates largely insist that the progress of science and civilization brings out the sense of Scripture; and we submit whether their writings do not throw a flood of light on the relation of antagonism which the apostle Paul represents as existing between "the wisdom of men," and the mysteries of salvation by the cross of Christ. And whether the man who now studiously rejects from the little that he does believe the divinity and atonement of the Son of God, is not in the succession from those Greeks to whom the preaching of the cross was "foolishness," because it could not be subjected to "rational

* Jowett, in Essays and Reviews.

criticism," and who would not hear him after he mentioned the "resurrection," because no such thing was dreamed of in their philosophy. "Reason and faith," which God hath joined together in the constitution of the human soul, and whose union and mutual service he has ordained as the necessary condition of acquiring both earthly and heavenly wisdom, are by rationalistic unbelief put asunder, and set in relations of hostility to each other: and because the transcendental mysteries of redemption cannot be demonstrated from premises within our own reach, or do not reveal themselves immediately to our intuitions, they are repudiated as incredible and absurd.

That this is most unreasonable may be seen in its assuming what can never be shown to be true, viz., the impossibility of supernatural communications from God to men—an impossibility which all the positive evidences of Christianity go to disprove.

It is not to reason, but to the false relation in which reason is placed, and the perverted use to which it is applied, that the revelations of the gospel are opposed. As far as reason sees, it is our guide; when it reaches the boundary of its discoveries, faith in a well-attested revelation from God comes to our assistance, and opens a vista of supernal glories, in which are things that eye hath not seen nor ear heard, nor man's heart in all its questionings and criticisms has ever conceived. The one supplements the other. In the graceful allegory of Henry Rogers: "Reason and Faith are twin-born; the one in form and features the image of manly beauty; the other of feminine grace and gentleness; but to each of whom, alas! is allotted a sad privation. While the bright eyes of Reason are full of piercing and restless intelligence, his ear is closed to sound; and while Faith has an ear of exquisite delicacy, on her sightless orbs, as she lifts them heavenward, the sunbeam plays in vain. Hand in hand the brother and sister in all mutual love pursue their way through a world on which, like ours, day breaks and night falls alternate; by day the eyes of Reason are the guide of Faith, and by night the ear of Faith is the guide of Reason." Enlightened Christianity appreciates and uses both; the advocates of a progressive theology, which leaves the Scriptures behind it while professing a qualified faith in their revelations, *enthrone Reason* as the supreme judge and the last and highest source of truth. The divinity within is the oracle they credit, the voice of the people is to them the voice of God.

And to the dark and dubious sayings of such an inspiration, they would remand for rest those who have wearied themselves in the greatness of their way, amid the literalities of Scripture and the jarring theologies of the church! Was ever a thought so preposterous? That man's moral nature is fixed and immutable in the essential elements that belong to it, such as the accountability and freedom of which it can never be divested, together with the sin which defiles the conscience and alienates the heart from God and blinds the understanding, we know well enough; but that its deliverances on the high and momentous questions which concern the nature, relations, duties, dangers, salvation, and destiny of man are the only certain, final, and permanent truths of theology, is something we have not been able to see, nor can we understand exactly what and where the oracle is that utters them. If it be the universal reason and conscience of the race, in what book are they embodied, and who has prepared a "harmony" of the gospels according to Zoroaster and Mohammed, or who has collated the books of Confucius with the book of Mormon, and who, out of the unwritten traditions of all ages and all climes, has gathered and stated the moral and religious truth in which all agree? Is there any such thing as this accepted creed of the universal reason and moral nature of mankind? As to the first principle of all theology, the being of a God, what does it amount to? The atheist says there is no God; the pantheist that there is no being but God; the polytheist that there are many gods; the interior tribes of Africa find their conceptions of a divinity realized in the conjurer who professes to bring them rain; the Christian bows down at "the throne of the King eternal, immortal, and invisible." If such diversities, contradictions, and absurdities arise under the tuition of man's moral nature and unassisted reason, in reference to the most fundamental article of religion, it is vain to seek repose in its teachings from the unrest of doubt and uncertainty.

It does not furnish the elements of an abiding and fixed theology. If, instead of trying to catch the voice of universal humanity, as it rises in the discordant speech of all nations, and echoes along the track of the centuries, we descend to sections, schools, coteries, and individuals, who assume to give forth the witness of reason and nature on the solemn problems of man's duty and destiny, what have we but a perfect Babel of contradictory opinions? Their only and absolute unity consists in a common opposition to evangelical truth.

A fallacy which vitiates all their speculations and reasonings is the assumption that the moral nature, the intuitional consciousness, or by whatever name it may be called, is, or can be, a source of transcendental truths which lie beyond the sphere of rational demonstration, and are not embraced in that of necessary convictions. It is a judge rather than a revealer; a faculty or a susceptibility to be educated and enlightened, not an oracle at whose feet we are to sit down; and though it be capable, as it is alleged, of developing only in certain directions and "to certain effects," the development ranges up and down on a scale which is nearly immense. "We have an original susceptibility of music, of beauty, of religion," it is said. "Granted," replies the writer already quoted, "but as the actual development of the susceptibility exhibits all the diversities between Handel's notions of harmony, and those of an American Indian, between Raphael's notions of beauty and those of a Hottentot; between St. Paul's notions of a God, and those of a New Zealander, it would appear that the education of this susceptibility is at least as important as the susceptibility itself, if not more so." We must, therefore, conclude that, repudiating the Divine authority of Scripture, or which amounts to the same thing, bringing its contents to the bar of reason to be condemned or approved, gives small promise of repose from the war of conflicting beliefs, and presents no sort of temptation to those who have cast the anchor of their hope and faith on the solid rock of God's eternal truth. The data of a fixed and immutable theology are contained in the revelations of Him whose omniscient eye at one and the same look pierced the recesses of our nature, and saw the "end from the beginning" of human progress, and who gave such discoveries of truth, in nature, manner, amount, in words even, as would be adapted and sufficient for all time, and for all the possible vicissitudes of the race. It needs no supplementary additions, admits of no subtractions, and denounces the woes it predicts on every one who mutilates it in either respect.

And to deny or doubt that on all vital points it is well and rightly understood, would approach very nearly to blaspheming its Author, by saying that he had given to the world a revelation of the way of life, which still left men in darkness, after the study and experience of two thousand years! Was ever Delphic utterance more ambiguous? If the aim had been to hide the truth under the pretence of making it known, could the success by any possibility have been more complete? The avowed design of God in speaking to men at all, the promise of the Holy Ghost to dwell with the church for ever, leading the disciples of Jesus into "all truth," and the historical fact, that those who have clung to the articles of faith in which evangelical Christians are agreed, have been "a peculiar people, zealous of good works," the conservators of truth and holiness on the earth,—all serve to assure us that "the truth as it is in Jesus has been found and understood, confessed and obeyed, and that in the happy experience of millions on earth, and of myriads in heaven, his prayer, that men might know "the only true God, and Jesus Christ whom he had sent," has received its blissful answer. While, therefore, we have "no faith in the infallibility of the church, we have unbounded confidence in the truth of what all Christians believe."*

II. But while we would thus "earnestly contend for the faith once delivered to the saints," and insist that truth is immutable as the God of truth from whom it emanates, and as the Scriptures in which it is expressed, and whilst with equal confidence we urge that the elements of a fixed and permanent theology exist in the doctrines which the faithful in all ages and in all parts of Christendom have embraced, we are not blind to the fact, and have no sort of reason for disguising it, that theology itself has a history which shows the alternate progress and decay of sound doctrine. This history is not that of truth in the abstract, but of truth in its relations to the mind of man; the object of intellectual apprehension and of faith, and subject to all the influences from without and from within which either

* Dr. Hodge.

facilitate or hinder its reception. This fact, in the nature of the case, has given rise to the most important branch of ecclesiastical history—that of doctrines—which "shows how the mind of the church has gradually apprehended and unfolded the divine truth, given in the Holy Scriptures, how the teachings of Scripture have come to form the dogmas of the church, and have grown into systems stamped with public authority."*

A progress like this implies a certain degree of imperfection, and, within certain limits, a degree of mutability in the church's views and statements even of the most fundamental doctrines; and shows how she has "struggled for centuries to find language sufficiently precise to express her consciousness respecting them."† She has come to the knowledge of the truth under a discipline analogous to that by which individual believers get an insight into the promises of the gospel, and come to the experimental knowledge of its strong consolations,—by the trials, and sorrows, and opposition she has met with in her progress toward the light and purity of her millennial state. A change of circumstances brings new truths to view, or at least sets them in clearer light, and in new relations to the system of doctrine and the life of the church. So much is this the case, that certain periods are famous for the triumphant vindication and establishment of some one great truth of the Christian system,—as of the person of Christ, original sin, justification by faith, and the doctrines of grace, as opposed to Arminian free-will, which are severally linked in history with the names of Athanasius and Augustine, with Luther and the Synod of Dort. Every creed in Christendom bears the marks of theological controversy, and carries in itself, in its language and form, the history of the period in

* Dr. Schaff. † Dr. Hodge.

which it originated. If there is, as Mr. Trench has shown, a "history in words," there is certainly a history in creeds and confessions, whose very terms are abiding memorials of the conflicts which gave them birth.

Among the causes which modify the form, and, to some extent, affect the substance of theology, we would not be disposed to assign a place of much importance to temperament and original differences of mental constitution.

Some have thought they could trace the influence of temperament even in the subjects treated by the different apostles, and have spoken of James as phlegmatic, of Peter as sanguine, of Paul as choleric, and of John as melancholic: but we judge that whatever may have been their physical conditions, it was not these, but the Spirit of God, that inspired their doctrines; and we feel quite sure that it is the depravity of the heart, more than any peculiarity of bodily or mental organization, that mutilates or prevents the clear perception and complete embrace of divine truth.

Nevertheless, something may be conceded to differences of race and nationality, and even to individual idiosyncrasies. Evangelical theology, as it exists in the mind of a Frenchman, or of a German, or of an Oriental convert, though identical in substance, is not precisely the same "formation" as in the direct, common-sense, and logical mind of the Anglo-saxon. With them, emotion, philosophic subtlety, and a glowing imagination shape and colour the truth: with us, a severe logic casts it into formal and definite propositions. And as it regards individual minds, theology, as a system of truth believed, and as a science developed, is not precisely the same thing as it lies in the conception and understanding of different persons. This is a necessary result of the imperfection, or at least the limits of the human mind: but it argues no imperfection of the truth; it is rather a mark of its divinity.

As Dr. Schaff has finely remarked, "The truth of the gospel, in itself infinite, can adapt itself to every class, to every temperament, every order of talent, and every habit of thought. Like the light of the sun, it breaks into various colours, according to the nature of the bodies on which it falls; like the jewel, it emits a new radiance at every turn."

A similar difference in the mode of apprehending truth, and, to a certain extent, also, in the substance of the doctrine apprehended, is caused by difference in the culture, taste, character, and spirit of successive and distant ages and generations.

Though that indefinite and impalpable thing called "the spirit of the age" is invoked to aid the cause of a lax and latitudinarian theology, and is used to unsettle and dissipate the old beliefs of the church, it is a matter of simple observation and history, that while the leaven of Divine truth pervades and assimilates the mass of our lapsed humanity, it moves in the channels which at any time it finds existing, employs the implements which civilization supplies to its hands, and becomes "all things to all men." Christianity not only uses different methods in its practical dealing with the work it has in charge, but it presents truth in new proportions and new phases, as providential occasions arise; now apologetic, then polemic; at one time dogmatic, at another practical. Each of these in its time is the best form of theology, and is of use in all succeeding time; but nothing is plainer than that if the peculiarity of one such period were carried into another, and truth exhibited in the same relations and degrees, it would be shorn of its power. Retaining its own changeless identity, it succeeds by "changing its voice," speaking in the tongue, and after the manner, and according to the taste of the times. Its image is not a granite rock, which lies immovable in its subterranean bed, the same in its every particle since it was melted and moulded into its final form by the internal fires of the globe. It is rather the limpid stream which meanders through the valleys, flows round the hills, and reflects from its glassy bosom the beauties of the adjacent landscape, and the glories of the over-arching sky.

In the ages past, the rise of heresies and errors has probably exerted more power in giving form and proportion to theology than any other single cause. In our times, it would seem that this predominant influence is exerted by the increase of Biblical learning and the progress of natural science. In all the requisite appliances for a critical and thorough study of the Scriptures, this century is greatly in advance of the past, and a new light has been thrown on the sense of Scripture, which, with inferior advantages, was hardly attainable: and what in this direction has been, is that which shall be. To conclude that no further additions will be made from the better interpretation of the Scriptures to the existing stock of Divine truth as contained in the knowledge and creeds of the church would be as presumptuous as to affirm that physical investigations had reached the *ultima thule* of their progress, that no more inventions in the useful or fine arts were to be expected, and that, in short, the material works of God were completely explored and comprehended. While the truth which is necessary to the being of the church and the salvation of the soul lies on the surface of Scripture, it is doing honour to God to believe that his word like his works is sufficient to occupy and reward the study of the church throughout her earthly history. Not only is philology directly tributary to the better understanding of the Bible and to the increase of our knowledge of Divine truth, but we must admit that the progress of the physical sciences since the incoming of the Baconian philosophy, and especially during the past half-century, has shed an indirect though important light on the meaning of some parts of Divine revelation. It is true that an infidel philosophy, and a science falsely so-called, have presumed to pronounce its statements ignorant and mistaken, and we should exercise the greatest caution in admitting the dicta of any science which appear to conflict with the natural sense of the word of God, yet we know that true science has not only disclosed an inexhaustible store of illustrations, but has revealed a fulness and a grandeur of meaning in particular passages, which could not otherwise have been detected. If when men thought that the earth was the centre of the system, the heavens declared the glory of God, and the nocturnal sky evoked the sublime strains of the Psalmist's praise, with what a widened reach of thought, and in view of how much grander displays of Almighty power and wisdom, do we exclaim, "O Lord, our Lord, how excellent is thy name in all the earth!" "When I consider thy heavens, the work of thy fingers, the moon and the stars which thou hast ordained, what is man, that thou art mindful of him; or the son of man, that thou visitest him?"

How far the amount and the forms of Christian theology may be affected by these and other causes, in the lapse of coming ages, the nature of the case forbids our knowing or even conjecturing. There are two limits within which it will be confined, whatever its amount. On the one hand it will be bounded by the truths of the gospel, which we certainly know, and will be built upon them, and on the other it will fall far short of the unclouded vision of the heavenly state. Between these limits there is a vast field to range over, and there is reason to believe that the spiritual knowledge of the church will increase with the passing centuries, until, in its millennial brightness, the knowledge of God which shall then fill the earth as the waters do the seas, will be distinguished as much for its depth, and clearness, and comprehensiveness, as for its universal prevalence. "The light of the moon shall be as the light of the sun; and the light of the sun shall be sevenfold as the light of seven days."

We should not, therefore, as it seems to me, be afraid of any possible advances either in secular learning or theological investigations, as if the foundations we stand upon might thereby be endangered; nor should we suffer the prejudice naturally begotten by the pretended discoveries of rationalizing and infidel progressives to close our eyes to the important truth which they distort and abuse.

In the sense and under the limitations suggested, progress is perfectly consistent with the staunchest conservatism: living in an age which boldly questions and freely criticizes every thing in morals, and politics, and religion, which the traditions of the past have delivered to the present, we need to be well established in the faith, and yet so far in sympathy with the spirit of progress as to welcome whatever comes to us with the clear attestation of truth; and be willing to learn the defects of our opinions even from our enemies.

The application of these views to the existing creeds and confessions of the church opens a field of inquiry of no small importance, and of considerable difficulty, not to say delicacy. That they embody the essential truths of the gospel, is what we have specially laboured to prove, and do most assuredly believe.

But that they are absolutely faultless, and of equal authority with the Scriptures, is what nothing but the narrowest and most benighted bigotry would pretend. The very process of their development amid temptations and conflicts with error, while it stamps them in their essence with the seal of divinity, involves the liability, if not the absolute certainty, of their being cast in moulds that are marred by human imperfection. The state of learning and philosophy at the time; the degree and kind of culture possessed by their framers; the particular controversies out of which the necessity of their formation arose, and the heresies at which they were aimed, impress upon them a strictly historical character, and involve, of necessity, a certain degree of one-sidedness. The logic, the learning, and the philosophy of the age leave their print upon them: this is inevitable, and it is of the nature of an imperfection. The substantial truth is there, but not in the words, forms, connexions, and proportions in which we find it in the Scriptures. As it respects the creeds of the several Christian denominations, the imperfection, and even the error, is patent on their face, in the contradictions they oppose to each other on points of secondary importance. The gospel is Divine; these are human; and in depressing them to the position which rightfully belongs to them, we only seek to exalt the word of God to its throne of supreme and sole authority.

Heretics hate creeds, because their own errors are therein condemned, and the truth is set forth in such sharp and pointed antagonism, that no refuge of ambiguity remains: for this purpose, as well as for the indoctrination of the church, they are of excellent use; the very spear of Ithuriel which disrobes the father of lies, though he were "transformed as an angel of light."

But there is a danger connected with their use. If the "form"—the type—"of doctrine in which our views and experience are moulded is that of the scientific theology of the creeds, instead of the inspired words and truths of the Scriptures, they will be so far more human and less divine, and the mere shape and order of truth will be likely to hold a place in our minds which should be assigned to its substance. This tendency is mainly confined to ministers of the gospel and students of theology, who study divinity as a science: and its influence is most frequently seen in young preachers, who are wont to use the scholastic nomenclature of the text-books, rather than the "words which the Holy Ghost teacheth." It is always done at a vast sacrifice of practical power and impression, though it may, perchance, save the interests of orthodoxy. The energy and Spirit of God are in the word of God as they are not in anything else. If all nature, art, history, and life be put in requisition to illustrate and win attention to their expression, let "no wisdom of words," no scientific stiffness and artificial niceties obscure their divine beauty, or impede their living power. The creeds savour of controversy; the gospel is a testimony, and needs not dialectic subtleties, but an earnest and tender proclamation. "Controversy," said Dr. Chalmers, addressing his theological classes, "may lead you to exchange the Scriptural for the scholastic style, so that instead of propounding a doctrine in those words which were devised by God for the direct instruction of the teachable, you may propound it in those words which have been devised by men for putting down the heresies of gainsayers:" this he regarded as an evil; and in one of his letters he enlarged on what he terms "the spontaneity and development of the immediate oracles," in contrast with "catechisms which, however correct in their dogmata, may not be correct in their general effect upon the mind."

If the scientific and controversial statement of truth is liable to objection on the ground of its one-sidedness and artificial jointing, much more detrimental to its impression and saving power is that "deceitful handling" which converts the gospel of Christ into a human philosophy. Instead of promulgating it as a Divine testimony, and demanding the "obedience of faith," for "the authority of God speaking therein," there is a constant temptation of the most seductive character to men of superior gifts, not only to throw their teachings into a philosophic form, but to find the very foundations of the Christian faith in an earth-born philosophy. Not content with seeking for illustrations and analogies, they must show reasons and arguments, and seem to feel as if a Divine declaration were hardly worthy of credence, unless backed by their own demonstrations.

Their theories of psychology, and metaphysics, and the moral government of God, are somewhat more fundamental in their apprehension and methods, than the inspired verities of Scripture, which must, accordingly, take their shape, adjustment, and expression from what underlies them. This precisely is what we understand the apostle Paul to condemn in terms the most emphatic, as that which makes the cross of Christ "of none effect." It is the "wisdom of words," and the "enticing words of man's wisdom" which "the wise" and "the scribe," and the "disputer of this world," would employ to express the doctrines of their own philosophy, but which as little befit the herald and teacher of gospel mysteries, as the cumbrous armour of the king was suited to the limbs and frame of the shepherd-boy who "assayed" to use them.

It imparts immense weight to the apostle's repudiation of the methods and principles of the Greek philosophy to know that he was schooled therein, and could have met its masters on their own ground. For one who is incapable of such speculations, it is no act of self-denial to ignore them, but in Paul it required a higher courage and a stronger resolution than was requisite for fighting with beasts at Ephesus, or laying his head on the block at Rome, to "preach Christ crucified in a crucified language," and in the presence of Epicureans and Stoics, to utter the deep things of God, "not in words which man's wisdom teacheth, but which the Holy Ghost teacheth." To do otherwise is to strip the gospel of its grand peculiarity as a system of supernatural truth, which the reason of man can neither discover nor prove. It is to substitute the authority of man for the authority of God, and to reject the element of its greatest strength—the faith which the soul reposes in the testimony of him who cannot lie. "A rationalistic Christian, a philosophizing theologian," as has been truly remarked, "lays aside the divine for the human, the wisdom of God for the wisdom of men, the infinite and infallible for the finite and fallible. The success of the gospel depends on its being presented, not as the word of man, but as the word of God; not as something to be proved, but as something to be believed."*

The pulpit, as an instrument of regeneration and life, is vitally conditioned upon a faithful adherence to these principles. Departure therefrom in the mode and spirit in which divine truth is handled may attract the superficial, and please the carnally-minded, but it will not prove "the power of God unto salvation." The word and not man's reasonings upon it is the hammer that breaks the flinty rock, the two-edged sword that pierces to the dividing asunder of soul and spirit, and is a discerner of the thoughts and intents of the heart. Our commission authorizes and commands us only to "preach the word,"—to proclaim the good news,—to "testify the gospel of the grace of God."

Thus shall we finish our course with joy to ourselves, with salvation to others, and with glory to the Lord Jesus Christ.

* Dr. Hodge, on 2 Cor. pp. 235, 236.

The views now suggested, of a conservatively progressive theology, satisfy two of the profoundest tendencies or instincts of a renewed mind, and are full of consolation. They leave the Christian in the assured possession of what he has, and give him the promise of ever-increasing knowledge. They satisfy the desire for absolute certainty, and for indefinite progress. If a suspicion could cross the mind that the great truths on which the new life has been fed should ever pale their brightness in the presence of other revelations, or that "the glorious gospel of the blessed God" should be found to have answered only a temporary use, and to have been but relatively true, it would send a thrill of anguish to the Christian heart. And if, on the other hand, a limit were assigned to our knowledge of God and truth, the future of existence would be divested of one of its principal charms, and would become almost an object of dread, instead of being, as it now is, radiant and glorious with all that inspires hope, and makes the Christian joyful in the prospect of immortality. That prospect is one of eternal progression in knowledge; and of the study of theology in a clearer light and in far other conditions than those which limit our view and retard our advances on earth. Now we are slowly and laboriously acquainting ourselves with the rudiments of the divine science; then we shall deal with its highest forms, and most recondite mysteries. Here it is night, there it is day. At present we are children in understanding, hereafter we shall be men.

With slow and unsteady step, we walk by faith; when faith is changed to sight, we shall move on with bold and rapid pace.

"Now we see through a glass darkly: but then face to face. Now I know in part, but then shall I know even as also I am known."

www.ingramcontent.com/pod-product-compliance
Lightning Source LLC
LaVergne TN
LVHW020227110826
845151LV00003B/849